USA FOOTBALL YOUTH COACHING HANDBOOK

TONY DUNGY
WITH JAMES A. PETERSON, PH.D.

©2018 Coaches Choice. All rights reserved. Printed in the United States.

No part of this book may be reproduced, stored in a retrieval system, or transmitted, in any form or by any means, electronic, mechanical, photocopying, recording, or otherwise, without the prior permission of Coaches Choice.

ISBN: 978-1-60679-414-2
Library of Congress Control Number: 2017959772
Book layout: Cheery Sugabo
Diagrams: Reggie Sugabo

Coaches Choice
P.O. Box 1828
Monterey, CA 93942
www.coacheschoice.com

DEDICATION

This book is dedicated to youth football coaches who make a positive difference in the lives of their athletes.

ACKNOWLEDGMENTS

First and foremost, we would like to express our appreciation to Steve Alic of USA Football for his extensive and thoughtful efforts on this book. We would also like to thank Joe Frollo of USA Football for his capable and fitting editorial input on the project. Finally, we would like to acknowledge Mike Aruanno, Steve Axman, Leo Hand, and Kenny Ratledge—football coaches extraordinaire—for their practical input and invaluable advice concerning the book. This book could not have become a reality without their contributions.

FOREWORD

Football has been a major influence in my life from my early playing days as a grade-schooler, then later as part of a state championship Morris Hills High School team in New Jersey and culminating in my years as a player on the fields of friendly strife at the United States Military Academy at West Point. Football played a critical role in my early development as a leader. It taught me the significance of the team, selflessness, resiliency, integrity, and the value of hard work and sacrifice. Football emphasized to me the importance of mental and physical toughness when overcoming adversity and the merits of exhibiting courage in all aspects of life.

Football was hugely significant in developing my character as a young man. It taught me the importance of and satisfaction found in being part of something greater than myself. It not only provided me the opportunity to attend West Point, but it also better prepared me for the many challenges which I would face there both physically and academically. Its influence helped develop me into someone others can count on—my teammates, my troops, my colleagues, and my family.

We live in an important time for football. The sport's advancements in player safety on all levels are under scrutiny. As the Chairman of USA Football, I am committed to continue to propel our work to make this exceptional team sport safer, smarter, and better. My ongoing focus is to help make certain that this unique facet of the American spirit continues to provide developmental growth opportunities for the youth of America.

In that regard, the *USA Football Youth Coaching Handbook* is a must-have resource for every coach who wants to be a positive difference-maker in the lives of our children. A comprehensive book that is chock full of information, insights, and ideas, the following pages feature easy-to-understand tips and techniques showing how coaches can develop their players—both on and off the field. This remarkable resource is the perfect companion for youth football coaches who do what they love and love what they do.

Raymond T. Odierno
Chairman, USA Football
General, Retired
38th Chief of Staff of the United States Army

CONTENTS

Dedication 3
Acknowledgments 4
Foreword: General Ray Odierno (Ret.) 5
Preface 8

SECTION I: LAYING THE FOUNDATION FOR SUCCESS **9**
1. Why do you want to be a coach? 11
2. What kind of coach do you want to be? 13
3. What do you want your team to achieve? 16
4. What are the key factors in the growth and development of youth? 20

SECTION II: PLANNING FOR SUCCESS **23**
5. What does it take to be a good coach? 25
6. What does it take to be a good teacher? 35
7. What is involved in building a coaching staff? 40

**SECTION III: DEVELOPING THE SKILLS AND TECHNIQUES
FOR ON-THE-FIELD SUCCESS** **45**
8. Sport-specific skills and techniques 47
9. Position-specific skills and techniques 55

SECTION IV: PUTTING IT ALL TOGETHER FOR SUCCESS **159**
10. How to develop a true team 161
11. How to develop an offensive system 166
12. How to develop a defensive system 184
13. How to develop a special teams unit 212

SECTION V: ENHANCING LIFE SKILLS FOR SUCCESS **231**
14. How to teach and reinforce values in your athletes 233

APPENDICES **237**
A. Glossary of Terms 239
B. USA Football National Practice Guidelines for Youth Tackle Football 253
C. USA Football Flag Rulebook & Player Pathway 259

About the Authors 271

PREFACE

This book was written to provide a roadmap to assist individuals who are involved in a commendable and noble endeavor—coaching youth football. In a step-by-step manner, it addresses many of the issues that youth football coaches, who want to make a difference in the lives of their athletes, will face at some point. In that regard, it emphasizes the fact that the role of a youth football coach entails more than simply teaching athletes the X's and O's of the sport. Such a role also involves helping athletes become better players, better teammates, and better people.

This book does not purport to provide the single "best" way to coach youth football. What it does advance is the premise that a number of factors collectively impact a coach's efforts to help ensure that his players will have a positive experience under his tutelage. Many of those factors are detailed and discussed in this book.

The expression that "no man is an island" also applies to this book. In fact, several individuals have helped turn this book into a reality, particularly Steve Alic (communications director at USA Football), Kristi Huelsing (managing director of book publications at Coaches Choice), and Mike Aruanno (who provided input and feedback on many of the X's and O's topics covered). In fact, we are indebted to the collaborative efforts of everyone who contributed to this book.

Finally, we are most grateful to anyone who has ever been involved in the great game of football—either as a coach or a player. Collectively, their efforts are part of the mosaic that is football. If this book assists those individuals who are associated with youth football in any way, then the effort to write it will have been worthwhile.

—TD
—JP

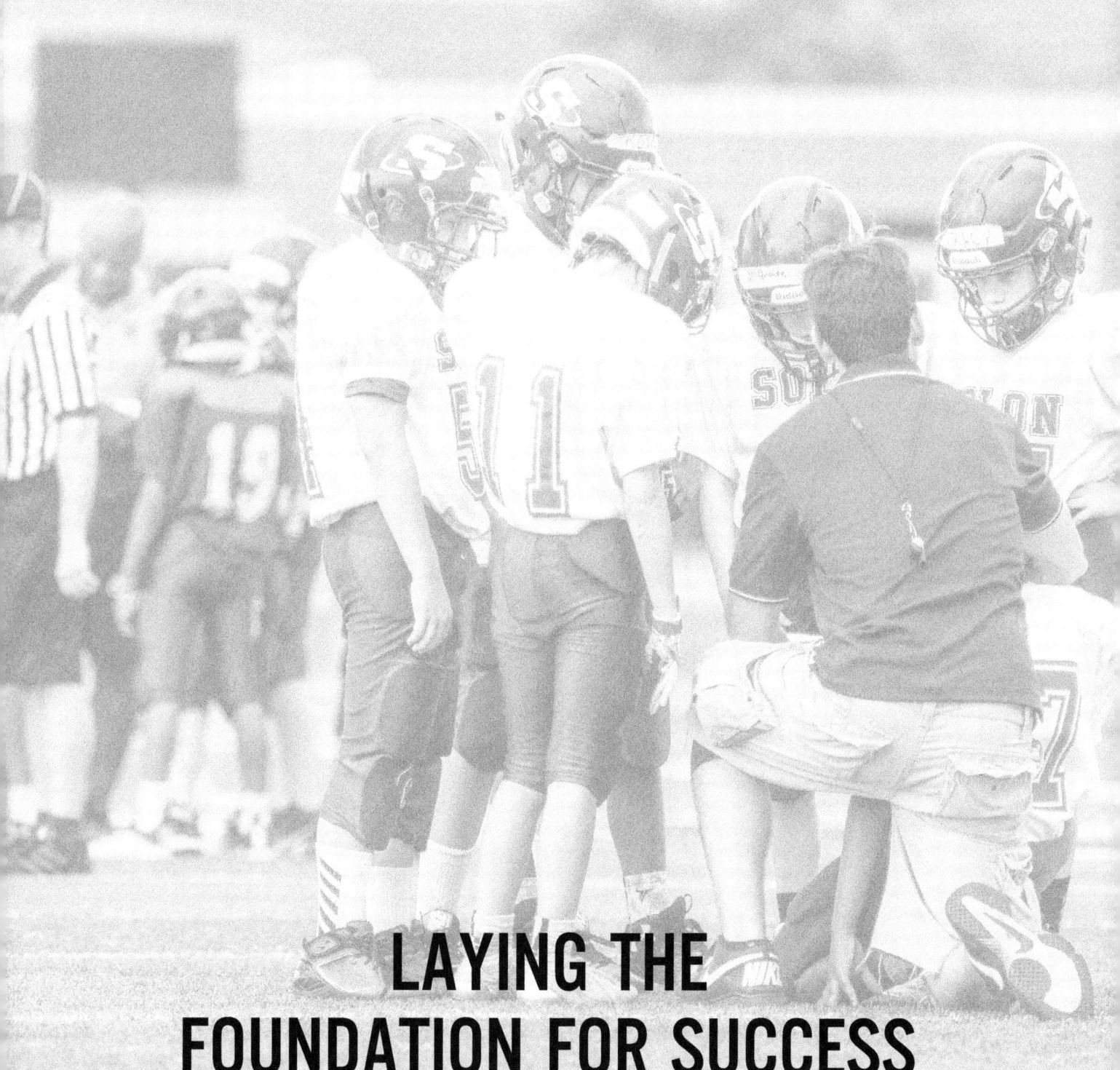

SECTION I

LAYING THE FOUNDATION FOR SUCCESS

CHAPTER 1

WHY DO YOU WANT TO BE A COACH?

One of the most rewarding things you will ever do is coach youth football. More often than not, your heart will swell with pride as you successfully take advantage of the opportunity to help frame how your young athletes navigate the pathway of social and physical maturity. You will also take great pleasure in providing your players with a positive experience that enables them to have fun playing a game that they love.

In reality, individuals want to be a coach for a variety of reasons (often a combination of several). Some want to embrace the chance to work with and help kids. Some want to coach their own kids. Others want to coach because of their love of the game. Still others want to be of service to their community. Some are intrigued by the strategy inherent in the game. Some like the teamwork the game encompasses. Others sign up because they want to experience what it's like to actually coach (i.e., lead a group of people, however young they might be, in pursuit of a common goal). The interest of still others is piqued by the challenges they perceive that coaching presents.

Arguably, the list of why someone might like to coach is not only virtually endless, it can also be somewhat complicated. The factors that influence one person to become a coach may not affect another, and vice versa. Furthermore, the reasons that lead a person to coach often change over time. What may matter to someone today may be irrelevant or less important to that same person tomorrow.

WHY DO YOU NEED TO KNOW WHY YOU'RE A COACH?

Whether you are getting into coaching youth football or you are already in coaching, if you do it for the wrong reasons, you probably won't enjoy it very much or be in it very long. The important point to remember is that, as a rule, the joy and sense of satisfaction in coaching must come from the day-to-day teaching and learning that impacts the development of your young athletes, as well as the day-to-day goals that are achieved each time you work with them.

The journey of a youth football coach is sometimes littered with hurdles and stumbling blocks. Your team won't win every game. The parents of your players may not always be accommodating and pleasant. You won't always have every resource you need to be successful.

Nonetheless, almost without exception, you will determine that your decision to become a coach was the right one. The growth you observe in your athletes, the joy you experience when things go as planned, and the sense of personal fulfillment that you have when your athletes refer to you by your befitting name ("Coach") will all contribute to your feeling of accomplishment.

All factors considered, coaching for reasons that are important and suitable to you will help reinforce your commitment to make the appropriate effort to perform the job to the best of your ability. Knowing why you're doing what you do can help you to be better able to handle any stress or frustration that may arise.

Ultimately, it will enable you to be better prepared to deal with the challenges that are inherent in the role of coaching youth football. As someone who is destined to have a positive impact on the lives of young athletes, you will be rewarded with well-deserved feelings of being a "difference-maker." What more could you want?

COACHING NOTES

- [ ] Be mindful that no single "right" reason to coach exists. In reality, a variety of factors can motivate an individual to become a coach.
- [ ] Be someone who applies the lessons you've learned in life to your efforts to better understand why you want to coach.
- [ ] Be aware that your primary responsibility as a coach is to help your athletes grow and develop as individuals.
- [ ] Be open to the fact that the reasons you feel you are coaching may evolve and change over time.
- [ ] Be passionate about both why you are coaching and what your role is as a coach.

CHAPTER 2

WHAT KIND OF COACH DO YOU WANT TO BE?

How would you like to be remembered as a coach? Ideally, you want to be the kind of coach who has a positive impact on the lives of the young athletes with whom you work. Wanting to have a positive impact (i.e., make a difference), however, is not enough. You also need a plan for turning your goal into a reality.

The foundation of that plan is your coaching philosophy. In essence, your philosophy is the *why* that underlies everything you will do as a coach. It is a reflection of why you are a coach, what your values and beliefs are, and what your goals (as a coach) are. It is also the primary factor in the kind of coach you are, including the type of teaching and learning environment you establish for your team.

DEVELOPING A COACHING PHILOSOPHY

Every coach has a philosophy, regardless of whether they know what it is. Their philosophy is what they believe will enable them to achieve their desired objectives. Accordingly, it is very important to understand that "winning" is not a philosophy. It is an outcome.

In order to develop your coaching philosophy, ascertain who and what you are and what you want to be in your role as a youth football coach. In that regard, you should ask yourself the following questions:

- What attributes make a good coach?
- Do you lack any of these traits?
- Do you like the kind of coach you are?
- Do you think children would like to have someone like you as their coach?
- How do you think current and former players would see you as a coach?
- How do you think the parents of your players view you as a coach?
- Do you actively solicit unbiased, objective feedback on how you are doing as a coach?
- Do you have a plan to identify and address any weaknesses you may have as a coach?

- Is how you are coaching consistent with why you are coaching?
- Is how you believe you should behave in your everyday life the same way you behave when you are coaching?

Once you have an honest impression of the kind of coach you are (or want to be), the next step in establishing your coaching philosophy is to determine what you hope to accomplish in your role as a coach. The following objectives are examples of commonly held coaching aspirations:

- Use football to teach life skills
- Make the sports experience fun
- Serve the community
- Help athletes grow as individuals
- Establish positive relationships with parents
- Be a positive example to others
- Provide an environment that enhances the athletes' love of the game
- Develop the sport and motor skills of athletes
- Use football to teach values
- Stay close to the game

More often than not, your attitude about the X's and O's (technical) aspects of the game is also an outgrowth of your coaching philosophy. With regard to how you want your team to play on offense, are you conservative or aggressive? Defensively, do you favor an attacking style of play or a bend-don't-break approach?

Another factor you should consider to help you develop your coaching philosophy is to think about coaches who have influenced you. They could be individuals who coached you at some point in your life, coaches you've read about, or coaches you've watched from a distance (e.g., television) over the years. What attributes of these coaches would you like to exhibit? What traits would you like to avoid having?

Using the aforementioned information as a guide (the kind of coach you want to be; the objectives you want to achieve as a coach; your beliefs about the X's and O's part of the game), as well as your feelings and observations about other coaches, you are essentially at a point where you can put your coaching philosophy in writing.

The key point to remember is that your philosophy should reflect who you are as a person. For example, a sample coaching philosophy might entail the following:

> *First and foremost, I believe that youth football should focus on fun and learning. It is my responsibility to coach in a manner that reinforces everyone's love and joy for the game. The athletes should learn not only the skills involved in the sport, but also lessons that will have a positive effect on other areas of their lives. Athletes should also be taught to put the team above individuals ... others before self. In addition, a community of players, coaches, and parents should be created to work together to support each other in establishing an enriching and uplifting experience for everyone involved.*

A SENSE OF URGENCY

Whatever time you put in determining your coaching philosophy will be well-spent. In fact, it will help save you time and energy as you go forward. All

factors considered, decisions will require less thought. Your judgment will be more considered and consistent. Actions will require less explaining. Avoid temptation to delay the task of developing your coaching philosophy. With regard to discerning your philosophy, the advice is straightforward—do it right and do it right now.

DEVELOPING A COACHING STYLE

If your philosophy is how you feel about things, your style of coaching is how you carry out your feelings. In reality, no one "right" style of coaching exists. Wrong ones, however, certainly do—coaching by fear and intimidation, for example. The key is to adopt a coaching style that is consistent with who you want to be as a coach (e.g., authoritative, cooperative, casual, etc.).

As a rule, the best youth football coaches tend to be positive, energetic, responsible, and caring. They have a values-based orientation that focuses on addressing the needs and interests of their athletes. They exhibit an ongoing love and respect for the sport.

COACHING NOTES

☐ Be aware that no substitute exists for the quality of person you are.

☐ Be someone who never forgets why kids really play football (e.g., have fun, be with friends, learn new skills, etc.) and plan your approach to coaching accordingly.

☐ Be passionate in your role as a coach; keep your enthusiasm level high; allow your athletes to feed off your energy.

☐ Be prepared; if something isn't working as planned, be prepared to either change it or try something else.

☐ Be open to input about how others view you as a coach; if their feedback indicates that a disconnect exists between how you are actually coaching and how you would want to coach, adapt to reality.

CHAPTER 3

WHAT DO YOU WANT YOUR TEAM TO ACHIEVE?

Coaches who want to make things happen set goals and objectives. As a rule, goals are positive statements that articulate what needs to be accomplished over time to achieve the "vision" that the coach has set for his team and program. Objectives, on the other hand, are clear, relatively specific statements, the completion of which will lead to the achievement of the team's goals.

Unlike objectives, goals tend to be purposely stated in broad generalities. Objectives, in contrast, are inclined to be short-range, challenging (but realistic) statements that focus on more immediate accomplishments. Collectively, goals and objectives help establish a direction for your program, define what resources will be needed, and help determine how, when, and where those resources will be used. They also provide a measuring stick for how well your program is doing and whether any changes may be needed going forward in what you're doing.

SETTING GOALS AND OBJECTIVES

The process of setting goals helps you choose where you want your program to go. It is a process that begins with careful and thoughtful consideration of what you want you and your program to achieve, and ends (hopefully) after a lot of hard work, with the attainment of a vision. In between, there are several well-defined, specific steps that are designed to help each goal become a reality.

Effective goal setting involves planning, preparation, and passion. Anything less may compromise what you would like to have your efforts as a coach achieve. Adhering to the following guidelines for goal setting can be helpful:

- ☐ Be decisive. Know what you want, why you want it, and how you plan to achieve it.
- ☐ Stay focused. Sustaining your focus can have a meaningful impact on the ultimate outcome of your goal-setting efforts.

- ☐ Anticipate and embrace failure. Expect failure to occur as a temporary setback on the pathway of progress. Try to grow from every experience you have—good and bad.
- ☐ Put your goals in writing. Don't rely on your ability to recall things.
- ☐ Plan thoroughly. Never underestimate the value of the expression detailed in the five Ps—"Proper planning prevents poor performance."
- ☐ Involve others. To the extent feasible, engage individuals whose knowledge, values, and compatibilities you respect help you achieve your goals.
- ☐ Be action-oriented. Be aware that achievement demands action on your part. Be a doer, not a spectator.
- ☐ Be realistic. Set goals that are attainable. Make sure that the necessary resources (e.g., energy, skills, talents, time, etc.) are available that can help place your goals within reach.
- ☐ Don't try to do too much. Don't set too many goals. Don't spread your energy or the program's resources too thin.
- ☐ Be adaptive. Keep shaping, molding, and adapting your goals, as appropriate, to your ever-changing circumstances as they actually exist, as opposed to how you would like them to be.

In contrast to goals, objectives are the core of your plan to achieve your goals. You need to set as many objectives, as is appropriate to your situation, to successfully reach your goals. Similar to goals, there are certain steps you can adopt to enhance the likelihood that your objective-setting efforts will be effective, including the following:

- ☐ Keep it simple. Focus on setting objectives that you know can be achieved in the allotted timeframe.
- ☐ Be specific. Know exactly what the objective entails and how it will contribute to your goals.
- ☐ Establish a clear understanding of how an objective may be related to other objectives and goals you may have. Align each objective with the broader vision you may have for yourself and your program.
- ☐ Make each objective measurable. While this factor is not possible in all instances, it does enable you to know if/when you reach a particular goal.
- ☐ Break broader goals into smaller (mini-) goals. Doing so can help you make your objectives more specific and help you establish more detailed milestones to monitor your progress.

IDENTIFYING GOALS AND OBJECTIVES FOR YOUR PROGRAM

Setting goals and objectives you would like to have your program achieve should be a thoughtful process, based on honest reflection of who you are and what you would like your program to be. Since achieving the outcomes you intend for your program will not occur by chance, it is essential that you devote an appropriate amount of effort to the process.

One of the biggest challenges you will face is the inherent complexity involved in defining goals and objectives for a youth football program that are specific, measurable, and realistic. Some factors are subjective in nature; others are objective. Some

are quantifiable; others are not. Some are tangible; others not so much.

Just as individuals coach youth football for a variety of reasons (as was noted in Chapter 1), different individuals tend to have different goals and objectives concerning what they want their programs to achieve. The following lists detail the broad range of reasons that coaches often give for what they want their programs to accomplish:

☐ Goals:

- To enhance the love that their kids have for the game
- To help their kids be better prepared for challenges they may encounter outside of football
- To inspire their kids to do more than they previously believed was possible for themselves
- To enable their kids to learn how to appropriately handle the "joys" of victory and the "agonies" (and disappointments) of defeat
- To give back to the community (e.g., sense of pride, excitement, connection, emotional link, etc.)
- To instill an awareness and appreciation in their athletes for being physically active
- To provide an opportunity for the parents of their athletes to connect with their children in yet another area of their kids' lives
- To give their athletes a variety of values-based experiences (e.g., accountability, responsibility, mindfulness, teamwork, leadership, etc.)
- To afford their kids the chance to have fun and experience the joys of competing against others
- To have a team that is well-prepared in all facets of the game (offense, defense, special teams)
- To have young athletes who exhibit self-discipline, regardless of the situation
- To have a team that merits the respect of others (e.g., opponents, parents, members of the community, etc.)
- To be successful

☐ Objectives:

- To win "X" number of games
- To have an offense, defense, and/or special teams unit that is one of the best in the league
- To have a group that is one of the least penalized teams in the league
- To have an offense that gains an average of "X" number of yards per game
- To have a defense that is among the best in the league in points allowed
- To have a special teams unit that does not give up a return for a touchdown all season
- To have a team that is one of the best in the league at fumbles recovered
- To have a team that is one of the best in the league in takeaways

SUCCESS ENTAILS MORE THAN WINNING

Too many people, including some coaches, place too much emphasis on winning as the core factor in success. In their minds, to paraphrase Pro Football Hall of Fame coach Vince Lombardi, "Winning isn't everything, it's the only thing." They don't realize that success is not always about winning. In fact, it is usually much, much more.

Truth be known, "winning" is seldom given by young athletes as the main basis for their interest in playing a team sport. Rather, they cite "having fun, being with their friends, and participating in a game they love" as their primary reasons for playing.

As their coach, while winning may be somewhat important to you (who doesn't like to win, if for no other reason than to help validate the effort that everyone is putting into the program?), it certainly shouldn't be nearly as important to you as having a positive impact on the lives of your athletes. Not only do you instill the joy of playing youth football in your athletes, you also help facilitate their development, both on and off the field.

Arguably, given the time and effort involved in coaching youth football, it would be logical to assume that your decision to become a coach was made for reasons that you perceived as appropriate. Like most of your colleagues in a similar situation to you, coaching youth football is a calling ... a call to be a difference-maker ... a call that involves a higher purpose than winning ... a call to which you responded.

COACHING NOTES

☐ Remember that you have a unique opportunity to help frame how your kids will think about things long after your season is over.

☐ Be aware that program success has several dimensions.

☐ Never underestimate the importance of having fun in the eyes of your players.

☐ Know that every child (athlete) is different and that this uniqueness may require you to adjust your approach and expectations.

CHAPTER 4

WHAT ARE THE KEY FACTORS IN THE GROWTH AND DEVELOPMENT OF YOUTH?

Human development is a process entailing behavioral, cognitive, emotional, and physical growth and changes that occur over the course of an individual's lifetime. Being knowledgeable about what changes and behavior are relatively normal during each transition stage can go a long way in helping a child to successfully manage the changeover. It can also help shed light on how they learn, what they should be expected to learn, and what they are actually able to learn.

As a coach, it is important that you have a basic understanding of the developmental characteristics of your players, given the fact that you must work differently, for example, with eight-year-old athletes than with 12-year olds. You may also find that it is necessary to utilize a different tact to teach the same skill to two players of the same age. A list of common developmental characteristics of different age groups is presented in Figure 4-1.

As Figure 4-1 illustrates, certain attributes are common to kids at each age level. Although individuals may differ in the rate at which they develop, the order of the stages does not vary:

- Infancy (birth to 2)
- Early childhood (ages 3-8)
- Middle childhood (ages 9-11)
- Early adolescence (ages 12-14)
- Middle adolescence (ages 15-18)

The key point to remember is that each stage is distinct. Each phase is characterized by abilities, attitudes, and priorities that tend to be qualitatively different from those preceding, as well as those following, it.

It is also important to be aware of the fact some needs and interests are universal to all children to help ensure their successful growth and development. Such a list encompasses a number of factors, including the following:

- Be accepted by individuals of different ages (peers and authority-figures, alike).
- Become increasingly independent.
- Experience a positive self-concept.
- Experience a sense of adventure.

Age (years)	Sensory and Motor Development	Cognitive Development	Physical Development	Suggestions for Coaching
3–5	Limited coordination and balance. Fine motor skills still developing.	Short attention span. Easily distracted. Not good at cooperation.	Growth rate slows: bodies start to grow taller and thinner.	Show them how to perform skills and activities. Keep instruction time short. Provide lots of fun activities.
6–9	Improved posture and balance.	Cooperation improves, but still have short attention span (1–5 minutes). Difficulty in remembering multiple instructions.	Longer arms and legs can give a gangly appearance. Enjoy testing muscle strength and skills.	Focus on fundamental skills. Keep rules and instructions simple. Teach verbally and visually in 20- to 30-minute increments.
10–11	Able to balance automatically, but this ability can decrease with the onset of puberty.	Improved concentration. Can follow multiple instructions.	Increased body strength. Improved coordination and reaction time.	Can offer verbal instructions for fundamental and advanced skills. Instruction time can be increased to 30–60 minutes.
12–14	May be awkward and clumsy due to rapidly increasing growth.	Begin to grasp abstract and symbolic concepts. Understand long-term consequences but often do not believe they will be affected by them.	Many teens experience a growth spurt between the ages of 11 and 14. Sexual characteristics begin developing.	Kids are acutely self-conscious and easily embarrassed at this age, so when possible, take them aside to offer correction and discipline.
15–18	Boys continue to develop strength and agility after puberty; girls tend to level out.	Gradually develop the ability to think in sophisticated, abstract ways. Have a better understanding of concepts like morality, consequence, objectivity, and empathy.	By 15, most girls have reached or are close to their adult height. In boys, the big growth spurt starts about two years after puberty.	This age group desires respect, autonomy, and leadership opportunities. Give them opportunities to run practices, develop and call plays, etc.

(© Dr. George Selleck; used by permission)

Figure 4-1. Developmental characteristics of different age groups

- Experience success in what they attempt to do.
- Give and receive attention.

In order to be as supportive as possible in the growth and development process of your athletes, it is absolutely essential that you are cognizant of certain fundamental points, including:

- Every child is unique and special.
- Children develop at their own pace.
- Each stage of development entails different markers.
- All developmental characteristics will not be observed in all kids at the same age or at the same stage of development.
- Age is not a perfect predictor of maturity (e.g., a task or activity that is well within the capability of one of your players may be too difficult to handle by another child of the same age).

- Growth can proceed at a different rate in various development areas within a particular child. For example, one of your players may be above average in his physical growth, but below average in his emotional or social growth.
- One size does not fit all. You may need to take a different approach to each developmental area in order to help a child reach his potential.
- Kids are *not* miniature adults.

UNDERSTANDING YOUR ATHLETES

Effective coaching begins with understanding. Understanding why you coach. Understanding what is the best approach for you to take to achieve your coaching-related goals. Understanding what your players need and expect from you as their coach. Understanding what's important to your athletes.

With regard to being aware, to a degree, of some of the basic attributes of your players, get to know them better. Talk to them and ask about their interests, their dreams, what excites them, what bugs them, etc. You could also try to better understand their culture, including their social and economic environment. Figure 4-2 provides an overview of several of the most relevant characteristics of the athletes you are likely to be coaching in our ever-evolving society. One of the most important takeaways from the list for you as a coach, is that your athletes are not the players your father may have coached. Over time, the world has not stood still and will not stand still. The times are changing ... and so should you.

Characteristic	Effect
Under more pressure to succeed	Stressed out, materialistic, and more likely to cheat to get ahead
More likely to be latch-key kids or come from single-parent families	Little experience with authority and structure and may rebel when you try to impose these things on them
Raised in a self-indulgent, child-oriented climate	Inflated sense of entitlement; expectation to be given things without working to earn them. For example, an athlete may expect to be named a starter just because he has been playing for a few years—even though younger players may have stronger skills.
Living in a fast-moving, turbulent society	Confusion, cynicism, apathy
Specializing in a single sport at increasingly younger age; participating in year-round seasons	Overuse injuries; burnout; may view sports as work (as opposed to fun)
Participate in sports that are almost always organized and supervised by adults	Fewer opportunities for kids to develop creativity and leadership qualities (adult-driven vs. child-driven)
More leisure-time opportunities (e.g., video games, computers)	Less active and easily bored

Figure 4-2. Characteristics of some athletes in today's society

SECTION II

PLANNING FOR SUCCESS

CHAPTER 5

WHAT DOES IT TAKE TO BE A GOOD COACH?

In reality, no two football coaches are exactly alike. For that matter, neither are any two football coaches whose programs are doing well. Sometimes, these differences are relatively subtle, on other occasions (think: Jim Harbaugh versus Bill Belichick), not so much. More important than how some successful coaches may seem to be dissimilar, however, is what coaches who are thriving in their role have in common … which is considerable. For example, most successful football coaches tend to share certain characteristics, including the following:

- Consistently behaves in a professional manner.
- Exhibits a "can-do" versus a "make-do" attitude.
- Realizes that perhaps his most important role as a coach is to be a difference-maker in the lives of his players.
- Knows that the best coaches are great teachers.
- Is able to handle both wins and losses with class.
- Is well-organized.
- Has realistic expectations of his players.
- Knows that one of a coach's major jobs is to make a player better than the athlete thinks he can be.
- Makes a concerted effort to ensure that his players understand the material he presents to them.
- Is fully cognizant of the fact that it is more important that he is respected by his players, than liked.
- Understands the importance of "character" in his players.
- Realizes that he often has to re-teach material in order to have it be learned.
- Knows that while he will not always get along with every one of his coaching colleagues, everyone must be tolerant and professional.
- Understands the value of soliciting feedback from his players.
- Is always looking to improve as a coach—every practice, every day, every season.

- Tries to make every meeting he has with a player or the team as time-efficient and productive as possible.
- Focuses on getting the most out of his team's practice time.
- Never equates activity with achievement.
- Knows how to motivate his players to get them to consistently play at a relatively high level.
- Pays great attention to detail.
- Works to develop certain factors in his players, including unity, pride, and total effort.
- Lets his assistant coaches know that he is always available to talk to them.
- Tries to help his assistant coaches, to the degree feasible, to achieve their coaching-related goals and objectives.
- Encourages every one of his assistant coaches to become "a student of the game."
- Undertakes a proactive approach with regard to ensuring that his players grasp the importance of doing well beyond football (athletic, academic, home-life).
- Makes sure that members of his staff have a clear understanding of what their on-field and off-field responsibilities are.
- Coaches his coaches (i.e., makes sure that every one of his assistants not only understands his duties, but can perform them in a manner that will lead to success).
- Knows that one of his major responsibilities is to develop his players to be leaders.
- Is a master teacher.
- Places an emphasis on special teams play.
- Understands the value of being prepared.
- Makes it clear to the parents of his players that he is fully aware that he is given responsibility for their most prized possession—their children.
- Enjoys being around and helping his players.
- Places the focus on the importance of the "team," rather than the individual.
- Knows that there is no substitute in life for truth, trust, and integrity.
- Spells out his expectations for each of his players.
- Develops a sense of authentic confidence in his players.
- Teaches his athletes to play with discipline and poise.
- Does not allow setbacks to detour him from what he believes.
- Is guided by a sound and well-thought-out philosophy.
- Knows that he is accountable for his actions.
- Is able to delegate responsibilities to members of his coaching staff.
- Demonstrates a level of persistence to keep the experience fun.
- Is able to overcome adversity.
- Periodically undertakes a probing self-inventory to self-assess whether his aspirations, visions, missions, priorities, and actions are where he wants them to be.
- Teaches the rules of the game to his players.
- Emphasizes the importance of not being penalized during the game.
- Teaches his players to respect one another as people, while also demanding effort and performance from each other.

- Is aware that his players are often a mirror of their coaches.
- Is a good communicator with his players.
- Knows that a player's mind has a vital effect on his performance.
- Is a good listener.
- Does whatever is necessary to ensure good communication between himself and his staff.
- Places great importance on staff togetherness.
- Knows that one of the best ways to take care of the big stuff that affects his program is to stress the "little" things (i.e., take care of the small stuff).
- Knows that being successful entails more than simply winning.
- Uses his time efficiently.
- Emphasizes player safety at all times.
- Makes sure that players' equipment fits properly.
- Knows the importance of avoiding turnovers.
- Emphasizes ball security in all three phases of the game—offense, defense, and special teams.
- Prepares his team to handle special situations during the game (e.g., red zone, goal line, etc.).
- Teaches his players to give effort at all times.
- Has a system for maintaining, servicing, and keeping track of all of the equipment for his program.
- Never allows his players to become dehydrated during either practices or games. Water is not a reward.
- Is aware that things will not always go as planned.
- Is able to make appropriate adjustments in his team's strategic plans, particularly at halftime.
- Is able to make difficult decisions.
- Solves problems.
- Is guided in everything he does by a strong set of personal values.
- Practices what he preaches.
- Has the ability and willpower to control his own behavior.
- Is committed to the process of being a lifelong learner.
- Is a critical thinker.
- Creates a team culture that facilitates teamwork and team spirit.
- Has a systematic plan in place for sound clock management during the game.
- Sees the "big picture."
- Is passionate about doing whatever he can to help his team be its best.
- Knows why he is coaching.
- Is aware of what he is trying to accomplish in his program.
- Loves coaching and loves football.

A GET-IT-DONE MOSAIC

Successful coaches can be viewed as mosaics—they possess a unique variety of traits, characteristics, insights, and acumen that collectively enable them to fulfill roles as coaches in a capable, competent, and caring manner. It is important to note while the specific mosaic of one individual may differ in both composition and configuration from another person's, which may result in them taking different approaches to handling similar issues, they both can thrive. In other words, no one size (mosaic) fits all scenarios.

Just as successful individuals can differ in a variety of ways, so can the situations in which coaches find themselves. Different demands, different challenges, different approaches to addressing them. As noted previously, regardless of the obstacles confronting you, an appropriate level of caring, passion, and preparation is essential to overcoming them. You may encounter any number of hurdles on your personal journey to becoming a good coach. Four of the more problematic areas are establishing standards and expectations for your athletes; communicating with your players; motivating your athletes; developing rapport with your players; and possibly coaching your own child. Each of these issues has its own set of challenges and nuances.

ESTABLISHING STANDARDS AND EXPECTATIONS FOR YOUR ATHLETES

When some people hear the words standards and expectations, they believe that they're interchangeable. They're not. To a youth football coach, a standard is a baseline bar that each of his players are to meet with regard to behavior or effort. An expectation, in contrast, denotes either how the coach anticipates something will turn out or how he would like it to.

☐ Standards

As a coach, standards are about knowing who you are, what's important to you, what's not, what your boundaries are, and what's tolerable. As a rule, setting and having standards can provide a variety of benefits, including the following:

- Set the tone for the program.
- Provide a basis for preparation and accountability.
- Enhance the understanding of everyone in the program (players and coaches) concerning what constitutes appropriate and acceptable behavior.
- Augment the ability of the coach to judge and make decisions about either behavioral- or performance-related issues.
- Furnish a framework for the coach to be better prepared to exert ethical leadership.

No single process for setting standards exists. What one coach deems appropriate, another may find unsuitable. While one coach may choose to engage his players to shape his program's standards, another may prefer to form them independently.

Standards are usually set in concert with the overall plan that a coach has established for his program. These standards must be consistent with the goals and objectives he has instituted. They must also be congruent with the values he holds dear for his players, as well as for himself.

☐ Expectations

One of the most effective steps that a coach can undertake to improve the behavior, ability to learn, and motivational level of his athletes is to set positive expectations for them. These expectations can also help serve as building blocks for the personal growth and development of each player. Over time, these expectations can become self-fulfilling prophecies.

☐ Standards vs. Expectations

The basic underlying difference between a standard and an expectations is illustrated in the following examples:

Making practice:

- Standard—missing more than "x" practices unexcused will bring a consequence.
- Expectation—with the exception of an excused absence, players are counted on to attend every practice.

On-the-field behavior:

- Standard—engaging in troubling actions (e.g., fighting with an opponent; being disrespectful to a game official; etc.) will result in "x" discipline.
- Expectation—it is presumed that players will conduct themselves in a positive manner.

Off-the-field behavior:

- Standard—performing in a way that is counter to the values-related goals and objectives of the program will result in "x" discipline.
- Expectation—all players should behave in a values-oriented fashion.

Being a team captain:

- Standard—in order to be a team captain, a player must meet specific criteria.
- Expectation—a team captain is expected to command the respect of others and act in the best interests of the team.

COMMUNICATING WITH YOUR PLAYERS

The ability to communicate effectively is one of the most indispensable skills any individual can have, including a youth football coach. Effective communication involves more than simply knowing what to say or the words to use. Less than 10 percent of communication is verbal.

Skillful communication can be accomplished in several different ways, including verbal communication (face-to-face, telephone), listening, writing, feedback, memory, and non-verbal communication. While all successful coaches don't communicate in exactly the same manner, almost all of them have the ability to employ most of these channels. Similarities also exist in the way capable communicators connect with each other. The following suggestions can help ensure that your message is conveyed properly and received, as well as understood, as you intended:

- ☐ Be a good listener. Listen to learn, not to defend.
- ☐ Be open-minded. Be willing to change your mind, based upon what you hear.
- ☐ Avoid coming across as a one-dimensional communicator. Be aware that effective communication runs in both directions.
- ☐ Keep your communication efforts simple. Don't meander or muddle your message by making it complicated. Know your audience.
- ☐ Be in the present. Don't mentally jump ahead to plan your reply.
- ☐ Get to the point. Be concise. Don't beat around the bush.
- ☐ Think before you speak. Organize your thoughts.
- ☐ Choose your words carefully. Use positive action words.
- ☐ Enunciate. Avoid sloppy diction.
- ☐ Use proper grammar. Don't diminish your ability to get your message across clearly and effectively.

- ☐ Be aware of the fact that much of your communication is wordless. Focus on the tone you use, how loudly you speak, your body language, etc.

- ☐ Use an appropriate level of formality or informality when communicating with your athletes. Given that you're the adult in this situation, act like it.

- ☐ Project success. Speak with the expectation of success. Remember that you don't just sound like you feel, you also tend to think the way you sound.

Verbally communicating with young athletes can present its own set of challenges—some of which are unique to this age group, others that are common to virtually all ages. Among the tips for communicating with kids are the following:

- Do what you can to ensure that your kids are looking directly at you when you're trying to communicate with them.
- Speak in a calm voice.
- Periodically, ask questions to players to check their understanding.
- Demonstrate, whenever possible, what you want the kids to do.
- Use a combination of praise and constructive criticism when correcting players. Begin with a positive statement, follow with constructive feedback, and end with encouragement.
- Correct only one factor at a time. Focus on the behavior or the skill that is the issue at hand.
- Avoid using "you," whenever possible; rather use "I" or "we" statements.
- Always exhibit respect for your audience (e.g., your athletes and their parents).

MOTIVATING YOUR ATHLETES

How to effectively motivate athletes is one of the most discussed, disputed, and vexing topics in sports. Every coach, including youth football coaches, only wishes that he had a "miracle wand" that could somehow motivate each of his athletes. Unfortunately, it doesn't exist.

Wand or not, one of the most important responsibilities of a youth football coach is to motivate athletes to buy into the vision that the coach has established for the team. It is the coach's job to create an environment in which players believe in what they're doing, believe in each other, and are willing to sacrifice for each other and the collective good of the team.

The core issue is understanding what a coach can do to establish such an environment. Although no single step or strategy exists for motivating every athlete, several factors can help you trigger desired attitudes and behaviors in your young athletes, including the following:

- ☐ *Learn what drives your players.* As noted previously, most young athletes typically play for one or more of three reasons— for fun, to be with their buddies, and to participate in a sport that they love. It is also important to remember that other factors can also have a motivational influence on an athlete, such as a strong desire to succeed or a deep-seated fear of failure.

- ☐ *Motivate through challenges.* As a rule, many individuals, including kids, tend to look within themselves for an "I-can-do-this attitude" when faced with adversity. For a coach, the key is to make every challenge positive and motivational, rather than a threat. A threat,

by its very nature, is negative and can lead to the athlete being preoccupied with the consequences of failing.

- [ ] *Treat each player as a unique individual.* Find out why he is playing youth football and what he wants to get out of the experience. Always keep in mind that the factors that motivate one athlete may be slightly different than those that inspire another.

- [ ] *Employ goal-setting.* Work with your athletes to set, strive for, and achieve a series of small wins (objectives) over the course of the season that can help turn the vision of the team, as well as their personal dreams, into a reality.

- [ ] *Handle circumstances in a constructive manner.* Encourage an atmosphere in which failure and mistakes are perceived by the players as a normal and necessary part of the learning process and are to be expected, grasped, and taken in stride.

- [ ] *Use recognition.* Let the players know when they give a significant effort, do their job, etc.

- [ ] *Be a model of motivation.* Show that you truly care about what is going on. Arguably, motivation begets motivation. Be aware that simply going through the motions is one of the surest ways to dampen player excitement.

- [ ] *Be a salesman.* Sell your athletes on the values you hold dear, including hard work, the pursuit of excellence, the necessity of sacrifice, etc. Help your players understand the what, how, and why something is worthwhile to them, to their teammates, and for the program.

- [ ] *Be positive.* Focus on the good in your athletes. Look for opportunities, rather than obstacles. Care about the needs and interests of your players. Help unleash the hidden potential that exists within every kid.

DEVELOPING RAPPORT WITH YOUR PLAYERS AND THEIR PARENTS

Rapport is typically defined as a state of harmonious understanding with another individual or group of people that tends to help make communication easier and more effective, as well as to help make a positive connection. On occasion, rapport happens naturally. In those instances, you "hit it off" or "get along well," often because common ground exists.

Rapport, however, can also be built when encountering new people (e.g., your athletes and their parents), even if sufficient common ground may not be present. As a rule, you can develop it by the things you do. Fortunately, the actions required of you aren't all that difficult to undertake. It is also important to remember that rapport is not something that can occur by announcement.

Building rapport can be hard work. You should not assume that your players or their parents will have a meaningful connection with you or respect you simply because you are the coach. All factors considered, you need to be positive. Desire a positive relationship with your athletes and their parents, develop an understanding of what you can do to make those circumstances happen, and then execute your play to help turn your expectations into a reality.

- [ ] Rapport with your players

Several good reasons exist for you to work on establishing rapport with your athletes, including the following:

- Enhanced level of motivation. As a rule, players who feel rapport with their coaches are much more likely to be more motivated.
- Enhanced level of comfort. Athletes tend to be more engaged, open, and frank with coaches with whom they have rapport. They also are better able to communicate with them.
- Enhanced level of satisfaction and trust. Athletes who have rapport with their coaches are more supportive of the program, feel better about their participation in the program, and tend to have more trust in their coaches.

Once you decide to establish rapport with your players, you have a variety of steps that can be helpful. Among the more effective factors are the following:

- Show respect. You must exhibit respect for your players, the team, and how you handle your role as a coach.
- Have a caring attitude. You must care about your athletes, not only as players, but also as individuals.
- Be approachable. You must create an environment in which your players feel comfortable in approaching you directly.
- Have integrity. You must be someone your athletes perceive as being someone who has unwavering adherence to moral and ethical principles.
- Be positive. You must exhibit a level of passion, enthusiasm, and confidence in everything you do.

☐ Rapport with the parents of your players

View parents as your allies and an important part of the team. Although a few of them, on occasion, will not understand why their child is not playing more or is playing in a less-prominent position than one they would prefer, there are things you can do to help them be a positive force in your program. This includes the following:

- Let parents know that you are aware of your responsibility of taking care of one of the most valuable things in their life—the welfare of their child.
- Let the parents know what to expect with regard to how you coach, what the program entails, and the role they can anticipate their child having on the team. This is typically communicated in a pre-season letter or email or in a pre-season meeting. Let the parents know why and how you do things (e.g., disciplinary matters).
- Let parents know how they can help ensure that their child's participation in youth football is positive.
- Have an open-door policy. Encourage parents to share their concerns with you. Be a good listener. Never forget that they probably know a whole lot more about their child than you do.
- Keep parents in the loop. Let them know when their child is doing well or is experiencing problems.
- Employ appropriate body language. Certain non-verbals can have a significant impact on creating and maintaining rapport, such as body positioning, eye contact, facial expressions, and tone of voice.
- Be an ambassador. Be passionate and positive. Learn parents' names. Greet them with a smile and a handshake. Whenever appropriate, express your gratitude to them for their support and involvement, particularly allowing their child to play.

COACHING YOUR OWN CHILD

Coaching a youth football team can be challenging. When your own child is playing on your team, this demanding task can become even more difficult. If you decide to coach your child, you need to try to understand what that situation will entail for both of you. The following tips can help foster a great experience:

- ☐ *Get the input of your child first.* Before deciding to become your child's coach, ask him to help you compile a list of positives and negatives about the possibility.

- ☐ *Separate the coach and parent roles.* Create an environment that minimizes any potential emotional conflict or confusion with regard to these two roles.

- ☐ *Take off your coach's hat at home.* When you're a parent, be a parent. Provide unconditional love and support. Try to refrain from bringing something that happened on the practice field or in games home. Try to talk about things other than football.

- ☐ *Be prepared.* Be aware that just because you're a good parent, doesn't mean that you'll be a good coach. Do you know the game? Do you know how to teach it? Will you be able to provide a positive experience?

- ☐ *Be fair and equal at all times.* Avoid giving preferential treatment to your child. Don't be overly tough in an attempt to prove that you're not playing favoritism.

- ☐ *Communicate openly and honestly with the other parents.* When dealing with team issues (whether they involve your child or not), handle those situations quickly, ethically, and responsibly. Use your moral code to guide you.

- ☐ *Reflect on what you do and how you do it.* When in doubt, ask yourself when dealing with your child, if what you're doing is what you would do if this player was someone else's child.

Over and above the challenges inherent in coaching your child in youth football, there are also several benefits that coaches can gain from the experience, including:

- ☐ You'll have the opportunity to spend more time with your child. Ideally, the experience will entail a treasure trove of fun and happy memories.

- ☐ You'll forge new skills. You will gain an appreciation for what it's like to coach a group of kids and you'll also serve as a role model for your child outside of your comfort zone.

- ☐ You'll gain a sense of pride and accomplishment. If you coach for the right reasons and in the right manner, you'll achieve personal gratification and satisfaction, knowing you've had a positive impact on the development and life of your own child (as well as others).

- ☐ You'll experience the joys of coaching. The No. 1 reason kids give for playing football is because it's fun. In a very similar vein, so is coaching. As a coach, you'll take great pleasure in a job well done, as well as being a difference-maker.

COACHING NOTES

- ☐ Understand that participation in sport has been linked to a variety of positive outcomes. The type of coach you are will determine how strong these outcomes appear.

- ☐ Be aware that a variety of steps can be undertaken to better relate to your players and their parents. These things may entail some extra time and effort on your part, but the end result will be well worth it.

- ☐ Recognize that the ability to communicate effectively is one of the cornerstones of being a good coach. You need to master the art and practice of skillful communication.

- ☐ Accept the fact that kids have changed over the years. These are not your father's players. In fact, they probably don't have as much in common with the kids you grew up with as you would otherwise expect or would like. Tailor your communication and motivational approaches to the present times.

- ☐ Know that coaching your own child has its own set of inherent challenges and obstacles. You need to understand that, as a coach, maintaining a positive parent-child relationship is not completely under your control.

- ☐ Be cognizant of the fact that kids are not miniature adults. They differ physically, anatomically, physiologically, mentally, emotionally, and socially. Their world view is different. Being a good coach requires you to be aware that these differences exist and to adapt your approach to coaching appropriately.

CHAPTER 6

WHAT DOES IT TAKE TO BE A GOOD TEACHER?

Some youth football coaches seem to be naturally effective teachers. Others have to constantly strive to improve their teaching skills. Regardless of which group you feel best represents you, it is virtually impossible to overstate the importance of teaching. As legendary former UCLA basketball coach John Wooden once stated, "If you can't teach, you can't motivate. If you can't motivate, you can't coach."

A football coach who is a great teacher is someone his former players will remember and cherish. Great teachers inspire their athletes to give a maximum effort, to never settle for less than their best, and to be all that they can be. Great teachers have a long-lasting impact on the lives of their players.

THE QUALITIES OF AN EFFECTIVE TEACHER

Over the years, considerable discussion and debate has been undertaken concerning the key traits of a good teacher. There are numerous qualities that enable an individual to be an effective teacher. Every teacher is different. Each has a unique blend of qualities. On the other hand, every good teacher, to a degree, tends to possess a combination of some or all of the following traits:

- ☐ Accountability. You hold yourself to a relatively high set of standards and expectations.
- ☐ Adaptability. You are willing and able to change as circumstances dictate.
- ☐ Caring. You are fond of your players and try to do whatever you can to help them succeed.
- ☐ Creativity. You do whatever you can to teach in a manner that is engaging and effective.
- ☐ Dedication. You devote the necessary time and effort to help ensure that the teaching process provides each of your players the best opportunity to learn.
- ☐ Determination. You are committed to reach (teach) all of your athletes, no matter the challenges and barriers.

- ☐ Empathy. You can relate to the fact that not every child learns at the same rate. Some athletes may require more effort on your part.
- ☐ Engaging. You are able to teach in a manner that is fun, fresh, and productive.
- ☐ Evolving. You continuously look for ways to improve the skills in your teaching toolbox.
- ☐ Fearless. You are willing to think outside the box and try anything, within reason, to be a better teacher. You are virtually immune to criticism.
- ☐ Generosity. You are willing to donate your time and energy to help out wherever a need is recognized.
- ☐ Inspirational. You have the ability to get your players to buy into what you're asking them to do, as well as become what you want to be (as individuals). You are capable of making a lasting impact on your athletes.
- ☐ Joyful. You have a positive attitude, which is reflected by the good mood and sense of enthusiasm you exhibit every day.
- ☐ Kindness. You have a kind nature, disposition, and spirit.
- ☐ Knowledge. You have a thorough grasp of what you're teaching.
- ☐ Organization. You have a systematic plan for your team (of which the teaching process is an integral part) to which you adhere. You have clear objectives concerning what you teach.
- ☐ Passion. You love what you do and do everything feasible to be a good teacher.
- ☐ Patience. You see the whole picture, and feel that sometimes learning is a marathon, rather than a sprint. You never give up on your players.
- ☐ Resilience. You don't let adversity stop you from achieving your teaching goals.
- ☐ Resourceful. You find ways to make things happen, regardless of the circumstances.
- ☐ Trustworthy. You have the ability to get others around you (e.g., your players and their parents) to believe in you and what you are doing.

BEGIN AT THE BEGINNING

For every group of athletes you will coach, roughly one-third are going to "get it," virtually no matter what you do. They're talented, self-disciplined, and self-motivated, and even if you are one of the worst coaches in the world, they probably would still perform relatively well. A smaller group of players—two or three, for example—will never get on board with what you're doing. In the middle, however, is that larger group of athletes who could go either way, depending on your actions. It's that group you need to really concentrate on, because the bulk of your success, as a teacher, will come from these athletes.

How do you reach that group? You need to start from where they are—not from where you think they should be or from where you want them to be. For example, if the majority of your youth football players do not have a firm grasp of the fundamentals—blocking, tackling—then it won't do any good to start off with diagramming plays, no matter how strongly you believe they should have already learned the fundamentals before playing for you. You need to begin where your players *are* (needing help with the fundamentals) before you bring them up to where you want them to *be* (knowing how to execute plays from your playbook).

LEARNING STYLES

Effective coaches recognize that teaching sport skills to young athletes involves more than just showing them what to do and having them do it. Players learn in a variety of ways, and a teaching method that works for one person won't necessarily work for another. The four main learning styles that you need to be aware of are visual, auditory, kinesthetic, and combination.

☐ *The Visual Learner*

For the visual learner, learning is most effective when presented visually. Visual teaching techniques include using demonstrations, utilizing visual aids (e.g., videos, pictures, charts), or visually highlighting important aspects of the surrounding environment (such as when a football coach points to the numbers on a player's jersey and says passes should hit the receiver in the numbers). Consider the following tips for visually demonstrating a skill:

- Make sure everyone can see what you're doing.
- Perform the skill slowly, then at full speed.
- Focus on the key points of the movement.
- Have your athletes practice the skill immediately after the demonstration.
- Encourage athletes to practice the skill mentally.
- Provide feedback that is clear, positive, and specific.

☐ *The Auditory Learner*

For the auditory learner, learning is most effective when information is spoken and heard, as in lectures, group discussions, or audiotapes. Verbal guidance (telling players what to do) is usually used in conjunction with visual guidance (showing players what to do). Perhaps the only time you can get away with using verbal guidance alone is when you are working with an exceptional player or players who have played the sport for a long time.

When you offer verbal guidance to a player, you need to make sure your instructions are:

- Clear
- Accurate
- Precise
- Relevant
- Simple
- Highlighting the important cues of the skill

To make sure you are getting your verbal message across, ask thought-provoking questions and insist on thoughtful answers. Encourage your players to think for themselves by:

- Giving them "think time." For example, say, "I'm going to ask all of you a question and I'm going to give you a minute to think about your answer, before I call on you."
- Asking more "why" and open-ended questions.
- Asking your players to respond to others' questions (e.g., "Tom, what do you think about what Sam just said?").
- Calling on the players who don't raise their hands, as well as the ones who do.

☐ *The Kinesthetic Learner*

For the kinesthetic learner, learning is most effective when it's "hands-on" (i.e., physical demonstrations). This style is sometimes called "manual" teaching. Manual teaching involves using your body or a mechanical object to aid the athlete. For instance, a youth football coach might hold his extended hand over the backside of one of his offensive linemen who is trying to get into his stance, in order to reinforce the instructional directive that he

shouldn't extend his rear too far upward. The main advantages to using manual teaching methods are that they help build the athlete's confidence and reduce fear about performing poorly. They can also help athletes improve their timing and develop special skills. On the other hand, the potential exists that athletes could come to rely too much on manual assistance and—like a child who refuses to have the training wheels removed from his bicycle—fear the thought of performing without assistance. Performing a skill with manual assistance doesn't necessarily give the athlete correct feedback about the forces that would normally be acting on the body. Thus, the feedback the athlete is receiving could be incorrect and could lead to bad habits in the future.

☐ *The Combination Learner*

For the combination learner, learning is most effective when it is presented in a combination of visual/kinesthetic/auditory methods—such as explaining a play verbally, then diagramming it, and subsequently having the athletes perform it. While it's impossible to tailor your teaching to fully meet everyone's learning style, striving for a balance of instructional methods will help ensure that all of your players are learning enough to keep them interested and engaged in the process.

THE LIFEBLOOD OF LEARNING

Mistakes are part of learning. Without an understanding of the fact that making mistakes is a natural part of the game and learn from them, athletes may never reach their potential. Making mistakes, however, is often a painful process that must be handled carefully by the coach for athletes to turn their mistakes into learning tools. Coaches who rip into their athletes when a mistake is made not only embarrass the athlete, but they also demean themselves.

When you see an athlete make a mistake, give him immediate encouragement. In this instance, the following principle applies: If you are sure the athlete knows how to correct the mistake, encouragement alone is sufficient. To tell an athlete what he already knows can be more counterproductive than helpful.

On the other hand, if the athlete doesn't know how to correct the mistake, then you need to provide constructive, corrective instruction. Be encouraging and positive. Don't focus on the bad thing that just happened. Focus instead on the good things that will happen if the athlete follows your instructions. Your instructions should contain the following three elements:

- Start with a compliment. "Way to hustle. You really went after the ballcarrier."

- Give the future-oriented instruction or correction. "If you stay on balance, I know you will be able to contain the running back next time."

- End with another positive statement. "Hang in there! You're working hard. It will pay off for you!"

This technique is called giving your player a "positive sandwich" (two positive communications wrapped around the instruction). Such statements are designed to make the athlete positively motivated to perform correctly rather than negatively motivated to avoid failure and disapproval.

STRATEGIES FOR GOOD TEACHING

All factors considered, a lot is known about the characteristic of good teachers. Without question, the issue is relatively complex; however, many of

the traits that may be very effective in one situation may be less operative in another. The combination of attributes that cause one youth football coach to be a capable teacher in one set of circumstances may not be as potent in another. In other words, the "best way" to teach has yet to be identified.

Efforts to better understand the "essential nature of learning," however, have identified core teaching principles that help ensure the success of a coach's teaching endeavors. The following suggestions can make how you teach more effective:

- ☐ Establish the relevance of the content. Explain why the players need to understand and master the material. Craft a teaching strategy that will enable the athletes to learn.
- ☐ Help your athletes feel that they can successfully learn the material. Don't make the subject seem more demanding than it is.
- ☐ Utilize the power of feedback to motivate them to learn. Be constructive. Be positive. Allow your athletes to demonstrate what they've learned in different ways.
- ☐ Establish clear goals for the teaching. Tell your athletes up front what they will learn and explain how it will outline their responsibilities.
- ☐ Create an environment in which learning is most likely to thrive. Just as all learners are not the same, neither should be your teaching methods.
- ☐ Grow as you go. Learn what works for you as a teacher and what doesn't. Be open to adapting and adjusting your approach to become a better teacher. Coaches evolve. What worked for you as a teacher last season may not be as effective this year. Circumstances change. So must you. Progress involves extending your comfort zone.

COACHING NOTES

- ☐ Be aware of the fact that communication and teaching go hand-in-hand.
- ☐ Accept the fact that it's one thing to know how to do something; it's another thing to be able to teach it effectively.
- ☐ No game was ever won by what the coach knows; rather, it's what his players have learned.
- ☐ The better you prepare and present material to be taught, the easier it will be for your athletes to learn.
- ☐ Create a learning environment in which your athletes understand that learning is a process and that mistakes are a natural and integral part of that process.
- ☐ Demonstrate an understanding and in-depth knowledge of the material you are teaching and convey it to your athletes in a way that facilitates learning.

CHAPTER 7

WHAT IS INVOLVED IN BUILDING A COACHING STAFF?

The importance of having a good staff cannot be overemphasized. As the leader of a youth football program, you are responsible for a variety of tasks. To help ensure that these are done right, surround yourself with competent assistants. Accordingly, you need to be diligent in determining how you build your coaching staff.

Such an effort requires systematic planning on your part. As part of your plan, know how many assistants you'd like to have, what qualities you would like your assistants to possess, where you might be able to find these assistants, what steps you will take to locate them, and what you anticipate doing to help ensure they have the insight and skill to teach young athletes. Once you've identified your assistants, decide what their on-the-field and off-the-field duties will be and what you plan to do to make your staff a cohesive group.

HOW MANY ASSISTANTS?

The number of assistants you have will depend on a variety of factors. For example, does your team's league limit the number of assistant coaches you may have? How difficult will it be to find individuals who are willing to *volunteer* their time and energy to be an assistant coach? From a philosophical basis, is there an upper limit on the number of assistant coaches that you'd like to have? How many assistant coaches would you feel comfortable managing?

WHAT QUALITIES WOULD YOU LIKE YOUR ASSISTANTS TO HAVE?

Given the fact that when you select your assistants, you're building your "team," you need to choose them wisely. Rather than viewing the process of

building your staff as a torturous hardship, regard it as an opportunity to make your program better. To paraphrase Jim Collins in his best-selling book, *Good to Great*, your underlying objective in this regard is to get "the right people in the right seats on the bus."

Who are the right people? The answer to this question is straightforward: obtain the "best" possible assistants for your program. To a degree, your options for someone being a part of your staff will depend on your circumstances. How many coaches will you have? How qualified are they? Have written a description of each assistant coaching position you want to have?

Ideally, you know what attributes you want in your assistants. For example, you want your assistants to know the sport. Not only would you like your assistants to be proficient in the technical aspects of the game (e.g., skills and fundamentals), you should also prefer that they have a working knowledge of the strategic facets of the game (e.g., the tactics). It is essential that your assistants are good teachers and that their teaching and coaching style is consistent with yours.

In addition, your assistants should possess strong moral character (e.g., integrity, honesty, trustworthiness, loyalty, respectful, etc.), as well as have social values that are consistent with yours. Values such as being team-oriented, having a resolute work ethic, being punctual, being committed/dedicated, etc. are examples of traits that you might like your assistants to have.

HOW CAN YOU FIND ASSISTANTS?

Once you decide how many assistant coaches you are looking for and what characteristics you want them to possess, your next step is to develop a strategy for finding them. There are several sources into which you might tap, including the following:

- Coaches who are currently on the staff
- Someone your existing coaches might know
- Parents of your current or former players
- Someone from the physical education staff at a local elementary or middle school
- A contact from the league in which your team plays
- A contact from the staff of sports reporters at your local newspaper
- Someone from one or more of the local high school programs
- Colleagues who love football and enjoy working with kids

WHAT STEPS SHOULD YOU TAKE ONCE YOU IDENTIFY SOMEONE TO BE YOUR ASSISTANT?

Having determined whom you would like to be a member of your staff, your next step might be to interview them (ideally in person). Share your expectations for them in their role on your staff. It can also be helpful if you share your coaching philosophy to make certain that they are comfortable with it.

HOW CAN YOU INFORM YOUR NEW ASSISTANTS?

Once you've identified your assistants, determine what you need them to know about your program and how you might share that information. The following tools can be helpful:

- Policies and procedures with a code of ethics for staff and parents
- A playbook for each of the team's units (offense, defense, special teams)
- Casual staff meetings
- One-on-one meetings with you (as the head coach)

HOW CAN RESPONSIBILITY BE DELEGATED AMONG ASSISTANTS?

Being a head coach is a big job. It is essential that you delegate as many responsibilities as you reasonably can to your staff. You also need to hold your assistants accountable for what they have been assigned to do. It is important that your assistants are aware of what is expected of them.

One common area of delegation involves assigning responsibility for coaching the players who are part of the offense, defense, and special teams. An assistant may be assigned one or more of the following position groups:

- ☐ Offense:
  - Quarterbacks
  - Running backs
  - Receivers
  - Offensive line
- ☐ Defense:
  - Defensive line
  - Linebackers
  - Defensive backs
- ☐ Special Teams:
  - Kicking game (general)
  - Coverage game
  - Return game

Each phase of the game also may need a coordinator.

On occasion, assistants also assume responsibility for a variety of non-coaching duties, such as:

- Inventorying and maintaining the equipment
- Scouting (for older teams)
- Practice and game field maintenance
- Scheduling
- Sports medicine
- Organizing meetings
- Organizing and conducting team social events

For the good of young athletes, USA Football recommends youth football organizations have all coaches certified through its Heads Up Football program. Created by USA Football, Heads Up Football establishes important evidence-based practices through a comprehensive approach to teach and play the sport. The American College of Sports Medicine, the American Medical Society for Sports Medicine, and the National Athletic Trainers' Association, among other leaders in athletics and medicine, support this education-based program.

Heads Up Football instructs coaches on health and safety protocols, as well as on on-field fundamentals, including:

- Proper equipment fitting
- CDC concussion recognition and response
- Sudden cardiac arrest protocols
- Heat preparedness and hydration protocols from the Korey Stringer Institute
- Shoulder tackling and blocking

To learn more about Heads Up Football and to enroll into the program, visit www.usafootball.com/headsup.

HOW CAN YOU FACILITATE GOOD HEAD COACHING/STAFF COMMUNICATION?

One of the most important things you can do as a head coach is to invite free and open communication between yourself and your assistants. Failure to do this can stifle the exchange of ideas and information; make assistants feel that their opinions don't matter; and discourage the process of free-thinking.

As the head coach, you can foster strong communication among your staff in the following ways:

- Encourage a nurturing atmosphere for the staff to develop the best solutions and answers.
- Encourage free-thinking in every area.
- Make it clear that there is no such thing as a "dumb" question, answer, or suggestion.
- Show confidence and pride in your assistants, instilling a culture that they all help make the team successful.
- Make an effort to stamp out miscommunication.

COACHING NOTES

☐ Have a defined process for building your staff.
☐ Think outside the box when searching for assistants.
☐ Consider assistants' ability to teach.
☐ Establish a clear accountability process.
☐ Establish and maintain two-way communication with your staff.
☐ Be aware that one of your responsibilities is to help your assistants evolve and grow as coaches.

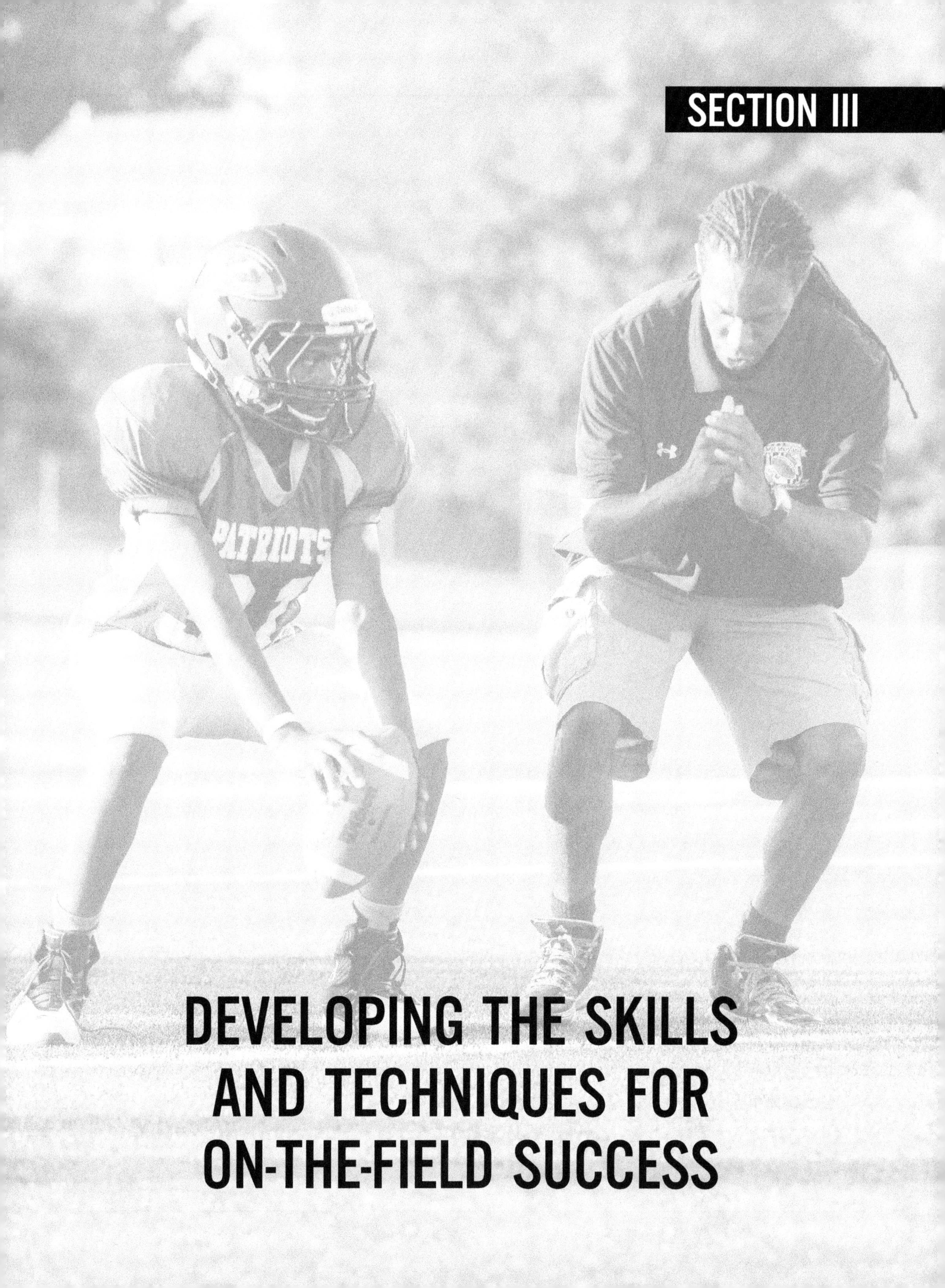

SECTION III

DEVELOPING THE SKILLS AND TECHNIQUES FOR ON-THE-FIELD SUCCESS

CHAPTER 8

SPORT-SPECIFIC SKILLS AND TECHNIQUES

At its very essence, football requires that players master two basic skills—tackling and blocking. USA Football is at the forefront of the effort to help ensure that these two skills are taught safer and more effectively on high school and youth levels. This chapter details the basic fundamentals that are involved in each technique and includes drills to help players develop these skills.

TACKLING

The Basic Fundamentals

It is vital that players on defense develop the ability to tackle safer and smarter. For some, the skill may be learned relatively easily. For others, mastering the techniques may be more of a challenge. USA Football recommends that every youth coach teaches his players to perfect the following five basic fundamentals of tackling.

- *Breakdown.* The foundational starting point for all movements and drills
- *Swoop.* Coming to balance prior to contact
- *Near foot.* Having correct body posture at the moment of impact. The head and eyes are up, while using the front of the shoulder as the point of contact.
- *Uppercuts.* With the head to the side and out of the contact zone, the defender should throw double-uppercuts and grab cloth on the back of the jersey to secure the tackle.
- *Shoot.* Exploding through the hips to generate power, the defender performs an ascending tackle.

The following overviews detail how each element should be taught:

☐ *Breakdown:*

This fundamental is where all athletic movements begin. It should be taught by utilizing a sequential four-element process:

- *Feet.* Have the players stomp their feet shoulder-width apart, setting a solid base from which to work. Their weight should be on the balls of their feet.
- *Squeeze.* Emphasize a big chest, as the players squeeze their shoulders back, which will help produce a flat back.
- *Sink.* Bend at the knees to get into a strong athletic position. Keep the back straight, the shoulders over the knees, and the knees over the toes.
- *Hands.* Bring the hands out front, ready to go— nice and relaxed.

Each player should have his knees bent, his feet shoulder-width apart, and his upper body in a 45-degree forward lean. His chin and eyes should be up, and his weight on the balls of his feet—not on the toes.

☐ *Swoop:*

Defenders need to cover ground in order to run down the offensive player with the ball and make the tackle. Once they get in position to make the tackle, they need to come to balance and regain the necessary low-pad level. Teaching this aspect of tackling involves three directions:

- After running a few yards in open field, have the defenders take quick, choppy steps to bring their body under control, while continuing to gain ground toward the ballcarrier.
- Once the defender is within striking distance of the ballcarrier, have the defender widen his base and sink his hips, while regaining a good football position as contact nears.
- As the moment of contact nears, have the defender lead with his left or right foot, depending on which side he has leverage, to align same foot, same shoulder.

☐ *Near Foot:*

After closing on the ballcarrier, have the defender take a short, downhill power step, which establishes the leverage and power a tackler needs at impact. Teaching this aspect of tackling involves three directions:

- Start the defender in a balanced stance, with a bend in both knees.
- Have the defender keep his head and eyes up, with his shoulders square to contact. His back should be flat, with his spine in line.
- On the coach's command, have the defender step with either his right or left foot, depending on which side he has leverage. He should step forward with the foot to the same side contact will be made.

☐ *Uppercuts:*

Once contact is made with the shoulder, have the players uppercut—not wrap—to secure the ballcarrier and being taking him to the ground. Teaching this aspect of tackling involves three directions:

- To practice this element, have the defender set up in front of a horizontally held bag with a right- or left-foot lead, as if the near foot fundamental has already been performed.
- Have the players forcefully club both arms in an uppercut motion, with their thumbs up and their elbows down.
- After the uppercut, have the defenders secure the tackle by grabbing cloth (the back of the ballcarrier's jersey). His elbows should be tight to the ballcarrier's side.

Tacklers should be made to run through the uppercuts for five yards in order to accentuate the need to finish the tackle.

☐ *Shoot:*

The player's power should come from his hips. Young athletes should be taught how to tap into that power source by exploding open and upward through the hips to make contact, with his explosiveness grounded in the strength of his core (trunk, hips, abdominals). Teaching this aspect of tackling involves three directions:

- Starting from a kneeling position in front of a bag or other soft surface, have the defenders keep the laces of their shoes on the ground to ensure that their power is coming from their hips, not jumping.
- At the coach's command, have the players sink and then shoot to drive from their hips.
- While driving open and up, have the defender throw double-uppercuts in order to bring their hips through the motion and generate additional power.

As players advance in their level of proficiency, coaches can stand in front of the bag and flash a number of fingers, while the players are performing the drill. Athletes call out the numbers to ensure their spines are in alignment and their heads are up and their eyes are open.

Tackling Drills

Once your players understand and can perform the five fundamentals of tackling, your next step is to identify and implement developmental drills to teach the skill in action. The following four drills are designed to be performed in phases—initially against an imaginary ballcarrier (i.e., against air), then against bags or another soft surface, and finally progressing to player-on-player contact, according to USA Football's nationally endorsed youth football practice guidelines (Appendix B).

☐ *Leverage Drill:*

Leverage is a key element in tackling. It puts the defender in the strongest position to bring a ballcarrier to the ground. Through leverage, players can create beneficial angles from which to initiate contact and make a tackle. You can teach your players how to establish leverage with the following drill:

- Starting from a proper two-point stance and with an appropriate amount of distance for the player's skill level, have the defensive players change speeds appropriately—shuffle, run and gather, sprint, stop and go—to practice closing the space on a ballcarrier and staying in alignment with the near hip.
- Have each defender keep his near foot and near shoulder closest to the ballcarrier's target hip slightly forward, while closing the distance to declare proper leverage and force the offensive player in one direction.
- Once the defender is within the contact zone, have the defender swoop to near foot and maintain a strong base and ensure that his footwork remains under control, while striking with the same foot and same shoulder.

* Through leverage, defensive players can target a ballcarrier's hip from anywhere on the field, while covering ground and maintaining the proper position to close cutback lanes and gain the advantage on contact.

☐ *Form Tackle Drill:*

A form tackle is a traditional leverage tackle, with a near foot and near shoulder strike to a contact point above the waist of the ballcarrier. You can teach your players how to execute a form tackle with the following drill:

- Starting close to the ballcarrier and already in a swoop-and-near-foot position, have the defender target the near pec of the ballcarrier's as the strike point.

- With his head and eyes up, have the defender keep his spine in line, while maintaining a strong posture, which allows the defender to transfer power into the opponent from a near foot position.

- Have the defender perform a strong shoot and uppercuts into the ballcarrier, which will allow the defender to grab cloth, secure the tackle, and reverse the ballcarrier's momentum.

- Finish the drill by having the defender drive his feet through contact to take the ballcarrier backward.

* After players develop an understanding of tackling from close quarters, you can add some distance between the defender and the ballcarrier to work on doing multiple skills within a form tackle.

☐ *Thigh-and-Drive Tackle Drill:*

For shoulder tackles with a target area below the waist, it is important that defenders maintain leverage with a near foot and near shoulder position. Often referred to as "eyes through the thighs," this lower strike zone targets the area between the player's hips and the knees.

- Starting from a near foot kneeling, and slightly offset position, have the defenders strike through the near thigh.

- Consider putting a marker (e.g., a sticker or piece of tape) on the bag or soft contact surface you are using to represent the ballcarrier's thigh level.

- Have the defenders punch their arms around the legs (bag) to wrap and squeeze, trapping the legs together.

- Have the tackler drive through the legs of the offensive player, while maintaining a strong posture and keeping his head up to take the ballcarrier to the ground.

* After players develop an understanding of how to tackle from their knees, you can raise them up on their feet from close quarters, eventually adding some distance between the defender and ballcarrier to work on doing multiple skills within a thigh-and-drive tackle.

☐ *Thigh-and-Roll Tackle Drill*

This below-the-waist shoulder tackle is just like the thigh-and-drive, only, in this instance, the defender is finishing off with a roll to the leverage side in order to bring the ballcarrier to the ground.

- Starting from a near foot kneeling, slightly offset position, have the defender strike through the near thigh.

- Consider putting a marker (e.g., a sticker or piece of tape) on the bag or the soft contact surface you are using to represent the ballcarrier's thigh level.

- Have the defender punch his arms around the legs (bag) to wrap and squeeze, trapping the legs together.

- Have the defender always roll to his leverage side, winding up on top.

- After players develop an understanding of how to tackle from their knees, you can raise them up on their feet from close quarters, eventually adding some distance between the defender and the ballcarrier to work on doing multiple skills within a thigh-and-roll tackle.

BLOCKING

Blocking is one of the most basic skills in football—one that every player needs to be taught. USA Football recommends teaching a blocking technique that is designed to help foster safer play, properly engaging with a defender, driving with the legs, and maintaining correct body position, while reducing helmet-to-helmet contact. USA Football breaks down this skill into five basic elements:

- *Stance*. The foundational platform for all blocks off the line
- *Get off*. The initial two steps for all blocks—a short positional step, followed by the contact step
- *Strike*. Explosive contact with the hands, front of the shoulder, upper arm, or forearm—not the head
- *Stick*. Rolling the hips into the defender, while staying low and taking away space
- *Finish*. Short, strong power steps to take the defender backward

The following overviews detail how each element should be taught.

☐ *Stance:*

Whether starting in a two- or three-point stance, have the players begin in a solid, fundamental position to perform a correct block. Line the players up in rows or straight across. Have players exaggerate their movements to ensure that they have both the knowledge and the feeling of what being in a proper stance looks and feels like. Teach the stance as follows:

- *Feet*. Have the players stomp their feet to get them comfortably shoulder-width apart.
- *Slide*. Have the players slide their foot on the same side of the body, where the hand will go down (for a three-point stance), back to the instep of the lead foot.
- *Squeeze*. Have the players bring their shoulder blades back and lock them into the correct posture.
- *Sink*. Have the players bend at the waist and knees to come down with forearms on thigh pads.

* Take your time between each command to ensure that the players are complying with your instructions.

☐ *Get-off:*

The first two steps that a blocker takes can be the difference between success and failure. No matter what blocks are utilized in your team's scheme, the initial footwork is the same. Teach the get-off as follows:

- From a proper three-point stance, have the player keep his head up and backside down.
- On your command, have the blocker take two short quick steps from heel to instep, about four to six inches each.
  ▸ The first step should be either setting the angle of contact or an up-and-down timing step.
  ▸ The second step should land before contact and should be in the direction in which the blocker is going.
- Keeping a wide base and a flat back, make sure that the blocker's head remains up through the motion, with both of his feet on the ground before contact.

* Once players have mastered a straight-on block, adjust the drill to block at a 45-degree angle or open up into another type of block.

☐ *Strike:*

It is critical that young athletes learn how to make initial contact on a block with their hands, as opposed to using their helmets. For this drill, have players begin as if they have already come out of their stance and have executed a correct get-off. Accordingly, from a two-point stance, teach the strike as follows:

- Staying tight inside, with their thumbs up and their elbows in, have the players strike inside the opponent's body, below the base of the shoulder pads.

- Have the players finish the block, with their hands above their eyes so that they aren't standing up on contact. Their elbows should stay bent, not extended.

- As a blocker strikes, look to see if the defender (or the player holding the bag) rises. The goal is to lift the defender's chest with pad-under-pad, raising the defender's center of gravity and gaining control.

* The action of striking should be explosive and powerful. The same drill can also be used to teach initial contact with the front of the shoulder, upper arm, and forearm—but never with the head.

☐ *Stick:*

Once initial contact is established, blockers should then look to set the block by rolling their hips into the defender, while staying low and taking away space. Teach the stick as follows:

- Have the blocker start with his arms extended and his hands already in place, in a position that a proper strike would be delivered.

- Have the blocker take a short power step forward, bend his elbows, and snap the hips up and into the defender, driving him back.

- Have the blocker maintain a wide base as he rolls his hips and stays compact to take away space between himself and the defender.

☐ *Finish:*

Once the blocker is in control and has position, his next task is to finish off the block. Taking short, strong and powerful steps with cleats in the ground, he should drive his defender backward and out of the play. Teach the finish as follows:

- Following a strike, have the blocker start with a wide base, his elbows bent and his hands in a strong thumbs-up position.

- On your command, have the blockers press up on the defender's chest, while taking short, choppy steps forward on his instep. He must keep off his toes.

- Continue to observe the blocker's body and hand position throughout this phase to emphasize control.

- As the defender gives ground, have the blocker press forward, and control and direct the defender's movements by taking short powerful steps through the whistle.

Blocking Drills

Once your players understand and can properly perform the five basic elements involved in fundamentally sound blocking, identify and run drills to teach the skills in action. The following four drills can be performed initially against air (e.g., an imaginary ballcarrier), then against bags or another soft surface, and finally progressing to player-on-player contact. Again, design your practice plan within USA Football's nationally endorsed youth practice guidelines (Appendix B).

☐ *Quarter Eagle Drill:*

One of the most valuable attributes an offensive lineman can possess is the ability to move quickly, while maintaining a good football position and proper distribution of his weight. This drill entails the following:

- Have the linemen assume a two-point stance, facing you, and position them spread out in front of you.
- On your command, have them make about an eighth of a turn to their right, then back to the center (facing you), left, center, right, etc.
- Make sure that the players turn sharply, while keeping their feet on the ground and pivoting in place.
- Complete the drill by having your players sprint forward for five yards on your signal.

* Do not allow the players to hop when moving. Make sure that the players keep their cleats on the ground as much as possible.

☐ *Push-the-Leader Drill:*

Leverage plays a key role in almost every skill and technique that players perform on the football field, including blocking. Conducting this drill entails the following directions:

- Have the linemen pair up and stand in front of each other, facing in the same direction.
- Have the lineman in back assume a proper run-blocking demeanor, while the lineman in front squats down and provides resistance.
- On your command, have the player behind push the player in front like he would push a car.
- Execute the first few repetitions in a straight line. After both players have mastered the straight-line push, have the front player provide resistance, while shuffling from side to side.

* Make sure the player pushing (the back player) maintains a flat back. Have both players accelerate their feet and maintain contact during the shuffle phase of the drill.

☐ *Move-to-Improve Drill:*

Offensive linemen need to control their body and come off the ground quickly. This drill is run as follows:

- Have the linemen form three lines, facing you, and assume a three-point stance.
- On your command, have the players sprint five yards, at which point they should put their right hand down, with all of their weight on it.
- Then, have the players pivot 360 degrees, get up, and sprint five more yards.
- Have the players repeat the drill, but this time, have them ground their left hand.
- After the left-handed spin, have the players do a forward roll and come up into a five-yard sprint.

* Emphasize that each player should get off the ground as quickly as possible and then move forward quickly while under control.

☐ *Zigzag Drill:*

Proper footwork off of the line of scrimmage, squaring the shoulders and maintaining proper body position enable offensive linemen to protect the passer. The following drill is designed to strengthen pass blocking skills:

- Have linemen pair up and have one of them assume a proper pass-set position, with his hands behind his back.
- On your command, have the other lineman move toward the lineman in the pass-pro set position, zigzagging toward him, while emphasizing moving laterally.
- Have the lineman in the pass-pro set maintain an inside position by employing proper footwork.

* The alignment of both linemen can be modified so that the player assuming the pass-pro set can work on various aspects of his footwork, particularly the initial states of his pass-pro set.

FLAG FOOTBALL

Unlike tackle football, blocking and tackling are prohibited in flag football. Instead, the emphasis is on players learning and executing basic aspects of the sport (e.g., running, passing, receiving, moving, etc.). USA Football's rules for flag football are presented in Appendix C.

CHAPTER 9

POSITION-SPECIFIC SKILLS AND TECHNIQUES

Every position on a football team has a defined role. Each position requires specific skills and techniques to play it. The following sections detail the basic skills and techniques that each position on both offense and defense entails. They also feature a series of developmental drills for each position. It is important to note that this information is simply a guideline for what you should look for and do in teaching your players. Differences in physical, motor, and mental maturity and ability exist between kids that, on occasion, may require you to modify what and how you coach.

OFFENSE

Quarterback

The quarterback is arguably one of the most important, if not the most important, players on the offensive side of the ball. The basic tasks involved in playing this position include assuming the pre-snap stance; receiving the snap; handing, tossing, or quick-pitching the ball off; faking; and passing the ball.

☐ *Assuming the Pre-snap Stance*

Under-the-Center Stance:

- Plant the feet slightly less than shoulder width apart. Wide stances cause hitch steps.
- Stand flat-footed with his heels slightly off the ground.
- Stand as tall as possible, while still staying comfortable (head up, chest out, knees bent). Having visibility of the entire field is important.
- Keep his arms comfortably bent (never straight-armed and tense).
- Press the middle finger of his top hand tightly along the seam of the center's pants, with his fingers spread comfortably.

- Thrust his bottom hand down and back at an approximately 135-degree angle. His thumbs will be over the top of each other, with the bottom thumb protruding out an inch or so further than the top one.

Shotgun Stance:

- Line up five-and-a-half to six yards deep, depending on the preference of the offense.
- Position the feet shoulder-width apart, even—not staggered—to allow him to step either to his left or his right.
- Bend the knees slightly. He should not be lock-legged, and as a result, flat-footed.
- Be ready to react in case of a poor snap.
- Once he is in position to receive the snap, have him extend his hands out to the center, with the palms down and his fingers comfortably spread and pointed upward.
- Be sure to lock his eyes on the football in the center's hand(s) in case of a miscue or an early snap by the center.

☐ *Receiving the Snap (for a Right-Handed Quarterback)*

From Under the Center:

- Place the right hand firmly up under the center's backside, making it the top hand.
- Widely spread the fingers of the top hand to press up against as much of the center's pant cloth as possible.
- Face the palm of the top hand down, parallel to the ground.
- Place the middle finger of the top hand directly on the seam of the center's pants.
- Spread the thumb of the top hand out so that it is nearly parallel to the line of scrimmage.
- Position the thumb of the bottom hand so that both hands mesh comfortably.
- Offset the knuckles so that the bottom hand is slightly behind, or under, the top hand.
- Create upward pressure under the center's backside with the bottom hand.
- Be aware that on a proper snap, the football breaks the heels of the quarterback's hands, thereby forcing them to envelop the ball naturally.
- Once the hands receive the ball, draw the ball to the quarterback's stomach (i.e., "the third hand").
- Adjust the ball for proper fit.

From the Shotgun:

- From the start, lock in his focus and maintain his level of concentration.
- Once the quarterback signals that he is ready for the ball to be snapped, either by raising his hands or one leg, lock his eyes on the football. He must actually see the ball begin to move in the center's hand(s) as the snap is initiated.
- See the ball leave the center's hands.
- Follow the flight of the ball all the way to his own hands.
- Catch the football with his fingers (not his palms), in order to immediately gain control of the ball.

☐ *Handing, Tossing, or Quick-Pitching the Ball Off*

Handoff:

Photo 9-1

- Secure the ball against his stomach until the moment of delivery into the ballcarrier's "pouch."
- Immediately find the spot in the ballcarrier's stomach that is the center of the pouch, two inches above the ballcarrier's belly button.
- Concentrate so intently on the aforementioned spot throughout the handoff action that he actually attempts to see the ball make contact with this precise spot.
- Preferably, use a firm, two-handed handoff that enables security and control of the ball all the way from the snap to the ballcarrier's pouch.
- If a one-handed exchange is utilized, firmly press the ball on the handoff spot, parallel to the ground.
- Be aware that the handoff is actually made in two stages:
  ▸ First, push the ball up against the spot, with both hands on the ball and with the back of the inside hand (the one closest to the ballcarrier's body) actually placed directly on the spot.
  ▸ Second, push the ball up against the spot with the outside hand, as the inside hand slides out from behind the ball.
- Make all handoffs as deep behind the line of scrimmage as possible.

Tossing/Quick-Pitching:

Photo 9-2

- Be aware that the ball on a quick-pitch must quickly get to the ballcarrier, who is already well outside the quarterback. A toss, on the other hand, is not as rushed, since the ball can easily be tossed to a point that leads the ballcarrier, so that it hangs a bit as he catches up to it on his own path. All factors considered, a soft, end-over-end, tumbling toss is recommended.
- Be cognizant of the fact that a toss or a quick-pitch can be executed from either a front-out opening action or a reverse-pivot action.

- Regardless of which action is used, maintain a level-shoulder position to ensure a consistent delivery and follow-through.
- When executing a straight-arm toss or quick-pitch, sight the ball to the delivery point by peering over the fingertips.
- Have his palms "take a picture" of the exact spot to which he wants the ball to be delivered. On either a toss or a quick-pitch, this spot should be one-and-a-half yards in front of the ballcarrier, belt high.
- Avoid lowering the ball from his stomach area after receiving the center snap, before he delivers the toss or quick-pitch. Such a "hitch" can lead to poor execution.

☐ *Faking*

- Make the faking action look like normal execution of the play.
- Avoid over exaggerating the faking action.
- Be aware that the appropriate fake depends on the design of the offensive play.
- On a two-handed handoff fake, place the ball in the faking back's pouch and ride toward the line of scrimmage, until which point the quarterback must withdraw the ball.
- On a one-handed handoff fake, position the ball just above the juncture at the top of his leg and the bottom of his stomach. Sit the ball on the soft bottom of his stomach to preclude interference with the movement of the leg.
- Use the free hand to fake the handoff into the faking back's pouch.
- Ride in the pouch as long as the body movement away from the mesh point will allow.
- Initiate his movement away from the mesh point as soon as the faking back clears the quarterback's intended path.
- Do not be too eager (e.g., pull out too quickly) to carry out the rest of the action on the play.
- Keep the level of his shoulders as consistent as possible, beginning at his pre-snap stance (e.g., don't raise his upper body too high).

☐ *Gripping the Ball on a Pass*

Photo 9-3

How a quarterback grips the football will vary among players. A smaller-handed quarterback will hold the ball closer to the end of the ball, while the larger-handed player will grip it more toward the center. Wherever he grips the ball, he still must do the following:

- Spread his fingers wide to help with control and the spiral.
- Extend his index fingers toward the end of the ball.
- Place his last three fingers across the laces.
- Wrap his thumb comfortably around the ball to produce a firm, comfortable grip.

☐ *Setting Up to Pass*

Photo 9-4

Setting up requires some form of dropback movement to a launching point, a coming under control, and a stopping action. The quarterback must assume a cocked position of the back shoulder and hold of the ball so that a quick and fluid release can be performed. The launch point is back away from the line of scrimmage and usually inside the tackle-to-tackle area. From this area, the quarterback with launch (or throw) his pass from a fixed (or "set") position, while remaining stationary. Throwing on the move (e.g., a sprint-out pass) entails a separate set of guidelines.

Dropback movement to a set position can take the form of a variety of set-up actions, depending on the team's philosophy of the set-up action. Regardless of which set-up action is preferred, the key considerations are the depth and speed of the dropback action, throttling down and stopping, and assuming the cocked throwing position. The following factors should govern the set-up:

- Be aware that the depth and speed of getting to the launch point are extremely important. Dropback actions typically involve taking a three-, five-, or seven-step drop.
- Be cognizant of the fact that no matter which set-up method is used, a quarterback's vision will be enhanced by a quick, deep set-up that gives him more time to view the situation in front of him.
- Know that whatever dropback action is utilized, the first one, three, or five steps of the dropback are intended to get maximum depth behind the line of scrimmage. The last two steps, no matter how many steps he drops back, are always the same—used to throttle down and plant (i.e., stop) with the back foot.
- On the plant step, make sure he is in the cocked position, ready to throw, with the majority of his body weight on his back foot, ready to be transferred to his front foot during the delivery or launch action.
- Hold the ball in a gathered position (i.e., gathering in all parts of the body in preparation for the action of transferring the body weight from the back foot to the front foot and channeling the body's momentum into the delivery of the ball).
- Place the free hand on the ball during the set-up action for better ball security.
- Fully cock the shoulder of the throwing arm.
- Position the back elbow up and away from his body to help produce a level carry of both shoulders.

Three-Step Drop (for a right-handed quarterback):

The three-step drop is employed in the quick passing game.

- Step #1 (separation step): pivot on his left foot to gain as much distance as possible with his right foot.

- Step #2 (crossover step): cross over his right foot with his left, planting this foot, getting ready to throw.
- Step #3 (balance step): release the ball quickly after coming to balance.

Five-Step Drop (for a right-handed quarterback):

The five-step drop is used in the medium-length passing game.

- Step #1 (separation step): pivot on his left foot to gain as much distance as possible with his right foot.
- Step #2 (crossover step): cross over his right foot with his left, planting this foot, gaining as much distance as possible.
- Step #3 (control step): bring his right leg behind his left, trying to get more distance and to establish control, while getting ready for his next step.
- Step #4 (crossover step): dig in and plant, while thinking about the area to which he will throw the ball.
- Step #5 (balance step): come to balance, before releasing the ball.

Seven-Step Drop (for a right-handed quarterback):

The seven-step drop is utilized in the long passing game. This drop is merely an extension of the five-step drop. All the drop steps are identical, except an extra crossover and control step are added in the middle to make it a seven-step drop.

☐ *Delivering (Throwing) the Ball*

Having sound throwing technique is essential for any quarterback. The following factors apply (in this instance, for a right-handed quarterback):

- Point his toes just to the left of the delivery spot to help direct his total-body motion to the targeted spot.
- As he steps forward to throw the ball, swing his hips around on the same plane to help whip his upper torso, and eventually his arm action, in the same direction.
- Transfer his weight from his back foot to his front foot, once the front foot is planted on the ground in order to regain his body balance.
- Be aware that the action of his hips (e.g., the degree to which they open to the target spot) will actually affect his forward step. Over-opening his hips can lead to the ball being overthrown. Closing his hips can be counterproductive to his efforts to pass the ball in a fluid manner.
- When passing the ball, release it as high as possible to allow a full range of motion of the passing arm, as well as to help enable the pass to clear the raised hands of the defensive line (Photo 9-5). Keep in mind that the individual style of passers must, to a degree, be accommodated to enable them to practice their own most efficient throwing technique.

Photo 9-5

- Remember that the throwing action of the arm should be one continuous, coordinated two-part motion:
  - Cock the ball in the area of the back shoulder, and yet still slightly in front of the body. Draw the elbow back so that the upper arm is approximately parallel to the ground.
  - Begin the forward motion of the delivery by extending the free hand and arm outward toward the target spot to start the motion of leading with the chest. Try to drive the ball with the chest by sticking out (or leading with) the chest to strengthen the delivery.
- Keep the wrist of the throwing arm firm and straight during the delivery to help avoid a wobbly pass.
- Release the ball with a screwball delivery action in which the thumb is pronated down toward the ground so that the palm is also facing downward.
- Snap the ball off with a snapping action of the wrist, as well as a full extension (or lock) of the elbow to help put extra zip into the release.
- Make sure that the index finger leaves the ball last.
- Focus on and execute a proper follow-through (Photo 9-6). Be aware that momentarily, where the index finger points as the ball is released is where the ball will go. As the ball is released, have the hand and arm continue to follow through across the body and down toward the ground. Simultaneously, pronate the hand (i.e., rotate the thumb and palm down).
- Keep in mind that the ultimate key to achieving a higher trajectory on a pass is the throwing elbow, since its position directly correlates to the forward throwing motion of the ball. The release of the ball must be higher and earlier.

☐ *Passing (Throwing) on the Move*

Passing on the run is employed in the sprint-out, roll-out, and bootleg. The underlying premise of throwing the ball on the run is that the upper-torso action of the passer must be separated from the running action of his legs. Passing on the run involves the following considerations:

- Ideally, from the chest up, all of the quarterback's throws should look the same.
- Once he starts his move-out action, be sure that he accelerates as fast as possible to break the containment. Threaten the line of scrimmage, threaten the secondary, and get away from any interior pursuit.
- Take his first three to six steps, depending on the timing of the route used, at top speed, with the ball carried in front of his sternum in a position to best accommodate the run action.
- On his fourth to eighth step (depending on the timing of the route, and whether he is right-handed or left-handed), cock the ball and be ready to throw.

Photo 9-6

- Keep in mind that the cocking action is no different from the cocking action in the set-up position, except that the ball should be held slightly higher and the elbow should be positioned to help accommodate his running action.
- Cock the passing shoulder in a position where it won't have to be moved back any further to initiate the throw.
- Place the strain on the stomach area, given that the chest of the quarterback should be facing the target of the pass.
- Be sure that his upper torso is ready to pass the ball, without the aid of his legs and feet.
- Ideally, have him gather his feet to help adjust the direction of his body to a point where he, at least, opens up his hips toward the target.
- For a right-handed quarterback, attempt to step toward the target with his left foot, whether he is moving left or right, and then roll over his front, right foot as he throws.
- Fully extend and lock his throwing elbow when throwing.
- Remember to emphasize the follow-through of his index finger, when he is moving to the side opposite his throwing arm and has to pass back toward the inside, instead of out toward the flank, where his run action is threatening.
- Be aware that a five- or seven-step timed, move-out throw to his right will necessitate him taking one additional step to his left to enable him to roll over his right foot on delivering the pass.

☐ *Quarterback Drills*

Air Dribble Drill:

This drill is designed to work on the quarterback's ability to grip the football. One football per quarterback is required to conduct this drill.

- Have him hold the ball out in front of his body.
- Then, have him drop the ball and reach down to catch it before it falls to the ground.
- Next, have him return it back to the original hold position.
- Have him repeat the exercise as many times as he can in 30 seconds.

* He should work both hands equally. Once he becomes adept at the skill with both hands, two footballs can be used simultaneously.

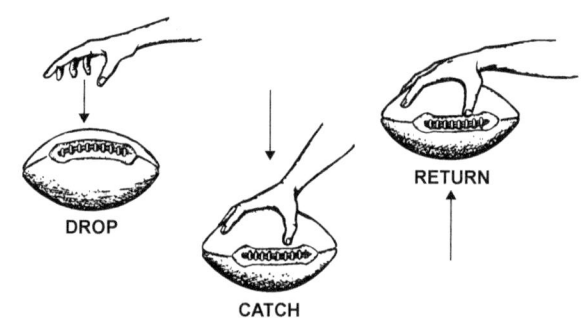

Figure 9-1

Run Delivery Football Drill:

This drill helps quarterbacks practice footwork to deliver the football in the quarterback-ballcarrier exchange on a run play. The drill requires one ball per quarterback and, preferably, a lined field.

- Have the quarterbacks line up so that they can go all at once or in rapid-fire order, one at a time.

- Have the quarterbacks practice the steps of each run play in the offense "on-air."
- Have each quarterback practice the exact stepping action for both the run play exchange and any faking action.

* Make sure that the quarterback does not lift up and down during his stepping action, helping him deliver a level, from-the-belt-buckle exchange.

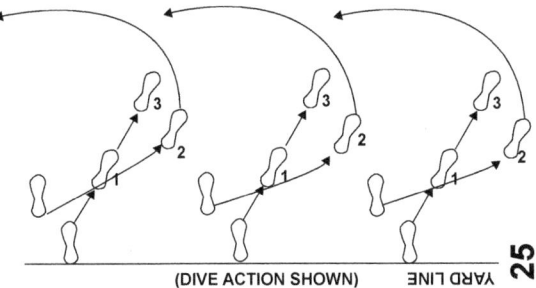

Figure 9-2

Quick Release Pass Drill:

This drill is designed to develop the ability of the quarterback to release the ball quickly when passing from a set position. One football per quarterback is required to conduct this drill.

- Align two receivers seven yards apart, 12 yards from the quarterback, with a defender positioned equidistant between the two.
- From a straight dropback and set-up position, have the quarterback wait for the defender to break one way or the other to cover one receiver or the other.
- At that point, have the quarterback attempt to complete a quick release pass to the open receiver before the defender can react and bat it down or intercept it. Note: the defender must take two steps toward the initial receiver before he reacts to the ball.

* Be sure that the quarterback's throwing arm is fully cocked so that there is no delay in his delivery. He should combine the quick release action with the proper index finger follow-through.

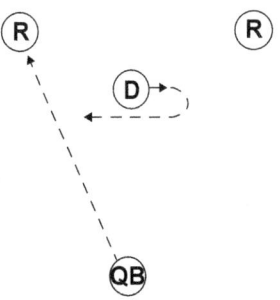

Figure 9-3

Circle Drill:

This drill is designed to teach the quarterback to throw on the run, while maintaining the proper body position. One football per pair of quarterbacks is required to conduct this drill.

- Pair the quarterbacks with one football between them and position them 10 to 15 yards apart.
- On the coach's (your) command, have the quarterbacks circle in a counterclockwise direction, passing the ball back and forth to each other.
- Then, have the quarterbacks change direction and throw passes to each other, while moving in a clockwise direction.
- Continue the drill until all quarterbacks have thrown a predetermined number of passes.

* Make sure that the quarterbacks keep the ball above their shoulders as they circle, as well as draw their hips and square their shoulders as they throw a pass. Emphasize the importance of adhering to the proper mechanics when passing.

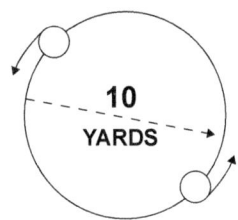

Figure 9-4

Running Backs

Every coach would like to have running backs who possess all of the essential ball-carrying skills. However, these skills need to be developed. Focus on having your running backs master the following skills: the stance; the takeoff; the ball exchange with the quarterback; receiving the pitch/toss; ball security; faking; running techniques; dragging a tackler; catching a pass; and blocking.

☐ *The Stance*

Depending on the system you use, running backs will start in either a two-point or three-point stance. Each stance has its benefits. A back in a two-point stance can better see the defensive alignment, which can help his run angles. A back in a three-point stance is more explosive and harder to pick up by the defenders before the play unfolds.

Two-Point Stance:

In a two-point stance, the running back should:

- Be balanced (i.e., not leaning forward or back or pointing left or right).
- Place extra weight on his push off foot, without showing it (e.g., if he were going to take a toss to his right, more weight should be on his left foot).
- Place his palms flat on his thighs, with his fingers pointing down.
- Have his head up and his chest out, surveying the defense; he should not be hunching over.
- Have all of his body parts straight ahead, with his feet perpendicular to the LOS.

Three-Point Stance:

In a three-point stance, the running back should:

- Distribute his weight evenly between the down hand and both feet; the fingertips of the down hand should be on the ground, not on the knuckles.
- Have his back parallel to the ground.
- Be consistent with the stagger of his feet (never more than heel to toe).
- Put the forearm of his free hand across his knee in a manner that it can quickly slide up to the stomach and form part of the handoff pouch.

☐ *Takeoff*

In a takeoff, acceleration is created with a powerful push off the planted foot and reaching maximum stepping distance with the lead foot. The concentration should be on the power foot or pivot foot. The elbows should be kept close to the body upon takeoff. Running backs should take off like an airplane, without standing up out of their stance.

The three types of takeoffs of the lead foot should be practiced extensively, first with the right foot and then with the left:

- Straight ahead, which would be used on a dive play
- 45 degrees, which would be used on an off-tackle play
- 90 degrees, which would be used on a sweep or toss play

A counter step involves a running back taking one step in the opposite direction he is going, looking the same way he steps, and then using a jab-step as his new pivot foot goes in the other direction.

☐ *The Ball Exchange With the Quarterback*

On running plays involving the running back, the quarterback takes the snap and then hands the ball off to him. In this instance, the running back creates a pouch that is the target for the quarterback's handoff. This task involves the following considerations for the running back, including:

- Establish the pouch by making a lateral "V" position of the arms, so that the ball can be placed on the spot by the quarterback, two inches above the back's belly button.
- In the pouch, lift the bottom (or outside) hand to the belt buckle area, palm up, with the pinkie close to the belt buckle and fingers spread almost taut, so that they do not interfere with the handoff.
- Whip the top (or inside) hand upward to raise the inside elbow as high as possible, so that it does not interfere with the handoff.
- Turn the thumb of the top hand inward and downward to help raise the inside elbow.
- Avoid looking at the quarterback's handoff action.
- Be aware that the explosive takeoff toward the landmark (i.e., the ballcarriers initial aiming point) is designated by the design of the play.
- In order to ensure a consistent mesh point for the handoff every single time a specific play is run, make sure that the ballcarrier never varies or veers from the designated course until after the handoff has been completed.
- Avoid hunching over as the pouch is formed to receive the handoff.

- Remember that the running action of the back and the formation of the pouch are two separate entities.
- Never attempt to carry the ball with two hands in front of the body.
- During the exchange, keep the head up, while reading the "hole" and the defense.
- After the ball has been handed off, fold or close the arms over the ball, trying to envelop the ball, so that it ends up in the armpit of the lower arm. Every carry must be in the armpit, with the hand over the other part of the ball.

☐ *Receiving the Pitch/Toss*

The techniques used to receive the various types of pitches or tosses are basically the same. The only real difference involves positioning the hands to receive the ball. Since the arrival of the ball can vary greatly with each of the pitch or toss techniques, one overall technique should be developed for the reception of all pitches and tosses. Key points to teach are:

- Fully concentrate when receiving a pitch/toss.
- Focus his eyes on the ball in the quarterback's hands—as it is carried by the quarterback, as it leaves the quarterback's hands, as it progresses, and as it reaches his hands.
- Form a basket with his hands, into which the ball will fall.
- Form the bottom of the basket with the inside hand.
- Curl the thumb of the inside hand downward to prevent interference with the pitch/toss.
- Face the ball with the outside hand to serve as a backstop to prevent the pitch/toss from going past him.

- Be sure that the fingers are open and spread, just as they are in a normal handoff.
- Be sure to look the ball into his hands.

☐ *Ball Security*

Photo 9-7

Ball security is one of the most important tasks a ballcarrier can perform. This task typically involves two situations—when carrying the ball and when switching the ball from one hand to another.

Carrying the Ball:

- Envelop the ball with the hand, fingers, arm, and armpit.
- To the degree possible, limit the amount of the ball that is showing.
- Cover the tip of the ball with his spread fingers, which should help force the ball in the armpit, like a vice.
- Wrap the elbow around the ball to maximize coverage of the ball.
- When in traffic, use a two-handed carry—one hand to keep the ball tight in the armpit, the other hand over the ball to help protect it.

Switching the Ball From One Hand to the Other:

Typically, when the ballcarrier is in the open field, and defenders are coming in their pursuit angles, the ball should be switched to the sideline arm to protect it from contact. The switch takes place through the following steps:

- Passing through the two-arm carry, have the carrying arm force the ball into the other armpit, keeping it secure throughout the switch.
- Never attempt a switch if a defender is even remotely close to him.

Faking:

Faking a handoff is extremely basic. The player doesn't do anything differently than he would if he were to actually be given the ball. He hits the hole like he has the ball, lowers his shoulders, and gets someone to tackle him. Although this maneuver sounds simple, it is imperative that he practice this as much as any real handoff. Every detail of a real handoff needs to be carried out from the player's hands, shoulders, head, feet, and hips. The player who is executing the fake should:

- Never hunch over (backs with the ball don't hunch).
- Never clasp his hands together quickly out of the pouch (every defender will know it is a fake).
- Run full speed (faking backs have a tendency to quickly slow down).

☐ *Running Techniques*

The following are basic running techniques to teach to your backs.

Dive Technique:

A dive run means a back is hitting a hole with no lead blocker. This technique is used on dives, counters, draws, etc. The key to a dive run is hitting the hole as quickly and explosively as possible. The back should have a north/south mentality coming off his blockers. He should be at top speed when he hits the hole.

Freeze Technique:

The freeze technique simply entails that the ballcarrier runs directly at the defender. This strategic move is often done at linebackers. If the runner commits his direction too early, he will surely give up an easy tackle. The key is to make the defender flat-footed, therefore giving the runner the advantage.

End Running Technique:

The emphasis in this instance should be on north/south running. One of the biggest mistakes made by young running backs is that they tend to angle their running. Most outside runs are designed to create a run-lane up the field. The runner must read the blockers and choose the proper lane (i.e., outside the block or inside the block). At that point, he needs to have a north/south mentality.

Open-Field Running Technique:

As with any run, the most important thing for a running back to do when in the open field is explode in a north/south direction, while elongating his strides. All cuts should be executed off a north/south running lane. Remember, the more north/south he runs, the fewer defenders who will have a realistic shot at tackling him.

Spin-Out Technique:

The spin-out technique is used when the runner hits a pileup but still sees daylight to one side or the other. To perform this maneuver, the runner must be running north/south, as he hits the pile. His shoulders should be arching his back, and he should use the force of his hit to roll off in the direction he wants to run. Keeping his feet moving at all times is the key.

Dragging a Tackler Technique:

This technique is employed when a back is trying to get an extra couple of yards out of a run. It is performed by running north and south with short, choppy steps. A forward body lean and powerfully pumping knees high are hallmarks of effective rushers. The ball should be tucked securely when attempting this technique. Tackle attempts from other directions will likely be sustained as the runner churns for yardage.

☐ *Catching a Pass*

Running backs should work on their receiving skills, just like the wide receivers and tight ends. Refer to the "receivers" section of this chapter for detailed information and guidelines on how to properly catch a pass.

☐ *Blocking*

Depending on your offensive system, running backs may be required to block on certain plays (refer to Chapter 8 in this book for additional specific information concerning the recommendations of USA Football regarding blocking).

Isolation Block:

This type of block entails blocking a linebacker who is left isolated in the blocking scheme. It is best performed by using the freeze technique with the runner to put the blocker at an advantage. To execute the isolation block, teach the blocker to:

- Spring out of his stance.
- Aim for the lower part of the chest plate of the linebacker.
- "Throttle down," slightly just before contact.
- Stay in control and widen his stance.
- Punch up with the palm of his hands, just under the chest plate from a power angle (this action is referred to as 'stepping on the linebacker's toes').
- Thrust into the block, using the lower body.
- Upon contact, roll his hips under, while arching his back.
- Maintain contact with the linebacker as he drives him up and back.
- If the linebacker gets by him, execute a 'rip' move on the far side of his chest.
- Never lunge at the linebacker; rather, stay in control and focus on delivering the proper blow.

Kick-Out Block:

The kick-out block is usually performed on the defensive end. This block is used to set up a running lane into which the runner can cut back. Since most defensive ends have "read and contain" mentalities, the blocker needs to get to him quickly, before he reads the play. As such, the blocker should:

- Take an inside-out route at full speed toward the defender.
- Stay low.
- Keep his elbow up.
- Rip up through the inside part of the defender's chest.
- Follow through with his block.
- Be persistent.

☐ *Running Back Drills*

Handoff Pouch and Reception Drill:

This drill is designed to teach, or refine, the basic fundamentals of the quarterback-ballcarrier exchange. No equipment is required to perform the drill, which involves the following steps:

- Have a group of running backs jog aimlessly in a square/circle, 15 to 20 yards wide.
- While on the move, have them initially practice forming a perfect handoff pouch and then folding over an imagined handoff action.
- See that the handoff pouch is done right, e.g., inside elbow up, fingers spread (almost taut), hyperextended backward, the upper body's carry disengaged from the lower body's run action.
- Have the backs practice folding over the ball, without a jerking or clamping action.

* Be sure that the backs are keeping their eyes up while pretending to fold over the football, reading the blocking scheme in front of them. Check the action of the backs from numerous angles.

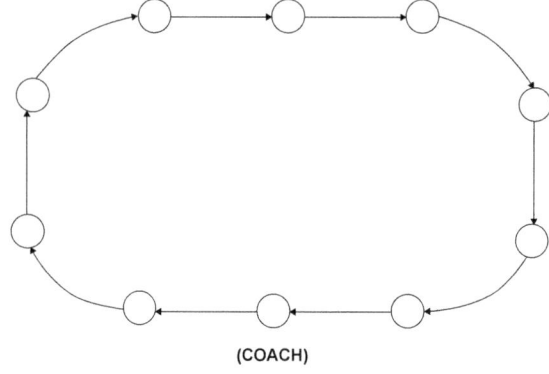

Figure 9-5

High-Knee, Step-Over Drill:

This drill is designed to develop the footwork of the running back, as well as to improve his agility. The drill requires five step-over dummies or tackling dummies to perform and involves the following steps:

- Set the bags up in a row, parallel to each other, one yard apart.
- Form the players in a line, five yards off the bags, facing forward.
- On your command, have the first player in line step over each bag. After he has cleared the bags, have the next player in line step over the bags.
- After each player has performed a repetition of the drill, repeat it by having each player, one at a time, step with both feet in between each bag.
- Have the players lift their knees high between every step.

* Be sure that the players have their heads up, facing forward, when doing the drill. Eventually, when they become proficient at it, they should be able to perform the drill without looking down.

Dive Action Drill:

This drill is designed to teach a ballcarrier how to read the block of his offensive lineman in a tight area. The drill involves a quarterback, a running back, a blocker in a three-point stance, and a defender, who is lined up over the blocker. The drill requires six items (e.g., cones, pinnies, etc.) to establish a marked-off, one-yard boundary on both sides of the blocker. The drill involves the following steps:

- Have the running back take a dive handoff from the quarterback that simulates a dive action in your team's offense.
- Have the offensive lineman block the defender over him.
- Have the defender try to make a thud tackle on the ballcarrier.
- Have the running back read the block of his lineman properly, by reading the backside and hips of his blocker and then making his cut.

* Be sure that the handoff is taken properly—the runner has his head up, and his eyes are focused on where he is running.

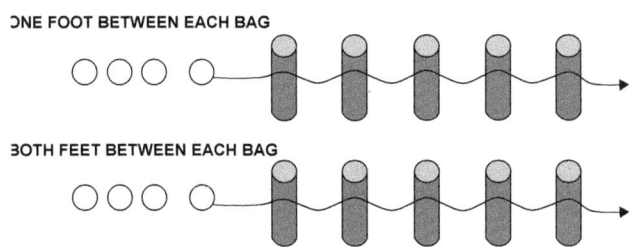

Figure 9-6

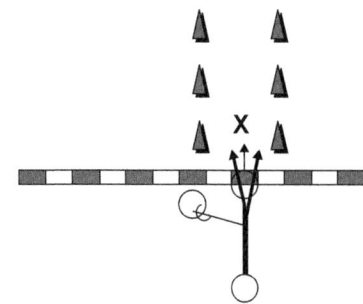

Figure 9-7

Ball Security Drill:

This drill is designed to teach the running back to protect the ball and deliver an impact when contact is inevitable. The drill uses a hand-held blocking dummy for each pair of players (a running back and a defender) participating in the drill, which involves the following steps:

- Have a running back, with a football secured in his left armpit, line up two yards from a defender, who is positioned on an angle to his right. Initially, the defender performs the drill with a hand-held blocking dummy.
- On your command, have the defender make a thud-type impact with the ballcarrier with the blocking dummy. Once the running back becomes proficient at the drill, the defender discards the dummy and makes contact with the ballcarrier.
- Have the ballcarrier drive into the defender with his right shoulder. Have the ballcarrier switch to a two-handed carry before contact.
- Perform three-to-four reps of the drill and then switch to the left side. The drill could also be performed with a defender on each side of the running back.

* Be sure that the running back uses a two-handed carry on every repetition of the drill. Have the ballcarrier keep his head up at all times and deliver a buck-up motion with each shoulder.

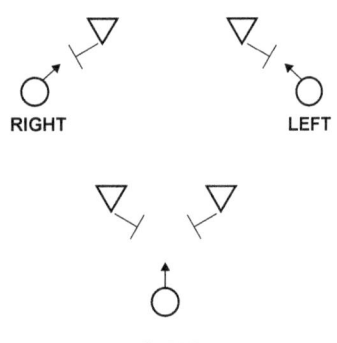

Figure 9-8

Wide Receivers

Wide receivers are a cornerstone of a passing offense. Effective wide receiver play includes a number of factors, including assuming the stance, reading the defense, getting off the line, running routes, catching the ball, and gaining yards after the catch. In addition, depending on the offensive system a team employs, wide receivers may also be assigned to block.

☐ *Assuming the Stance*

The most common stance for a receiver is a two-point stance, with the outside foot back. Assuming the proper stance is important for a receiver, enabling him to get the maximum burst as he explodes off the line of scrimmage into his route. While a good stance and start do not guarantee a good route and great catch, they are the first steps in that direction. More often than not, things generally don't finish right if they don't start right. The stance for a wide receiver should address the following:

- Stagger the feet front-to-back, with a comfortable lateral separation.
- Make the distance between the heel of the front foot and the heel of the back foot approximately the same as shoulder-width apart.
- Position the feet hip-width apart.
- Square the shoulders to the line of scrimmage and over the toes, so that the receiver has forward body lean.
- Bend the knees slightly.
- Point the toes of both feet straight ahead (note: the big toe of the forward foot may be slightly angled inside).
- Keep the head and eyes up.
- Flex the arms with the hands up.

One of the first issues that arises concerning the stance for a receiver is which leg should be forward in the stance. In reality, some teams leave the decision to the coach; others let the receiver decide. Obviously two options exist—inside leg up or outside leg forward. Of the two alternatives, having the inside leg up is the most common. Among the possible reasons for preferring one position to the other are the following:

Inside Leg Up:

- It gives all receivers a relatively uniform look so that the defense cannot use the stance as a clue to predetermine the route to be run.
- If the receiver is counting steps instead of yards to indicate the breakpoint on his routes, he will be in position to easily make the required break on the correct step and foot (e.g., the outside foot on a three-step slant).

Outside Leg Forward:

- The receiver has slightly better vision inside to the football.
- It enables the receiver to go in motion more fluidly.
- It provides a faster takeoff for inside blocks (e.g., crack blocks), because the receiver's stance is more open to his target.

☐ *Reading the Defense*

As the receiver comes to the line of scrimmage, he should think about several factors, including:

- Aligning outside (if in doubt, check with the line judge)
- Checking his splits (his alignment in relationship to the ball and his teammates)
- Looking over the defense and recognizing the coverage
- Deciding how he plans to release

When scanning the defense and initially reading the defense, the receiver needs to:

- Count the number of safeties and check their alignment.
- Locate if the linebackers and/or strong safety walked up (rover).
- Check the cornerback's alignment and eyes.

☐ *Getting Off the Line of Scrimmage*

A receiver can do a number of things at the beginning of his route with respect to the defense and/or a specific defender. One of the most important factors for a receiver is to get vertical push.

Vertical push is the ability to get downfield as quickly as possible to create problems for the defensive secondary. All factors considered, the further he gets downfield, the fewer number of defenders available to cover the whole field. In addition, by getting vertical push as quickly as possible, he forces the defenders to make reactionary adjustments. Of course, it helps if receivers have great speed, but the principles of vertical push can be utilized by any receivers who understand that they have to get downfield as fast as they can.

When a receiver is confronted by a defender who is lined up directly in front of him (anywhere from right in his face to three-to-four yards off of him), with the intent of making immediate contact to disrupt his route, the receiver can use a combination of techniques to achieve the fastest, smoothest release possible by minimizing contact with the defender. With regard to releasing, the following applies:

General Rules:

- On inside routes, release to the inside (relative to the line of scrimmage).
- On outside routes, release to the outside.
- Regardless of which direction the receiver releases, attack half of the defender's body, as opposed to squaring up on him.
- Do not allow himself to be manhandled or rerouted by the defender.

Stance-Related Factors:

- Shorten his stance when he realizes that he is going to be pressed by a defender.
- Bring his back foot closer to his front foot and bend his knees slightly more than usual.

Hands and Arms-Related Factors:

- Have his hands and arms ready to attack the defender's hands and arms.
- Have his arms flexed, his hands clenched, and his hands higher than the defender's hands (about six inches above the defender's hands, but not higher than his own eyes).
- Be aware that the keys to successful hand and arm movements include strength, quickness, and aiming point—the most important of which is quickness.
- Consider using a dip-and-release move (as described, in this instance, for an outside release), which involves the following:
  - As the defender brings his hands up to jam the receiver, the receiver swipes aside the hands of the defender with his outside arm and a clenched fist. Suggested aiming points vary from right above the wrist to the middle of the forearm to the elbow of the defender.
  - The receiver then dips his inside shoulder into the outside of the defender's body. The aiming point of the receiver's shoulder is the armpit of the defender.
  - Next, he rips up and through the defender's outside shoulder with his inside arm, which is flexed at a 90-degree angle. This motion is similar to a full-body uppercut in boxing.
  - As he delivers this ripping and punching-up motion, the receiver swaps hips with the defender by stepping with his inside leg immediately beside the defender and bringing his hips past those of the defender (i.e., he steps "through the defender"). He uses aggressive arm pumping to continue his escape.
  - Swapping hips is extremely important, because it allows the receiver to get back onto the stem of his route and forces the defender into a trail technique. If the receiver does not get his hips past the defender's hips, he allows the defender to be in a position to slow his route.
- Consider using a swim release, particularly as a change-up move, when a receiver is matched up against a defender who is shorter than him. As described for an outside release, a swim release involves the following:
  - The initial hand attack is the same as the dip-and-rip. The receiver's outside hand and arm swipe across to force the hands of the defender down and out of the way, as he moves to jam.
  - The difference involves the inside jam of the receiver, which comes up almost vertically and then pushes through past the head of the defender in the motion of a swimmer's crawl stroke.

- As the receiver's outstretched arm comes over the defender and makes contact with his back, the receiver pushes the defender back toward the line of scrimmage and uses the same motion to help propel himself upfield.
- He swaps hips and then uses aggressive arm pumping motion to continue his escape.

Footwork-Related Factors:

In order to successfully release, the receiver should combine one of the hand moves with effective footwork to get off the jam. It is imperative that the receiver gets vertical as soon as possible. He must have quick feet no matter what type of footwork he uses. Among the footwork options that a receiver has for releasing are the following:

- Speed release. A speed release is a fast release that involves quick hands but no initial directional fake with the feet off the line. The receiver's feet simply start the running motion, as his hands quickly strike the defender. The receiver should use the most effective angle to get by the defender and onto his route as quickly as possible. This technique is sometimes called an angle release. The angle of the path the receiver takes to release will differ, based on the route he is running and the leverage of the defender. On occasion, this angle will be only slightly off the stem of the route, and other times it may be a drastic angle. A speed release tends to work well for receivers who have extremely fast takeoff speed and power. For others, however, it can mean that they face a protracted battle at the line of scrimmage.
- Single-move release. In this release, the receiver takes a slight jab step forward in the direction opposite of the release. This step is not a step downfield, as if he were starting to run, but rather a small half-step accompanied by a slight head-and-shoulder nod in the same direction. The receiver then takes a regular burst step off the line of scrimmage with his other foot and incorporates one of the hand moves previously described. Of course, to be successful, the receiver must bring his hips parallel to or ahead of those of the defender (swap hips) to complete his release.
- Double-move release. The double-move is an advanced type of release. It is not the easiest to learn, and it must be done extremely quickly to be successful. When done properly, it can be a very effective way to beat the defender. In the following example, the receiver releases outside. First, he makes a small jab step outside, quickly followed by a jab step to the inside. Doing so guarantees enough cushion between the receiver and defender for the defender to see the double-move and be deceived by it. It is important that the receiver gives a head-and-shoulder fake in each direction, using as much hip motion as possible to help deceive the defender. The receiver incorporates his choice of hand moves. The last step is a burst step upfield and to the outside to being the route. The double-move is especially effective after a receiver has used the single-release move several times on the same defender. The double-move is also very effective on the goal line against man-to-man coverage, in conjunction with popular goal-line routes, such as slants or fades.
- Four-in-the-hole release. In this release, a rapid-fire movement is used to freeze defenders at the line of scrimmage. The name comes from agility drills that are done on a

speed ladder. In this drill, the player takes four quick pounding steps in one square (measuring approximately 20 by 14 inches) of the ladder, while vigorously pumping his arms in a running motion, before moving on to the next square.

Mimicking ladder work in this release, the receiver fires his feet up and down directly under his framework four times with quick and small motions. The four-in-the-hole release should be utilized with inexperienced receivers, while introducing hand moves. Footwork can be easily done on the first day of practice so they can then focus on the various hand techniques.

In game situations, this release tends to freeze the defender and get him back on his heels, as he assumes that the receiver is going deep. He also does not know to which direction the receiver is going to release. The limitation is that this release does not turn the defender's hips. As a result, the receiver could be a sitting duck for contact initiated by the defender.

Putting the Pieces Together:

While hand moves and footwork are discussed separately in this section of the chapter for reasons of clarity, they are obviously combined in any release move off of the line of scrimmage. In reality, most footwork techniques can be used in combination with most hand techniques, for example:

- Speed release and dip-and-rip
- Single move and dip-and-rip
- Single move and the swim move
- Double move and dip-and-rip
- Four-in-the-hole and the swim move
- Four-in-the-hole and dip-and-rip
- Four-in-the-hole and grab-and-punch

Initially, you should pick one or two release moves for your receivers and work those consistently in both directions. As your receivers gain experience, however, they can experiment using a variety of hand and foot combinations.

☐ *Running Routes*

The ability to make precise breaks in a route and separate from the defender is what can help make a great receiver. The receiver must concentrate on keeping his body lean and not giving the defender any clue as to which direction he will break to, and then accelerate out of the break, creating separation. As the receiver comes off the line of scrimmage, he should get his speed up to nearly full speed—yet controlled. It is important that the receiver not slow down before going into his cut. Three basic types of breaks are used by receivers—the speed cut, the comeback cut, and the breakdown cut.

The Speed Cut:

A speed cut, with correlating body movements, entails the following three steps:

- The receiver starts to break down with his foot that is on the outside of the break. If the receiver is breaking to his left, he will start to break with his right foot. This step is called a *pressure step* and is made at a 45-degree angle. At the same time the receiver should turn his head back to the quarterback to find the football.
- As the receiver leans into the route, he needs to take his second step and put it perpendicular to the sideline.
- His third step should be an acceleration step coming out of the cut.

It is important that the receiver be very smooth throughout the route, and accelerates out of the cut. This technique can take hours of practice, but once perfected, is difficult to defend in zone or man coverages. This type of cut is used on routes breaking to the outside that are usually no deeper than 12 yards, as well as on routes that break over the middle of the field. The speed cut can also be used when a receiver goes in motion and breaks upfield at the snap of the ball. In order to perform a speed cut, a receiver should:

- Turn his head back to find the ball the instant he plants his pressure step.
- Throw his left elbow back, at the same time he turns his head.
- Apply the pressure step at a 45-degree angle.

The Comeback Cut:

This type of break is used on curl routes and comeback routes. Although this route is simple to run, the techniques used by the receiver can make it more effective. Two critical steps for the comeback cut are as follows:

- *The four-step breakdown technique.* In approaching the *four-step breakdown*, the receiver is running at near full speed. He starts to break down with the foot that is on the inside of the break. In other words, if the receiver is coming back to his left, he will start to break down with his left foot. Most receivers break down with their outside foot. Breaking down with their inside foot, however, can be beneficial in two ways. First, breaking down to a complete stop, while running at near full speed, only takes four steps, not five. Second, by breaking down with the inside foot, the receiver keeps his shoulders square upfield, and keeps the defender at bay, not knowing which way the receiver is about to break.
- *A pressure step.* This step promotes separation from the defender. As the receiver starts out of his break with the *pressure step* at a 45-degree angle, he should already have his head turned back to the quarterback, as he pushes off his back foot toward the ball. Coming back toward the ball is extremely important, because it creates a separation from the defender. On occasion, the cornerback may have the receiver covered up to this point, but the receiver can create separation from the cornerback by coming back to the ball to finish the route off and make the catch.

To perform a comeback cut, a receiver should:

- Turn his head back to the ball, just as he hits his pressure step.
- Have great body lean, with his arms in a runner's position.

The Breakdown Cut:

The breakdown is a relatively simple break that is used primarily by the inside receivers on routes that break at 90-degree angles. This cut is very similar to the comeback cut in that it begins with the four-step breakdown technique. Instead of directly coming back to the ball, however, the receiver breaks at 90 degrees, either in or out. Two vital steps for the breakdown cut are as follows:

- The receiver starts to break down with the foot that is on the inside of the break. For example, if the receiver is breaking down to his left, he will start the break with his left foot. This is called the *breakdown step.*
- He should turn his head back to the quarterback at the same time the pressure step is applied.

When utilizing the breakdown cut, the receiver comes off the ball at near full speed. He runs downfield, being cognizant of where he wants to go and where the open area is going to be. Because the defensive back's main focus is on the wide receiver area, any moves the receiver uses tend to have little or no effect on the defender. The receiver can make his cut directly out of the break, or use a single or double-step move to beat the defender. As the defined breaking point, he should plant his *pressure step* at a 45-degree and, at the same time, turn his head back to find the football, accelerating out of the break, away from the defender. To perform a breakdown cut, a receiver should:

- Look directly at the defender.
- Position his shoulders over his feet, as he breaks down.
- Keep his arms in close to his body, while maintaining a running posture.
- As he hits his last step, turn his head back to find the football and break laterally.

The primary reason this technique works is that the receiver is separating from the defensive back very quickly into the open area. The receiver can also lean into his defender and prevent him from jumping the route.

Creating Separation:

Creating separation refers to the receiver's ability to break away from a defender just as the football is being thrown to him. The receiver should be catching the ball in space in order to gain maximum yardage after the catch. Creating separation requires the receiver to be in complete control of his body and run an effective route. This can take hours of refinement and instruction. The key point is that the receiver must develop the ability to separate from the defender. Creating separation requires that the receiver get into, and out of, his breaks cleanly and efficiently, which takes practice—lots of it.

☐ *Catching the Ball*

Photo 9-8

Catching the football is a vital skill for receivers. If they don't catch the football, a play is wasted, and the clock stops—period. Key points for catching the football are:

- Reach out to catch the pass (don't try to catch it against his body).
- Watch the ball into his hands.
- Catch the football with his fingertips.
- Catch the football, with palms up, when running away from the quarterback (unless the ball is thrown behind him—then he should come back and get it at its highest point, with palms out).
- When catching a pass in stride, always wait until the last second before reaching out for the football.
- Catch the football with palms out when running toward the quarterback (except if the ball is at his stomach or below).
- Use his body as a shield when going up for the ball in traffic.

- Catch the pass first, and then run for yardage.
- When the ball is in the air, go get it. Rather than waiting for it, he should come back to the football whenever possible.
- Catch the ball with two hands; rarely do receivers make one-handed catches consistently.

The ability to catch the football is predominantly mental, which means that anyone can become a better pass catcher with the proper technique, lots of repetitions, and the ability to focus on the football when the ball is in the air. This is accomplished in practice, as well as with lots of individual work.

☐ *Gaining Yards After the Catch*

The yards-after-the-catch (YAC), a.k.a. run-after-the-catch (RAC), is an important aspect of the receiver's job. The key components of YAC in the order that they occur include the following: secure the football, accelerate after the catch, gain yards, and protect the football.

Secure the Football:

Obviously, you can't have YAC without the "C." After the receiver catches the football, he must tuck the ball away while looking it all the way into his hands. The football should be secured in the tuck position before the receiver initiates other aspects of YAC.

Accelerate After the Catch:

One part of a receiver's YAC technique that should be included in every moving practice rep is turning quickly upfield and accelerating after the catch. Just as it is important to accelerate through the break, the receiver must accelerate after the catch to gain further separation from the defender. Accelerating after the catch can be enforced every day on every catch.

Gain Yards:

The receiver must determine the best way to gain as many yards as possible by running north and south, and executing escape moves before being tackled. The factors that a receiver uses to determine where and how to get upfield include:

- The route he is running
- The location of the defender(s)
- The position and momentum of the ball as he catches it

Among the general rules for gaining yardage after a catch are the following:

- If the receiver is already running upfield while making the catch, such as on a post or a fade, he should use his upfield momentum to keep running.
- If the receiver is running crossfield while making the catch (such as on a dig or cross), he should look for the quickest way to turn his crossfield path upfield to gain positive yardage.
- On routes where receivers are coming back to the football (e.g, stop and curl), they should first make as tight a turn as possible outside and away from defenders coming from the middle of the field. Once a receiver has become skilled at catching and turning outside, he may add a quick head fake to the inside to misdirect the closest defender before pivoting outside. If the ball's position causes the receiver to turn inside for the catch, however, he needs to use that momentum to continue his upfield progression, instead of changing direction to turn the long way around to the outside.
- On all types of routes, the receiver needs to be sure to run north and south as soon as possible after the catch, as opposed to moving laterally too far across the field.

- When two defenders are approaching a receiver, he should split the defenders ("catch and knife") and get as many yards as possible, instead of running crossfield to try to get around them.

Protect the Football:

When the receiver is in heavy traffic or is about to be tackled, he needs to secure the football with both hands to avoid fumbling. The preferred method is to use a running-back technique and squeeze the ball with both arms into the stomach area immediately before contact. He also can take his off hand and place it over the top of the football. In this instance, his hand comes clear across his body and double-secures the ball in his outside arm.

☐ *Blocking*

A wide receiver who can block can be extremely valuable to an offense. As a rule, not many runs gain a lot of yards without a block from the receiver. In order to be an effective blocker, the wide receiver should have a basic understanding of his team's running game. For example, he should know which hole the ball is being run through, as well as what the chances are for a cut-back run. The receiver should also understand the timing of the run. In other words, when will the ballcarrier be in a position to cut off the receiver's block? The receiver should also be familiar with how the running back will set up the receiver's downfield block. The running back should be able to accelerate past the receiver's block, or dip inside or outside to get the defender to commit one way or the other, enabling the receiver to take the defender where he wants to go. The stalk block is the most common block that wide receivers perform. (Note: Additional information on the recommendations of USA Football concerning blocking is presented in Chapter 8.)

The Stalk Block:

This block requires timing and technique, as opposed to brute strength. In the stalk block, the receiver should attack the man he is going to stalk block. As such, he should break down within three to five yards, before making contact. If the receiver runs with too much momentum toward the defender, the receiver will have a tendency to lunge at the defender, and miss the block completely. The receiver should sprint to an area in front of the defender, break down a bit, and then make the block.

On this block, the positioning and hand placement of the receiver will very much resemble an offensive lineman in a pass-blocking drill. The difference is that the receiver will not give up ground to the defender, but rather stop the defender's path to the ballcarrier, or any area to which the defender wants to go. The receiver should engage the defender with his arms extended to the chest area of the defender. The receiver should keep his hands inside the defender's shoulders and should not grab outside that area.

If the receiver needs to keep the defender from heading to the tackle box, the receiver should swing his rear to the direction to which he is preventing the defender from going, or wall off the defender, after the initial contact has been made. This type of blocking is most often needed when the ballcarrier is running between the tackles.

If the ballcarrier is running a sweep, toss, or pitch to the outside, the receiver should first make contact, and then push the defender wherever the defender first attempts to go. For example, on numerous occasions, a running back may set the receiver's block up by running to the inside of the receiver. The defender sees this situation and reacts by trying to run to the receiver's inside.

As the defender starts to the inside, the receiver will then swing his rear to the outside and, with the defender's momentum, take him to the inside. The running back will then bounce the play to the outside, which is free of defenders.

☐ *Wide Receiver Drills*

Drills can help your wide receivers develop their skills. It is your responsibility to select the right drills at the right time, in the right amount, and in the right way.

Partner Passing Drill:

This drill is designed to work on basic catching skills and the tucking-the-ball-away-after-the-catch techniques. The drill requires one football for every pair of receivers. Conducting the drill involves the following steps:

- Have the receivers pair up and face their partners at a distance of five yards. Each receiver in one line has a football.
- Start the drill by having the receiver throw the football to his partner in the other line. Steadily increase the velocity of the throw as the drill progresses.
- Have the receiver catch the ball with his hands out in front of his body as the ball is thrown to the middle of his chest.
- After a predetermined number of catches by each receiver, have the receiver throwing the ball vary the point around his partner's body to which he throws the ball.
- Next, have one line of receivers turn their backs to the other group.
- Then, have the receiver throw the ball over his partner's shoulder to simulate the fade ball.

* While this drill is being conducted, you should walk up and down the lines of receivers, correcting their technique.

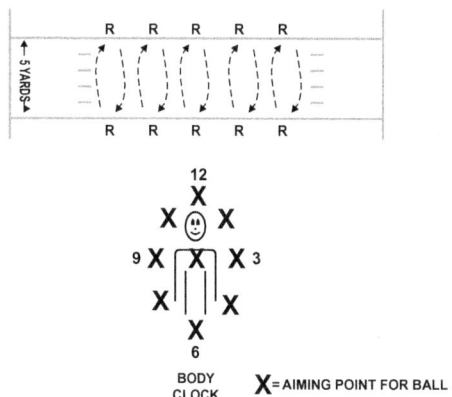

Figure 9-9

Reaction Drill:

This drill is designed to develop the ability of the receiver to react quickly to the flight of the football. Two footballs are required to conduct the drill. The drill is performed as follows:

- Position the receiver 10 yards from the coach (you), with his back turned toward you.
- To start the drill, shout "ball" and throw the ball to the receiver.
- Have the receiver quickly turn around, catch the ball, and tuck it away.
- The first time through the drill, have the receivers turn to their right; next time, have them turn to their left.
- Make sure the receiver turns his body 180 degrees in one motion.
- Have the receiver vigorously pull the elbow in the direction he is turning to help create momentum for the rest of his body to follow.

- Make sure the receiver immediately finds the ball with his eyes and quickly gets his hands in the correct position to catch it.

* Be sure that the receiver uses his eyes to look the ball all the way in, and tucks the ball quickly.

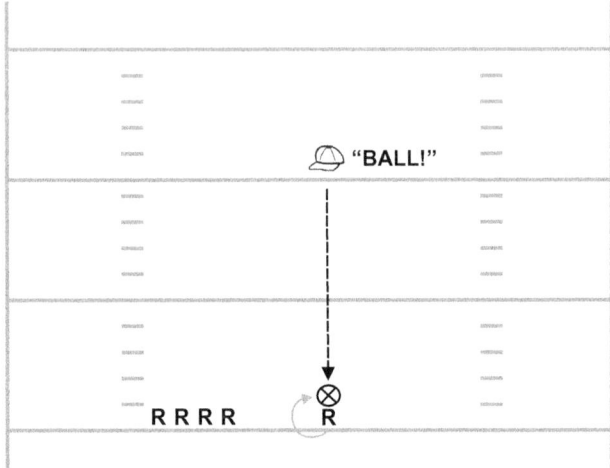

Figure 9-10

Swat Drill:

This drill is designed to develop the ability of the receiver to release against tight man or rolled coverage. A swat release involves a receiver using both of his hands to slap away the hand or hands of the defender. This move is used when a receiver has difficulty with the defender's strength. This technique enables the receiver to keep the defender's hands off of him. No equipment is required for this drill, which entails the following steps:

- Have the players position themselves in two lines—one line of receivers and one line of players who are simulating being defensive backs.
- Make sure that the defenders are in the ready position, with their knees bent and their hands extended at chest level, about 8-12 inches away from the receivers.
- On your command, have the receivers execute swat releases to either their right or their left.
- Have the receivers perform three releases in each direction and then change responsibilities with the defenders.

* Make sure that the receivers slap the hands of the defenders, while maintaining their proper running form.

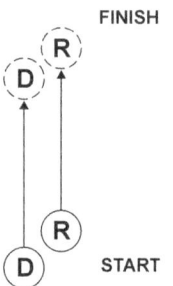

Figure 9-11

Comeback Drill:

This drill is designed to help receivers quickly plant a foot and come back toward the quarterback to catch the football, as well as to execute a quick cut and a burst upfield, once the reception has been made. A football is required to conduct the drill, which involves the following steps:

- Position the receivers in a line, side-by-side, with a quarterback set up to their right.
- To initiate the drill, have the receivers, one at a time, accelerate at full speed off the line and then make an appropriate cut toward the quarterback to catch a pass.
- Once the reception has been made and the ball tucked away, have the receiver plant and burst upfield to gain yardage (against air).
- Make sure that the receiver develops the habit of coming back to the quarterback as the ball is thrown.

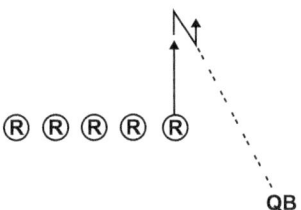

Figure 9-12

Offensive Line Play

Football is a game of fundamentals. No position group in football requires more discipline and technique than the offensive line.

All other factors being equal, teaching your players to master the fundamentals and techniques of offensive line play can help your team play to the best of its ability. Among the key aspects of offensive line play that you need to develop in your athletes are pre-snap fundamentals, run blocking, pass blocking, and blocking on the goal line. The center has a somewhat unique set of fundamentals to learn.

☐ *Pre-Snap Fundamentals*

Photo 9-9

As with any football position, the proper technique begins with the proper stance. As a rule, the ideal stance serves both run-blocking and pass-blocking techniques. In fact, a balanced stance gives players on the offensive line the ability to move in multiple directions without tipping off their assignment to the defense.

In essence, there are three basic stances that are utilized by offensive linemen: the three-point stance, which gives a player an opportunity to maximize his leverage when he is performing all of the tasks of blocking; the two-point stance, which some coaches believe enhances an offensive lineman's set-up move for pass protection—particularly dropback pass protection; and the four-point stance, which some coaches prefer for blocking on the goal line.

Three-Point Stance:

A balanced, three-point stance typically exhibits the following characteristics:

- A good base, including the following:
  - The feet should be positioned slightly wider that the width of the shoulders.
  - The feet should be placed close to a parallel position, not staggered.
  - The toes should be pointed forward.
  - The weight of the player should be centered on the inside of his feet.
  - The base should be centered in his hips and backside.
  - The player should be able to lift his down hand without affecting his balance.
- A proper power angle formed through the hips and shoulders, including the following:
  - The ankles should be flexed.
  - The heels should be on the ground (never raised).

- The knees should be ahead of the toes.
- The hips should be flexed, along with bending the knees and flexing the ankles.
- The hands in a position to set the proper demeanor including the following:
  - The thumb of the down hand should be positioned a few inches forward of the shoulders.
  - The weight of the lineman should be slightly forward on the fingertips of the down hand.
  - The off hand should be held open and placed on the side of the knee with the thumb pointing forward.
  - The off-hand elbow should be tight to the body.
  - The offensive linemen on the left side of the center ideally use a left-handed stance (i.e., left hand down).
  - The offensive linemen on the right side of the center ideally use a right-handed stance (i.e., right hand down).
  - The center may use a one-handed (i.e., three-point) stance or a two-handed (i.e., four-point) stance.
- The shoulders forming an adequate blocking surface, including the following:
  - The shoulders should be square to the line of scrimmage.
  - The shoulders should be parallel to the ground.
- The head and eyes leading the block, including the following:
  - The head should be positioned so that the upper screws on the helmet that connect the facemask to the headgear are facing forward.
  - The eyes should be focused straight ahead, as the blocker looks through the down defender.

Two-Point Stance:

A proper two-point stance exhibits the following features:

- The base:
  - The base should be centered in the player's hips and buttocks.
  - The feet should be positioned slightly wider than the width of the shoulders.
  - The feet should be positioned in a slight stagger, with the outside foot slightly back.
  - The toes should be pointed forward.
  - The lineman's weight should be centered on the inside of his feet—particularly on his inside foot.
- The power angle:
  - The ankles should be flexed.
  - The heels should be on the ground (never raised).
  - The hips should be flexed, along with the knees bent and the ankles flexed.
- The hands:
  - Both hands should be held open, with the thumb pointing forward and placed on top of the thigh.
- The shoulders and back:
  - The shoulders should be square to the line of scrimmage.
  - The lower back should be arched, with the shoulders pulled back and the back held in an upright position.

- The head and eyes:
  - The head should be positioned so that the upper screws on the helmet that connect the facemask to the headgear are facing forward.
  - The chin should be tucked back, so that the head is level.
  - The eyes should be focused on the defender whom the lineman is blocking.

Four-Point Stance:

A good four-point stance on the goal line is characterized by the following hallmarks:
- The weight is forward.
- The hands are slightly forward of the shoulders.
- The elbows are bent.
- The feet are balanced under the hips.
- The heels are slightly off the turf.
- The head and neck are bowed.

☐ *Run Blocking*

Run blocking is divided into three categories: man-blocking techniques; two-man blocking techniques, and pull techniques. When a blocker puts together the basic elements of an effective run block, he is said to be in the proper run-blocking position.

The Run-Blocking Position:

The proper run-blocking position is a combination of the correct body positioning and the blocker's movement during the "fit" stage of the block. A blocker fits with the defender at the moment of contact. A proper fit is a position that allows the blocker to maintain a sufficient blocking surface on the defender. The fit includes the stage of the block in which the offensive lineman maximizes his leverage. The proper run-blocking position is an important aspect of man blocks, particularly the drive block. A blocker exhibiting the correct blocking demeanor should demonstrate the following:
- Hips low
- Knees bent
- Ankles flexed
- Feet slightly wider than shoulder-width
- Lower back arched (i.e., hyperextended)
- Toes pointing outward
- Shoulders slightly elevated
- Elbows tight to the body
- Hands open, with the thumbs up

Optimal use of the leverage angle or power angle, from low to high, involves the following body position:
- The feet are flat—thereby maximizing the opportunity for contact with the ground.
- The toes are turned slightly outward.
- The knees are turned slightly inward.
- Hands to target. Depending on the type of angle desired, a flipper or both hands should be punched into the chest of the opponent in a low-to-high lifting fashion.
- The elbows remain tucked inward, while the thumbs point upward.
- Pad under pad. The shoulders of the blocker should be lower than the shoulders of the defender.
- The chin is kept level, so that the blocker's head remains level, while his neck is bowed.
- The head remains behind the plane of the chest, with the screws of the headgear facing forward.

Man Blocking:

Blocks categorized as man blocks are techniques used by only one lineman. The various types of man blocking include the following:

- Drive block
- Down block
- Level block
- Fan block
- Butt block
- Escape move
- Arc release
- Block release
- Alley block
- Reach block

• *Drive block.* Of all the man blocks, the most basic is the drive block. The drive block is at the core of the man-on-man struggle in the trenches. Mastering the techniques involved in the drive block is essential for an offensive lineman who is attempting to develop a complete repertoire of essential skills. As coach, it should be your objective to develop offensive linemen to defeat their opponents with a drive block. You should keep in mind that the outcome of most of the two-man blocking techniques usually depends on the movement created by a drive blocker.

The drive block consists of three main elements: the set to drive; the attack step; and the leverage step. The set to drive is the departure step of the offensive lineman (i.e., the first step of the blocker). This four-inch jab step serves as either a directional step or a settle step. The set to drive is a directional step that is used when the offensive lineman is firing off the line to meet the stunting defender. When the defender is not a threat to stunt, the set to drive is a settle step.

Setting to drive entails the lead foot grazing the turf to quickly plant and enhance the power of the offensive lineman's position. It is important for the offensive lineman to arch his lower back and flex his large muscle groups as he sets to drive. His eyes should focus on the target or the point-of-aim, as he attacks the neutral zone.

The attack step is the offensive lineman's second step. When drive blocking a defensive lineman, the attack step is executed just before contact is made with him. Ideally, the offensive blocker should make contact with the down defender after the blocker's third step; however, contact is usually made with the down defender after two and one-half steps. The attack step is also a tracking step. On the attack step, the blocker's inside foot steps toward the defender's inside foot, thereby putting the blocker on the track to strike the landmark with a full blocking surface. The attack step propels the blocker through the neutral zone, as the blocker gains momentum to hit through the defender.

"Hit through them, not to them" is a good phrase to use when coaching inexperienced offensive linemen. Beginning offensive linemen tend to stop at the moment of contact. When working with offensive linemen, you should note that while blocking is a fundamental part of football, it may not be a natural act.

Blocking should be taught in a manner that builds confidence, instills fundamentals, and puts each player in a position to succeed. One way of accomplishing this objective is to teach young kids to block through relatively soft dummies that are held with minimum resistance. In keeping with the concept of minimum resistance, you should refrain from standing on the blocking sled (if you use one) during repetitions. Indeed, many young players are not strong enough to explode through the heavier five-man and seven-man sleds. Standing on sleds only teaches the young offensive lineman to "hunker" on contact with the pad, thereby resulting in the development of major mechanical flaws and a possible negative mental mindset concerning blocking.

The next step (i.e., the third step) after the attack step is the leverage step. Against an outside-shaded defender, such as a 3 technique, the leverage step is made with the outside foot. The leverage step allows the blocker to gain depth and initiate the finish of the block. It is on this step that the blocker gets the lift on the defender as the fit is secured. You should coach your linemen to attempt to get the third step down before contact is made. The three-step progression must be made with four-inch strides, completed in rapid fire succession.

As the blocker completes his third step and engages the defender, he begins to attempt to gain lift on the defender. At that point, the blocker starts to apply his effort with regard to the "three-inch rule." Generally speaking, the three-inch rule can be used to determine a blocker's production.

The three-inch rule of offensive line blocking states that if the blocker can achieve a vertical dominance on the defender in a manner to knock him back off the line approximately three inches, the blocker will be successful in his block. In other words, after a blocker engages a defender, it is a matter of whether the blocker can achieve only three inches of movement. Considerable empirical evidence suggests that the success of a block is determined in the first fraction of a second. Almost without fail, a blocker who achieves three inches of movement and maintains a proper fit with the opponent will dominate the defender.

Lift is achieved primarily from the violent punch and thrust of the hands through the opponent's chest. Shooting the hands from the knee and ground causes the blocker's hips to snap forward on contact. As the hips snap forward, the feet must accelerate to chase the hips, thus providing even more momentum to the blocker's forward thrust.

By forcing the defender to elevate his head and pads, the blocker is able to finish the block. Once the defender elevates and the blocker begins to chase his hips by accelerating his feet, the defender becomes off balance and vulnerable to being knocked off his feet.

- *Down block.* A down block is an angle block toward the inside (i.e., toward the center). The down blocker will choose one of two landmarks to attack. The scouting report may dictate the choice of the landmark. Another factor to consider is the defender's technique during the last few scrimmage downs, or during the last scrimmage of a similar down-and-distance situation. Two landmarks are possible because a down defender will demonstrate one of two techniques. He may be a penetrator (i.e., a defender who attacks the line of scrimmage on the snap), or he may be a reader (i.e., a defender who sits on the line of scrimmage and reacts to the blocking scheme). A defensive penetrator has little regard for the particular blocking scheme. His role is to charge the line of scrimmage. By charging the line, the penetrating defender hopes to force your offensive linemen to tighten their splits.

In order to block a penetrator, the offensive lineman should aim for the opposite shoulder of the defender. The blocker should drive his outside arm and pad through the near shoulder of the defender, keeping the helmet and head away from contact. He must keep his hips down and his lower back arched, as he punches through the defender. The blocker should punch his inside hand to the chest of the defender, while he drives his outside hand under the armpit of the penetrating defender.

Driving the fist up through the near armpit of the defender forces the defender's near shoulder to elevate, thus increasing the likelihood of a pancake block. When punching through the near armpit of the penetrating defender, the blocker's outside hand should be kept open, so that he may wedge the armpit between his thumb and index finger. Positioning the outside hand to wedge the armpit gives the blocker an excellent feel of the defender's escape move. The hand locks in the defender, cements the fit, and prevents his escape.

A read-technique defender will attempt to anchor the gap and fight the pressure of the blocker. He will attempt to cross the face of the blocker and fight outside on a lateral plane. The read-technique down lineman is usually exceptionally strong in his upper body. Using his outside shoulder, this type of defensive lineman will dip and rip his inside shoulder across the face of the blocker to pursue toward the outside.

Since the read-technique defensive lineman doesn't move forward to any significant depth, the proper aiming point for the blocker is on a sharper angle from the blocker. The blocker doesn't fire out on a flat angle to block down on the reading defender. The aiming point against the reading defender is the defender's hip, not his shoulder. Because the inside reading defender will usually get an outside pull read by the inside blocker, the defender will be on the move toward the outside at the moment of the down blocker's contact.

If the down blocker were to aim for the defender's shoulder, the read-technique defender would gain several inches of clearance across the blocker's face. By aiming to the hip of the defensive reader, the down blocker can meet the defender with a secure fit, as the defender reacts to the outside pull read. The finish technique is the same finish technique that is used against the penetrator. The outside hand, arm, and shoulder provide a thrust and lift into the outside half of the defender's body.

The well-coached defender will keep his shoulders nearly parallel to the line of scrimmage, as he reacts to the outside pull. (If the defender commits the technique error of "facing up" to the blocker, he will be hit head on and easily pancaked by the down blocker's momentum.) The blocker should use his inside hand to punch across the defender's chest and grab cloth. His outside hand cements the fit and prevents the defender's escape.

If the landmark is correctly secured, and the fit is cemented, the down blocker can easily dominate the inside defender. By the same token, the size of the split should be directly related to the capabilities of the down blocker (i.e., the more skilled the blocker, the greater the split). For example, if a blocker is ineffective when down blocking, you should first consider cutting his split. For young players, it is particularly important that you build from success, instead of correct from failure.

This factor means that you should develop the down-blocking technique of young linemen from smaller splits. Developing an inexperienced lineman's down blocking technique from a tighter split gives him the opportunity to experience the feel of success. A smaller distance between the defender and the blocker allows the blocker to concentrate on his departure, position, and finish of the block. Working from inflexible, fixed splits is a waste of time, if your linemen aren't physically capable of controlling the split. You should concentrate on teaching the technique of the down block first, and then gradually widen the splits, as your linemen become more skilled at down blocking.

Some coaches install a system of splits, without taking into account the undeveloped down-blocking skills of younger linemen. These coaches are eventually forced to tighten the splits so that the

blockers can achieve their goal. Achieving the goal may then be complicated further by the blocker's fear of failure and lack of confidence, caused by his previous inability to control the larger split. It is much better to start with tighter splits and then progress to down blocking with wider splits.

Successful down blocking is a matter of the linemen adhering to several coaching points, including:

- Keeping the eyes and hands on target
- Keeping the hips down
- Keeping a proper run-blocking position
- Being able to redirect to prevent the defender's escape

• *Level block*. A level block is a backside-blocking technique used exclusively by a tackle. The level block is normally used by the backside tackle, when he happens to be aligned on the split side of the formation. When this scenario occurs, the defense will normally employ a stack alignment behind a weakside 4 and 5 technique tackle, if there is no weakside tight end. The stack alignment may be a loose-stack alignment or a vertical-stack alignment.

The level-blocking technique results in the offensive tackle moving on an upfield plane through the first two levels. The level-blocking tackle's assignment is to cut-off the pursuit of any defender who attempts to cross his face. It is important that the tackle step to a point between the set-to-reach landmark and the set-to-drive landmark, so that he can use only the outside half of his body to block the defender in his path. Ideally, the tackle wants to use his outside shoulder and flipper to slam the inside portion of the down defender, before proceeding into the second level.

The tackle's primary objective is to disrupt the pursuit of the defensive tackle and force him to go behind the block. Keeping the shoulders square as he moves upfield, the offensive tackle should immediately begin to search for the outside backer. The outside linebacker will likely hang for a moment, before he begins to shuffle inside to check cutback. This momentary hang-and-shuffle action gives the level-blocking offensive tackle an opportunity to rip up through the defensive tackle's inside shoulder and move up through the second level to cut-off the pursuit of the linebacker.

One of the most important points of emphasis of the level-block technique should be the need for the offensive tackle to chop his feet and widen his base, as he enters the second level. By cutting his stride length and widening his feet, the blocker positions himself in the proper run-blocking demeanor to wall out the shuffling outside linebacker. The choppy footwork and the wide base also help to ensure the timing of the tackle's arrival at the junction point. Once the tackle reaches the junction point, he should deliver a high "run-through" block, as he drives his outside shoulder pad into the chest of the outside linebacker.

An effective level-blocking technique involves the following actions:

- Taking the appropriate set to level block
- Keeping the shoulders square at all times
- Chopping the feet and widening the base when moving into the second level
- Preventing any defender from crossing a blocker's face

• *Fan block*. A fan block is an angle block toward the outside (i.e., away from the center). In this type of block, the blocker attacks the near hip of the defender. All factors considered, the fan block is one of the easier blocks to execute. This relative ease occurs because of the natural leverage angle created

by the defender's alignment and the defender's relative position to the hole through which the ballcarrier runs. When executing a fan block, the blocker must address the fact that a down defender will demonstrate one of two techniques. He may be either a penetrator—a defender who attacks the line of scrimmage on the snap or a reader—a defender who sits on the line of scrimmage and reacts to the blocking scheme.

In order to fan block a penetrator, the offensive lineman should pay close attention to his own mechanics in maintaining the proper run-blocking position. His feet should be slightly wider than his shoulders, and he should use his hands to punch, extend, and grab cloth on the chest of the defender. He must keep his shoulders on a lower plane than the defender's shoulders. His elbows should stay close to his body. It is particularly important that the fan blocker keep his face up, so that he doesn't become top-heavy in the block. Balance is one of the critical keys to executing an effective fan block.

On a fan block, the inside arm of the blocker is the dominant leverage arm. The fan blocker's inside arm fulfills the same role as the outside arm of the down blocker. Since both the fan block and the down block are angle blocks, the techniques are mirrored techniques. What the outside arm is for the down blocker is comparable to what the inside arm is for the fan blocker.

The fan blocker should drive his inside hand up through the near armpit of the defender. By punching to the armpit, the inside arm forces the inside pad of the defender to elevate. When one shoulder of a defender elevates, he becomes off balance, which makes him easy to topple. Since the inside pad of the outside-shade technique is his attack pad, driving the defender's inside shoulder upward removes his leverage.

The outside hand of the fan blocker punches to the inside number of the defender. The fan blocker should use his hand to grab cloth and control the defender. Extending the outside arm into the defender produces a lateral thrust. This thrust helps to facilitate the outward push of the blocker against the defender, thereby widening the hole. The outside arm also allows the blocker to feel the pressure of the defender.

Feeling the pressure of the defender cues the blocker to redirect his momentum and maintain contact. The inside arm provides the lift and forces an imbalance of the defender's posture; the outside arm assists in knocking the defender outward.

The wider the alignment of the defender, the flatter the attack angle the blocker should take. The placement of the set-to-drive step is dependent upon the defender's width and depth from the line of scrimmage. Staying on line to the defender's near hip is especially important for the success of the fan block. Firing out on too flat of an angle usually results in the defender easily ripping his outside shoulder across the face of the blocker. Firing out on too sharp of an angle usually results in the defender running behind the block to easily make the play. The fan-block technique is particularly sensitive to the blocker making the proper set-to-drive and attack step.

The components of an effective fan block include the following:

- A proper set-to-drive step
- A proper attack step
- Keeping the eyes and hands on target
- Maintaining a proper run-blocking demeanor
- Fighting pressure so that the blocker can redirect and maintain the fit

- *Butt block.* The butt block is a supplemental technique used with the set-to-reach step. Exclusively a backside-blocking technique, the butt block may appear to be slightly unorthodox. It is, however, an effective technique to use against a backside defender who attempts to "olay" behind the inside-zone blocker. (Refer to the next section for a detailed definition of the term "Olay").

  Similar to the level-blocking technique, the butt block is only used by the offensive tackle against a 50 defensive front structure. The tackle should not use the butt block, unless he is sure that a defensive lineman aligned on the backside guard is accounted for by a teammate. If the defensive lineman aligned on the guard is accounted for by rule, the backside tackle can freely use the butt-block technique when he steps to reach playside.

  The butt-blocking tackle uses his backside as the primary blocking surface. To use the butt-blocking technique, the tackle sets to reach inside, but plants and backs up into the playing defender. (The defender can be using an olay technique or simply attempting to run around the block, as he dips behind the tackle's backside.) When backing into the defender, the tackle will swing his backside arm as a large wing to hook the defender with his elbow.

  The finish position of the butt block involves a situation in which the blocker is facing upfield, and the defender is facing the backfield. They fit together closely at the hip—the tackle's outside hip to the defender's inside hip. To secure this hip-to-hip position, the tackle uses his outside arm to swing backward and pinch the defender between the back of his upper arm and his ribs. The tackle must then continue to shuffle his feet backward to maintain the fit, which is secured by his outside arm.

- *Escape moves* (olay and rip). Two basic inside moves are used to clear a defender. These moves are closely linked to the influence block, since they are both escape mechanisms for a blocker to slip underneath a defensive lineman and thus create an inside crease for a trapper coming from the offside.

  The first inside move to consider is the olay move. The term "olay" is a common term for a move used on both the offensive and defensive sides of the ball. It refers to a quick overhead, swimming motion by the arm opposite the direction in which the player is going. On offense, the olay technique is normally used as an escape move to the inside. It is more commonly used by a tight end, when he is escaping the clutches of the defensive end in order to release into a pass pattern. The tight end uses the olay technique to escape both to the outside and inside. For an offensive guard, the olay is an effective move to get to the inside and clear the trap bait.

  To olay, the guard must quickly swim his outside hand over the head of the defender. The olay move is made easier by the guard setting to drive (or pass setting the defender) and then immediately slapping the defender with his inside hand. The guard then drives his outside leg across the defender and swims his outside hand over the top. His outside hip must quickly follow his outside foot, as the guard crosses the defender's face. The olay is extremely effective in creating a crease for the trapper to exploit.

  The rip move is the more common escape move. As such, it offers its own unique advantages. First, the rip move is a slightly quicker escape move. The offensive lineman pushes hard off his outside foot and steps to a 45-degree angle inside with his inside foot. He rips his outside arm across the defender in an uppercut fashion, as he dips his outside shoulder.

Dipping the outside shoulder decreases the available surface area that the defensive lineman can use as leverage. The defensive lineman is trained to shoot his hands inside to the chest of the blocker. When the blocker's outside shoulder dips and twists across the defender, the defender has no surface to strike with his outside hand. A defensive lineman—even a well-coached one—tends to respond to the blocker's lowered shoulder by placing his outside hand on the back of the blocker's shoulder. The act of the defender placing his hand on the back of the blocker's shoulder actually assists the ripping blocker in gaining clearance to the inside. The defender will normally push against the back of the blocker's shoulder, thereby aiding him in crossing the blocker's face. Defensive coaches often work hard on training the defensive linemen to keep their outside hand low—under the ripping blocker's outside shoulder.

The blocker uses his outside arm to drive across the defender's body and to break free to the inside. Once the second step is completed, the ripping blocker will work upfield with his shoulders square. Executing his assignment, the escaping blocker will work up through the second level to either seal a linebacker or combo off of a 3 technique.

When a defensive lineman is aligned on an inside teammate, the ripping offensive lineman should use a glide step in finishing his escape. When no defensive lineman is positioned on the offensive lineman to the inside, the ripping lineman should take a more angular first step (i.e., flatter down the line of scrimmage). Stepping flatter into the line of scrimmage allows the ripping lineman to gain more clearance from the baited defensive lineman.

• *Arc release*. The arc release is a block used by the tight end to escape the defensive end and to release outside to block a second- or third-level defender. The arc release is also used by the tight end to get a wide release and to then run a vertical pass route into the seam of the secondary.

To execute an arc release, the tight end executes a sweep-pull technique to the outside. The bucket step of the outside foot creates distance from the line of scrimmage. Unlike the drop-step type of bucket step by a loop blocker in the fold-blocking combination, the arc-release bucket step includes a pivot and push off of the inside foot to gain width. The cushion created by the bucket step prevents the defensive end from getting his hands on the tight end. Adequate depth also allows the arc-releasing tight end to read the action of the secondary force. Once depth is gained, the tight end squares his shoulders and looks upfield.

Used primarily with an option attack, the arc release gets the tight end to the defensive flank, with a desirable degree of timing. As a blocker, the arc-releasing tight end's normal role is to work upfield to position himself so that he may hook the force defender. The force defender is the secondary defender who is responsible for turning the ballcarrier inside to the defensive pursuit.

• *Block release*. An escape mechanism used exclusively by the tight end, the block release allows the tight end to attack the defensive end, and then use his leverage to release cleanly into the pass pattern. The block-releasing tight end slams his shoulder into the defender. The tight end's head is kept to the side of the desired release. For an outside-block release, the tight end engages the defender with his inside shoulder. Once engaged, the tight end quickly disengages and releases into the pattern. A key coaching point of the block release is the tight end's leverage on the defender.

The tight end must deliver contact from his hips and hit upward through the defender.

• *Alley block.* The alley block is a backside, cut-off block that is carried up through the third level. Once a cut-off blocker has worked upfield to cut off the pursuit of the first- and second-level defenders, the cut-off blocker turns to sprint to the sideline. The width to which he sprints is dependent upon the width of the play called. If the play is a wide play (such as a sweep), the alley blocker should sprint further across the field, because the alley will be wider. When the alley is wide, the alley blocker should sprint across the field at a depth of approximately seven yards deep. He should intercept the alley just as the ballcarrier hits the alley, with his shoulders square. If the play is an off-tackle play, the alley will be tighter. When the alley is tight to the ball, the alley blocker will angle further upfield to enter the alley approximately 10 to 15 yards downfield.

The primary objective of the alley blocker is to enter the alley on a near-perpendicular path to the ballcarrier and blindside a third-level tackler. The most common recipient of an alley block is the free safety. A free safety usually attempts to fill the alley to tackle the ballcarrier. In filling the alley, the free safety intently focuses on the ballcarrier. The alley blocker can block the free safety as he attacks from the inside. The alley blocker should make sure that the momentum of his block is delivered from a position that is forward of the free safety to avoid the possibility of an illegal block in the back. Backside offensive linemen who hustle and master the alley-blocking technique will often turn a long run into a touchdown.

The free safety is often unaccounted for by the blocking scheme. The alley block can address this. The alley block can be performed by any backside-blocking technique blocker who eventually works his way through the second level. The alley block can be performed off of the inside zone or the fold block.

• *Reach (hook) block.* The reach block (i.e., hook block) is, by definition, an onside-blocking technique. It is technically the outside portion of the outside-zone block. To perform a reach block, the onside offensive lineman should set to reach. Setting to reach involves the blocker pushing off his inside foot and taking a set-to-reach step with his outside foot.

The second step is made through the middle of the defender, as the blocker rips his inside arm across the defender's chest. The blocker can use his inside arm as a flipper to rip with and secure the fit against the defender. The reach blocker's objective should be to initially overtake the defender in width. The reach blocker can then ride the outside shoulder of the defender, as he works up to the next level.

The reach blocker should use his flipper to push against the defender and prevent the defender from grabbing the blocker and pulling him to the ground. Lateral movement with outside leverage is integral to a successful reach block. The reach block is the mirrored blocking technique of the inside-zone blocking combination "zone" call. Both blocks are "J" blocks that are characterized by the blocker flattening his path to stop the defender's pursuit.

Two-Man Blocking:

The second major category of offensive line run blocks is the two-man black. Two-man blocks involve blocking techniques executed by two linemen,

working together as a tandem unit. Among the various types of two-man blocks are the following:

- Combo block
- Cross block
- Deuce block
- Double-team block
- Fold block
- Inside-zone block
- Outside-zone block

• *Combo block*. Also known as the bump block, the combo block is an excellent scheme to counter defensive stack alignments. The combo is nearly identical to the double-team block in that it consists of a post block and a seal block, executed by two adjacent offensive linemen. The primary objective of a combo block is two-fold—vertical movement of the down defender accomplished with an outside seal of the linebacker. The inside man (the post blocker) of the combo block drives his man backward, thereby winning the three-inch battle.

The outside man (seal blocker) glide steps inside and strikes the defensive lineman with the flat surface of his inside shoulder pad. The seal blocker's primary objective is to lift and turn the outside shoulder of the defender. This action opens the shoulders of the defensive lineman so that the post blocker can swing his hips to the outside and gain outside leverage as he drives the defender upfield.

When the defender's outside shoulder is elevated and twisted backward, the blocking surface is increased for the post blocker. The post blocker then needs only to slide his head and hips to the outside edge of the defensive lineman to gain outside leverage as he drives him upfield.

The dynamics of the combo block allow it to account for any action of the stacked defenders. This feature of accountability versus the stack games (stunts) begins with the set-to-drive step by the post blocker. The post blocker will set to drive with either his outside foot or his inside foot, depending upon the anticipated action of the down defender. If the defender is aligned in a position from which he could stunt inside, the post blocker sets to drive with his inside foot. If the defender is aligned in a definite outside shade, the post blocker sets to drive with his outside foot, because the defender is not a threat to successfully stunt inside. It should be kept in mind that the set-to-drive step—if properly executed—is only a four-inch step. The post blocker should keep his pads square at all times. Over-striding on the set-to-drive step inside will create a gap between the hips of the post blocker and the seal blocker.

The second feature of the combo block that provides accountability for the stack games is the hip-to-hip coaching point. Although the post blocker has some responsibility in maintaining hip-to-hip contact with the seal blocker, it is primarily the responsibility of the seal blocker to establish the hip-to-hip relationship. Once their hips make contact, the seal blocker should work to maintain this hip-to-hip relationship with the post blocker.

Maintaining hip-to-hip contact between the seal blocker and the post blocker guarantees the seal between the two blockers and denies the down defender the opportunity to split the blockers. If the down defender splits the blocker's hips, he can keep outside leverage on the post blocker and break the seal of the combo. It should be remembered that sealing the defenders inside is the second element of the two-fold objective of the combo block.

Achieving lift on the defender is one of the primary goals of the two blockers. Lift is accomplished when both blockers punch upward in an uppercut manner

to the defensive lineman's breast plates. Some defenders—particularly outside-shaded defenders—will attempt to drop to the ground when they recognize a seal blocker glide-stepping inside. This defensive technique can break down the integrity of the hip-to-hip seal, if the blockers are not hitting on the rise through the defender.

To hit on the rise, both blockers should use their near arm as a hook. The seal blocker should use his inside arm as a hook, while the post blocker should use his outside arm as a hook. If the blockers keep their shoulders square, the hooking technique with the near arms can catch the defender before he drops to the ground.

In this regard, an important coaching point to emphasize is that your seal blocker should stay engaged on a down defender, either until he feels vertical movement on the defender, or until he feels the defender stunt inside across the face of the post blocker. The uppercut-hooking technique by both blockers is discussed in greater detail in this chapter's section on the double-team block.

For the seal blocker to contact the outside shoulder flush with his inside shoulder pad, the blocker has to glide step. The glide step is a sideways step inside to the post blocker. A good glide step is made slightly upfield with the toes pointing forward. The step is enhanced by the blocker pushing forcefully off his outside foot.

A proper glide step keeps the shoulders square, as the seal blocker engages the defender, and allows the blocker to use his inside arm in the hooking manner described previously. The glide step is also the first step of an escape move used by a playside blocker on the trap.

As previously stated, a successful combo block achieves two primary objectives—the down defender is knocked off the ball and sealed inside, and the scraping linebacker is contained by the seal blocker. To engage the linebacker, the glide-stepping seal blocker must rip his inside arm and pad through the outside pad of the down defender. As he clears the defender, the seal blocker must look inside to pick up the angle of the linebacker's scrape. He should then adjust his path and chop his stride to join with the linebacker from a snug, outside-in blocking demeanor.

Two finishing techniques are available to the seal blocker. The seal blocker may either finish the combo block by driving his inside shoulder pad through the outside hip and thigh pad of the linebacker or finish the combo block by drive-blocking the linebacker with a good fit and run-blocking demeanor. If the seal blocker attempts to cut the linebacker, he should make sure he snaps his head up, as he delivers the blow to the outside hip of the linebacker.

A few additional factors should be considered concerning the seal-block combination. For example, the coaching points for the post blocker and the seal blocker should account for all possible defensive stunts. If the down defender stunts outside, the combo block turns into a double-team. When gliding inside, the seal blocker should keep his eyes on the near foot and hip of the down defender. If the defender's outside foot steps outward, the seal blocker can recognize the defender stunting outside. Once the seal blocker recognizes the outside stunt, he converts the combo block into a solid double-team block.

If the down defender stunts inside, the seal blocker can read the near foot and hip of the defender disappearing inside. The seal blocker can then immediately find the linebacker. Searching out the linebacker allows the seal blocker to immediately move to meet the linebacker in his path. When the down defender stunts inside, the seal blocker should use the drive-blocking technique against the linebacker. Such a defensive game characteristically has a tight scraping linebacker. In this situation, the face-up drive-blocking technique, with a good fit and run-blocking demeanor, is the better technique against a tight scraping linebacker.

• *Cross block.* The cross block is similar to the fold block in that two blockers cross paths to create a seam. However, that similarity is the only common ground between these two types of two-man blocks. Performed by two adjacent offensive linemen, the cross block is a blocking scheme in which two blockers perform angle blocks on two down defenders.

The blocker positioned on the outside of the tandem goes first, as he executes a down block. The inside blocker takes a position step with his outside foot, opening his shoulders so that his outside teammate has clearance for his down block. The inside blocker should jerk his outside elbow backward to open his hips as he position steps. His initial step is very similar to the first step of a G-block pull.

As the down blocker clears underneath the set of the inside blocker, the inside blocker should take his second step. As the inside blocker steps with his inside foot on the second step, he should reach to grab the outside cheek of the down blocker's buttocks. Using his inside hand, the inside blocker should pull himself forward on a tight angle off the tail of the down blocker. This reach-and-pull technique with the inside hand ensures a tight fit off the tail of the down blocker and a good inside-out path to the defender.

To finish the hybrid fan block-trap pull, the inside blocker aims for the near hip of the defender. Against a reading defender, the fit of the inside blocker's technique must be that of a proper fan block—not too flat and not too sharp. Against a penetrating defender who is ignoring the down block of the outside blocker, the fan block becomes a short trap pull. The inside blocker must kick out the penetrating defender with the trap-pull technique, using his outside shoulder to drive the defender outward.

The cross block is an excellent isolation scheme against an 4-4 even front. When facing a playside 3 technique tackle, with a playside 7 technique end, the cross block scheme is the favored scheme for splitting the "B" gap on the isolation play.

The cross block is also a great way to split the weakside of the defense from the one-back set, when the defensive front removes a linebacker to cover a running back who is aligned as a wide receiver. The trips formation can provide you with an excellent opportunity to use the cross block against the weakside of the defensive front.

An important coaching point with regard to the cross block is that it is basically a line call. This point refers to the fact that the block is called at the line by one of the two blockers. Since the block is usually executed by the playside guard and the tackle, the block is normally called by the guard, when he and the tackle are each facing a defensive lineman. The cross block should only be called when the inside blocker is facing an outside shade. If the inside blocker is facing an inside shade, the cross-block scheme is inappropriate.

When calling a cross block, the offensive guard must understand the relationship of the linebacker to the formation. For example, if a guard calls a cross block when the play is a base dive from a one-back set, he must understand that the near linebacker must be removed to a position outside of the offensive tackle-box.

• *Deuce block*. Appropriately described as an inside-out combo block, the deuce block is a two-man scheme that is used on the playside of the counter-trey play. The deuce block technique is also similar to the inside-zone block in that the inside blocker executes a "hanging" technique, as he drives the defensive lineman backward.

When properly executed, the deuce combination seals the down defender inside, while it carries him upfield. The deuce block begins a double-team, as the primary blocker sets to drive with his outside foot. The outside blocker initially blocks down on the defensive lineman, but quickly adjusts his technique to that of a backside blocker in an inside-zone combination.

Like an inside-zone technique and the combo block, the premium is on getting vertical movement against the defensive lineman. The inside blocker is the primary blocker as he initially uses a drive-blocking technique to engage the inside half of the defender's body. It is his responsibility to hang on to the defensive lineman until the outside blocker works his tail around to gain a face-up position on the defender.

The timing of the block is such that the outside blocker normally takes over the defender between the third and fourth step of the inside blocker's hanging-post block. The inside blocker can release off the hanging technique when he feels the outside blocker mesh with him and take over the vertical movement of the defender. In essence, the outside blocker bumps the inside blocker off to the inside and takes over control of the defender.

Once the outside blocker bumps the primary blocker to the inside, the primary blocker looks to seal the inside linebacker. The timing of the release of the primary blocker off the double-team normally puts him in a position to capture a linebacker who has diagnosed the counter trey and is redirecting his flow back to the playside. One important coaching point to the primary blocker's technique that should be emphasized is: If the primary blocker recognizes that a linebacker has prematurely recognized the counter flow and is scraping underneath the deuce block, the primary blocker must immediately disengage his vertical movement and come off on the scraping linebacker.

The most difficult defender to block in a pair of defenders is always the defender to the inside. Therefore, even though the inside blocker functions as the primary force of vertical movement against the defensive lineman, his ultimate responsibility is the linebacker. Some coaches refer to the technique of the inside blocker as a "peek" technique. The inside blocker can afford to hang on the down defender, as long as he peeks inside for the linebacker and sees no threat.

If the primary blocker feels that the inside linebacker is not a pre-snap threat, he alerts the outside blocker that he is hanging. If the primary blocker feels that the inside linebacker is a threat because of his pre-snap alignment, the primary blocker can alert the outside blocker with a "gap" call. When the inside blocker calls "gap," the outside blocker changes his technique from an inside-zone technique to a down block.

The gap call results in both blockers blocking inside with a down-block technique. The down-block technique allows the blockers to stop defensive penetration and caves the defensive line down to the inside.

- *Double-team block*. Without question, the oldest two-man blocking scheme in football is the double-team. The standard double-team involves both blockers getting the point of their shoulders together to form one large blocking surface. They work hip-to-hip, as they sweep the defensive lineman upfield. The double-team is ideally finished with the blockers driving the defensive lineman five to seven yards past the line of scrimmage.

Double-teams are commonly thought of as outside-in blocks. The inside blocker normally provides the post (i.e., lift and movement) to the combination, while the outside blocker secures the outside leverage and assists in the lift and movement. Inside-out double-teams are also effective schemes against the inside-shaded defender—particularly when the defense offsets the nose tackle away from the shade.

On an inside-out double-team, the outside blocker is the post blocker. while the inside blocker is the seal blocker who seals the defender out of the running lane. The outside blocker provides the lift and movement, while the inside blocker secures the inside leverage and assists in the lift and movement of the inside-shaded defender.

Two basic coaching philosophies are widely held concerning how to teach the double-team block. One philosophy strictly requires both blockers to sell out on the defender, sticking on him, regardless of his action. The more liberal philosophy of coaching the double-team calls for the double-team to convert to a combo block, if the defender stunts away from the hole—across the face of the post blocker.

Many coaches believe that a strict interpretation of the double-team is a waste of a blocker. If a defensive lineman stunts across the face of a post blocker, the seal blocker should stay on his vertical path and go up on the linebacker. In fact, an appropriate emphasis on the proper footwork and proper run-blocking demeanor can provide any team with a legitimate opportunity to successfully pick up any defensive stunt man-on-man.

With the exception of the single-minded focus on obtaining maximum vertical movement of the defender, the double-team blockers execute their technique in exactly the same manner as the combo blockers. Among the shared coaching points of the double-team and combo block are the following:

- Post block:
    - Execute with drive block coaching points.
    - Emphasis is on vertical movement.
    - Both hands uppercut punch through the defender to lift the defender's shoulders.
    - Win the three-inch battle.
    - Stick on the defender to work to gain playside leverage.

- Seal block:
    - Execute with a glide step (toes forward, over and up into the defender).
    - Postside arm rips upward in a manner of an uppercut to lift the defender's near shoulder.
    - Eyes read the near foot, knee and hip of the defender.

- Foot goes inside, and the knee and the hip disappear (i.e., the defender crosses the face of the blocker's teammate); the seal blocker goes up on the linebacker.
- Foot goes outside; the seal blocker sinks his hips and sticks on the defender.
- The defender's near shoulder is driven backward to open his shoulders and to maximize the blocking surface for the post blocker.

• *Fold block.* The fold block involves two adjacent linemen executing separate techniques with regard to a couple of factors—whether the fold block is an outside fold or an inside fold and whether the particular player is positioned on the inside or the outside of the tandem. The inside-fold block is characterized by a fan block outward by the inside player. On the inside-fold block, the outside blocker is responsible for looping around behind the inside blocker to get into position to drive block the linebacker. Keeping the shoulders square is an important coaching point for the loop blocker. Proper footwork allows the loop blocker to keep his shoulders square, as he "rounds the horn," underneath on the linebacker.

On an inside-fold block, the proper footwork for a loop blocker involves him taking a drop step with his outside foot. The drop step is made to the inside, as the blocker momentarily crosses his feet. He immediately follows with his inside foot stepping back to regain a good base. After the second step, the loop blocker is facing the line of scrimmage with his shoulders square. At that point, he is positioned two big steps behind the line of scrimmage.

The loop blocker is then able to read both the outward movement of the fan blocker and the filling action of the linebacker. Upon stepping backward with his inside foot, the loop blocker immediately drives off his outside foot to drive block the linebacker with a proper run-blocking demeanor. The loop blocker should attempt to fit closely off the tail of the fan blocker to junction the linebacker. The junction point of the linebacker's path is usually closely related to the backfield flow of the play. You should take care to include a simulation of the linebacker's expected flow when practicing the fold block. Inside-fold blocks are normally used with dive plays, which exhibit some form of counter-action.

On an outside-fold block, the proper footwork for a loop blocker involves him taking a drop step with his inside foot. The drop step is made to the outside as the blocker momentarily crosses his feet. He immediately follows with his outside foot stepping back to regain a good base. After the second step, the loop blocker is facing the line of scrimmage, with his shoulders square, at a depth of two big steps behind the line of scrimmage.

The loop blocker is then able to read both the down block and the filling action of the linebacker. Upon stepping backward with his inside foot, the loop blocker immediately drives off his inside foot to drive block the linebacker with a good run-blocking demeanor. He should attempt to fit closely to the tail of the down blocker as he rounds the horn to meet the linebacker.

The meeting point of the linebacker's path is usually closely related to the backfield flow of the play. You should take care to include a simulation of the linebacker's expected flow when practicing the fold block. Outside-fold blocks are normally used with stretch plays that are designed to hit off tackle or outside the end.

• *Inside-zone block.* The inside-zone blocking combination is an area-blocking scheme that seals off the backside pursuit. It involves two adjacent linemen blocking an area in tandem—one blocker acting as a frontside blocker and one blocker acting as a backside blocker.

The frontside blocker of an inside-zone combination sets to drive with the foot nearest the defender. His primary objective is to maintain playside leverage on the down defender, as he fits tightly with his backside flipper in contact with the defender. He should avoid being caught up with the defender, yet maintain pressure against the defender, as he works up to the next level.

Maintaining pressure on the defender with the backside flipper is called "hanging" on the defender. The hanging technique is the basic technique of the frontside blocker of the inside zone. The backside blocker can be alerted to the frontside blocker's use of the hanging technique by the "I'm hanging" call of the frontside blocker. The frontside guard makes an "I'm hanging" call when the linebacker is aligned away from the playside, either stacked or offset away from the call.

If the linebacker is aligned over the frontside blocker, the frontside blocker will make a "zone" call to the backside blocker. The zone call tells the backside blocker that he has the defensive lineman without any help. The point to remember is that the frontside blocker cannot afford to hang on the down defender, if the linebacker is aligned on the playside of the down defender. The zone call results in both blockers setting to reach the playside shoulder of the defenders. Instead of the emphasis being on the vertical movement of the down defender, as with the "I'm hanging" call, the emphasis is placed on cutting off the defender's pursuit.

The inside-zone blocking technique results in a moving wall that stops backside pursuit. It is an excellent combination scheme to create a cutback-running lane between the tackles. With the exception of the "zone" call, vertically moving (i.e., knock him off the ball) the down defender is the primary objective of the inside-zone combination. Key coaching points for the inside-zone blocking combination include the following:

- The frontside blocker taking a solid set-to-drive step into the down defender when hanging
- The frontside blocker keeping his playside arm free
- The frontside blocker using the flipper technique to hang into the defender, when appropriate
- The frontside blocker communicating the "I'm hanging" or "zone" call to the backside blocker
- The frontside blocker keeping his eyes open for the linebacker attempting to scrape over the top
- The backside blocker obtaining a good fit to the defender
- The backside blocker sweeping his backside shoulder upfield to get square on the down defender and gain playside leverage
- Both blockers pushing the defender upfield until the backside blocker takes over
- Both blockers gaining playside leverage on the linebacker and down defender

• *Outside-zone block.* An outside-zone block is a two-man reach block featuring a frontside blocker and a backside blocker. The outside-zone block is by definition an onside-blocking technique that has two independent parts—an outside blocker (i.e., frontside blocker) and an inside blocker (i.e., backside blocker). In reality, the outside-zone block

is a five-man block, because when one offensive lineman has an outside-zone block as his rule, all the other offensive linemen typically have the zone block as their playside rule. An excellent blocking technique for quick-hitting flank plays (e.g., toss sweeps, stretch, etc.), the outside-zone block is normally used at the point of attack, along with a massive backside moving wall sweeping over and up to the side of the play.

To perform an outside-zone block, the onside offensive lineman should set to reach. Setting to reach involves the blocker pushing off his inside foot and taking a set-to-reach step with his outside foot. The second step is made through the middle of the defender, as the blocker rips his inside arm across the defender's chest. He can use his inside arm to rip with the flipper and secure the fit against the defender.

The outside-zone blocker's objective should be to initially overtake the defender in width. The outside-zone blocker can then ride the outside shoulder of the defender, as he works up to the next level. The blocker should use his inside arm and hand to prevent the defender from grabbing the blocker and pulling him to the ground.

The technique of the block usually depends upon the defensive-front structure. For example, when the right guard recognizes a 30 defense, he faces a man over him. The guard also recognizes that the 30-defensive structure places a man on the adjacent tackle. (Note: "over" identifies a defender as a linebacker; "on" identifies the defender as a lineman.)

To execute the outside zone against the 30-defensive front structure, the right guard should set to reach and read the defensive tackle's reaction. If the outside play is called at the most opportune time, the 4 technique defensive tackle will be running an angle stunt inside or sparking inside. An angle-stunting 4 technique attacks on a direct line to the outside eye of the guard, whereas a sparking 4 technique attacks with an over-and-up move, with the defender keeping his shoulders square as he slides upward through the "B" gap.

The offensive guard's first step should be made to one of two landmarks. When expecting an angle charge by the defensive tackle, the guard should step to the tighter landmark (i.e., the tackle's near foot). When expecting a sparking tackle or a reading tackle, the guard should step to the outside foot of the tackle. In summary, the wider the defensive tackle's alignment, the wider the landmark should be.

The key to the first step is tied to the backside zone blocker's head placement. When performing the outside-zone block from an inside position of a blocking tandem, the blocker should attempt to get his outside earhole to the inside hip of his teammate. For example, the guard should attempt to get his outside earhole to the tackle's inside hip.

Once the offensive guard takes off to this landmark, he may adjust his angle upfield to gain leverage on an inside-stunting defender. Putting his near ear to the near hip of the outside teammate guarantees that the backside blocker can achieve outside leverage against the man aligned on the outside man.

The second step of the backside blocker is critical to achieving success against the inside-stunting defensive lineman. Against an inside-stunting defender, the backside portion of the zone should angle off his second step. Angling off the inside step entails the blocker adjusting the angle of his inside step to secure the proper fit and to establish the correct run-blocking demeanor. If the defender sparks inside, the guard takes a flatter second step as he slides outside, with his shoulders parallel to the line of scrimmage. Working to keep the shoulders parallel and securing outside leverage are the keys to successfully outside-zone block the sparking defender.

If the defender is angling inside on a direct path to the backside blocker's original alignment, the blocker's second step should strike more upfield. If the play is run to the wide hole, the backside blocker can simply run through the outside shoulder of the angling defender. To run through the angle-stunting defender, the backside blocker drives his inside shoulder through the outside shoulder of the stunting defender. Generally, the backside blocker's back foot should always step on or near a 45-degree angle toward the defender aligned on the outside teammate.

If an offensive guard is to properly read a 4 technique's reaction to the outside-zone combination, he must focus on the near foot of the 4 technique. If the foot points toward the blocker, the blocker knows that the defensive tackle is stunting inside. A veteran offensive guard can read the point of the foot.

If the defensive tackle steps to the inside, but keeps his toe pointed forward, he is running a spark. If the defensive tackle steps to the inside and points his toe on angle toward the guard, the defensive tackle is running an angle stunt inside. If the defender is playing a read technique, his near foot will step away from the guard, and his toe will point to the outside.

Upon reading the defender's toe pointing to the outside, the backside blocker can continue on his hook-shaped path upfield. The backside blocker's outside shoulder should rub against the frontside blocker's inside shoulder, as the two work outside and upfield as a tandem. Once the tandem is formed, the backside blocker can immediately feel the defensive tackle's reaction to the frontside blocker's set to reach. If the defensive tackle fights hard to the outside, the defender's near hip will disappear across the face of the frontside blocker. In this case, the backside blocker will have no blocking surface to secure on the defender. The backside blocker should then continue upfield on his hook-shaped path to angle off and cut down the second-level defender—the linebacker.

If the defender's near hip doesn't disappear, the backside blocker will feel an available blocking surface, as the defender hangs on the frontside blocker. When the defensive tackle hangs on the frontside blocker, the backside blocker should push the frontside blocker off the tandem-zone block and secure the fit to the outside hip and shoulder of the defensive tackle.

The backside blocker should secure the fit to the defender's outside by using his inside hand to grab the defender's chest and to pinch the defender into a secure fit between the blocker's head and backside shoulder. In this manner, the outside-zone block evolves from various one-man blocks along the line of scrimmage to a true two-man blocking scheme.

For an inside blocker, who is reach blocking a man on his teammate, the components of an effective outside-zone block include the backside blocker's responsibility to accomplish the following tasks:

- Set to reach.
- Throw the inside arm through the middle of the defender
- Read the near foot of the defender to determine if he is penetrating.

- Get his ear to the near hip of his outside teammate.
- Work upfield as part of an inside tandem against a floating defensive lineman.
- Keep the outside shoulder free and the inside shoulder fitted to the playside hip of the defender.

On the outside zone, the frontside blocker, who faces a defender playing on him, should step to reach, according to the width of the defender's alignment. If the defender is an inside shade, the blocker should set to reach with a vertical step (i.e., up the field). Versus an inside-shaded defender, the frontside blocker should step his outside foot to a point just outside of the defender's outside foot. He should keep the toes of his outside foot pointing upfield, as he steps to reach the inside shade. The blocker should then drive his inside shoulder through the outside armpit of the defender. His inside arm should be ripped upward in the manner of an uppercut punch.

The frontside blocker should get his inside arm's bicep under the outside armpit of the defender. Getting the bicep to this position lifts the outside shoulder of the defender. This punch knocks the defender's outside shoulder backward, while simultaneously tilting both of the defender's shoulders.

The tilt of the shoulders is caused by the upward thrust of the uppercut punch and the resulting lift of the outside shoulder. The shoulder tilt and the backward push of the outside shoulder result in the defender's chest opening. By opening the defender's chest, the frontside blocker gives the backside blocker an improved blocking surface—a surface conducive to getting around for outside leverage. This component of opening the defender's shoulders is vital to the two-man dimension of zone blocking the inside-shaded defender.

The frontside blocker in the two-man zone tandem block must not overstride the set to reach. If the frontside blocker steps too wide versus the inside-shaded defensive lineman, the backside blocker cannot properly punch through the defender's armpit. An excessively wide set to reach by the frontside blocker creates an unwanted spacing between the backside blocker and frontside blocker. Any type of gap or space between the two blockers will give the defender a crease through which he may split the two-man zone. The set to reach against the inside-shaded defensive lineman must be a tight vertical step, only inches outside of the defender's outside foot.

Once the frontside blocker punches through the armpit of the inside-shaded defender, he should throw his eyes to the second level to find the scraping linebacker. Every sound defensive scheme that uses an inside shade defensive lineman will support the inside-shade with a fast-scraping linebacker. The lead blocker of the outside-zone tandem must be on the lookout for a fast-scraping linebacker, as he rips through the outside pad of the defensive lineman.

The frontside blocker should flatten his path to the outside, as he rips through the inside shade. Flattening the path gives the blocker an opportunity to meet the scraping linebacker at his outside knee, hip, and shoulder. Once the frontside blocker meets the linebacker in his path, the blocker should drive with his inside shoulder pad driving through the backer's thigh and hip. The key to obtaining the proper fit at the meeting point is for the blocker to regain control of his body.

When a frontside blocker rips through an inside shade, he tends to become prone to overextend his power angle. Versus an inside-shaded defender, the frontside blocker should step with his outside foot to a point just outside of the defender's outside foot. He should keep the toes of his outside foot pointing upfield, as he steps to reach the inside shade. The blocker should then drive his inside shoulder through the outside armpit of the defender. His inside arm should be ripped upward in the manner of an uppercut punch.

The frontside blocker should get his inside arm's bicep under the outside armpit of the defender. Getting the bicep to this position lifts the outside shoulder of the defender. This punch knocks the defender's outside shoulder backward, while simultaneously tilting both of the defender's shoulders. The tilt of the shoulders is caused by the upward thrust of the uppercut punch and the resulting lift of the outside shoulder.

The shoulder tilt and the backward push of the outside shoulder result in the defender's chest opening. By opening the defender's chest, the frontside blocker gives the backside blocker an improved blocking surface—a surface conducive to getting his hands, hips, and shoulders around for outside leverage. This component of opening the defender's shoulders is important for the two-man dimension of zone blocking the inside-shaded defender.

A common error of the frontside blocker in the two-man zone tandem block is overstriding the set to reach. If the frontside blocker steps too wide versus the inside-shaded defensive lineman, the backside blocker cannot properly punch through the defender's armpit. An excessively wide set to reach by the frontside blocker creates an unwanted spacing between the backside blocker and frontside blocker. Any type of gap or space between the two blockers will give the defender a crease through which he may split the two-man zone. The set to reach against the inside-shaded defensive lineman must be a tight vertical step, only inches outside of the defender's outside foot.

Once the frontside blocker punches through the armpit of the inside-shaded defender, he should throw his eyes to the second level to find the scraping linebacker. Every sound defensive scheme that uses an inside shade defensive lineman will support the inside-shade with a fast-scraping linebacker. Therefore, the lead blocker of the outside-zone tandem must be on the lookout for a fast-scraping linebacker, as he rips through the outside pad of the defensive lineman.

The frontside blocker should flatten his path to the outside, as he rips through the inside shade. Flattening the path gives the blocker an opportunity to junction the scraping linebacker's outside knee, hip, and shoulder. Once the frontside blocker junctions the linebacker's path, the blocker should explode with his inside shoulder pad driving through the backer's thigh and hip.

The key to obtaining the proper fit at the meeting point is for the blocker to regain control of his body. When a frontside blocker rips through an inside shade, he tends to become prone to overextend his power angle and to be slightly forward in his demeanor. He must chop his feet on his fourth step—much as he does when he blocks the levels on the backside.

Chopping his fourth and fifth steps allows the blocker to reset his position to gain a proper fit at the point of engagement. Since this point usually occurs between the sixth and seventh step, the frontside blocker can easily reset his position before reaching it.

The frontside blocker's failure to chop his strides, after clearing the inside shade, will result in him losing the proper relationship in his path to the point of contact. Unless he chops his stride, the frontside blocker will either overrun the linebacker and allow him to cut underneath or lose outside leverage on the linebacker.

If the man on the frontside blocker is an outside shade, the set to reach is wider—slightly outside the playside shoulder of the lineman. His toe should remain pointed straight ahead, as the blocker sets to reach. On his second step, the blocker should punch his inside arm through the chest/armpit of the lineman. The inside arm should uppercut through the chest/armpit of the defender, as the frontside blocker plants his attack step (i.e., second step). The third step should secure outside leverage, as the frontside blocker works to gain width and depth.

The outside-shaded defender will likely attempt to fight to the outside in an attempt to keep his outside arm and leg free. The blocker should use his inside hand to grab cloth and pull himself to obtain the proper fit. If the defender continues to fight across the frontside blocker's face, the blocker should maintain contact on the defender, while working up through the first level to the second level.

Once the blocker enters the second level, he can push off the defensive lineman to flatten his path. Flattening his path gives the frontside blocker an opportunity to make a second block on a shuffling linebacker. If a linebacker doesn't show, the blocker should continue flattening his path, so that he can junction the path of a third-level defender, such as a free safety.

Riding the defensive lineman's outside shoulder through level one and flattening his path to cut a second- or third-level defender are ideal objectives for the frontside zone blocker. It is more important, however, that the frontside zone blocker never allow the outside-shaded defender to fight outside to regain the outside leverage. If a frontside zone blocker can overtake the outside-shade defender and maintain outside leverage, the likelihood of offensive success is relatively high.

For the frontside blocker of the outside-zone blocking tandem, the components of an effective outside-zone block include the blocker's responsibility to accomplish the following tasks:

- Set to reach.
- Uppercut punch the inside arm through the chest/armpit of the defender.
- Gain ground with the attack step through the chest/armpit.
- Accomplish the objective of the three-inch rule and obtain a vertical push on the defender.
- Continue to work outside and upfield as the blocker moves through the second level.
- Release and flatten to junction a second-level defender, as he enters the second level.
- Chop his feet and widen his base, as he enters the second level to regain the proper run-blocking demeanor and cut the linebacker.
- Continue flattening to the outside to junction a third level, if the second-level defender doesn't show.

For the frontside blocker who is performing an outside-zone block against a man over him (i.e., linebacker), the blocker must set to reach, just as he would set to reach against a wider down-technique defender. A linebacker naturally has a greater opportunity to flow on the snap prior to the frontside blocker reaching him. Therefore, the blocker must take the proper path after setting to reach. The proper path against a linebacker is a path that allows the frontside blocker to progressively close toward the linebacker, while maintaining a tight outside-leverage fit to the movement of the linebacker. Maintaining a tight fit to the linebacker's movement prevents the blocker from overextending his angle, thereby allowing the linebacker to plant and slip underneath the block.

The blocker's path to the point of engagement starts with a movement that is sometimes referred to as a J-step. The J-step terminology has its roots in the letter's resemblance to the desired path of an outside-zone blocker, as it might be drawn on a chalkboard.

The set to reach is a lateral step that provides some upfield momentum into the neutral zone. After the set to reach, the blocker should move in a near-vertical angle, as he proceeds to meet the defender. It is imperative that the frontside blocker keeps his eyes on the linebacker at all times as he moves toward him. If the linebacker bucket-steps, the threat of the linebacker slipping underneath the J-step is eliminated. As a result, the blocker may angle off his path slightly to intercept the bucket-stepping linebacker. If the linebacker steps sharply into the line of scrimmage, as he reads the play, the frontside blocker should keep his shoulders square and work up the field on a vertical path, thus preventing the linebacker from attempting to slip underneath.

Pull Blocking:

The third primary category of offensive line run blocks is the pull block. Pull blocks are characterized as techniques executed by a lineman pulling to either side. Among the various types of pull blocks are the following:

- Sweep hammer pull
- Trap pull
- Waggle/bootleg pull
- Horn pull
- Quick screen pull
- Reverse spin pull

• *Sweep hammer pull.* The sweep pull may be a short or a long pull. Short sweep pulls are pulls from the onside of the ball out toward the defensive flank. Long sweep pulls are pulls from the offside of the ball across the center to the playside. Sweep pulls are called "log blocks" or "wall blocks," when the pulling guard or tackle uses his inside shoulder to seal the defensive end inside. Sweep pulls are called "kick-out blocks" or "hammer blocks," when the pulling guard or tackle attacks the defender from an inside-out position. The hammer block—a specialized type of kick-out block used with the wing-T—was developed for single wing football and is still an effective method of creating the alley crease on the buck sweep series.

Sweep pulls differ from trap pulls in several ways. The biggest difference between a sweep pull and a trap pull is the angle of attack. The sweep-pulling lineman gains depth on his pull, while the trap-pulling lineman attacks on a flatter path into the line of scrimmage. The sweep pull can be either a log block or a kick-out block, whereas a trap pull is designed solely to be a kick-out block. The sweep pull is made off of a deeper pivot and a bucket step, while the trap pull is normally made of a sharp push flat down the line of scrimmage. Finally, the sweep pull is characterized by the blocker snapping his playside elbow around, so that his hand can slap his buttocks. In contrast, the trap pull is characterized by the pivot and handshake move of the blocker's lead hand.

The initial movements for both the short sweep log and kick-out blocks are identical. Only the finishing movements are different. The short-sweep pulling guard begins with a hard push off the inside foot, as he simultaneously rotates his toes inward. Rotating the toes of the push foot inward allows the hips to open to 90 degrees or more. When pulling right, the left foot is the push foot. The right foot is yanked backward, as the right elbow is jerked backward and to the left.

Young linemen can be trained to open deeply by having them attempt to slap the left side of their rear end with their right hand. This movement snaps their shoulders around and forces the hip to open. The right foot is also forced to bucket step, which is a key coaching point to sweep pulling. The bucket step forces the guard to pivot approximately 110 degrees, so that he is heading backward to some degree.

The second step crosses over to a point where the heel is directly in front of the toes of the bucket foot. The inside shoulder dips, and the guard gets his eyes to the target area as the bucket foot makes the third step and regains a normal base. On the fourth step, made with the inside foot, the guard gets his shoulders back to parallel with the line of scrimmage. At the point of the fourth step, the hammer-pulling guard and the log-pulling guard should be approximately two and one-half yards behind the line of scrimmage.

The sweep blockers gain depth for two reasons. First, they want to engage any penetrating defender through an outside gap. Second, they want to gain depth so that they can hit the line of scrimmage with their shoulders parallel to the line of scrimmage, while they read the edges of the alley.

It is on the fifth step that the short-sweep pulling guard's technique begins to take the identifying characteristic of being either a wall or a kick-out block. The log blocker should tighten his path into the neutral zone to fit tightly to the outside hip of the seal blocker.

It is between the fourth and fifth step that the hammer blocker analyzes the action of the force. The fifth step is made straight ahead, as the guard reads the relative positioning of the force. If the force is coming hard, the offensive guard plants the inside foot at a 45-degree step, thereby keeping the toe forward. The sixth step is a 45-degree plant step called the hammer step. The seventh step is made with the outside foot off of the 45-degree hammer step. The outside foot is a 90-degree step to a point where the guard may meet the upfield shoulder of the force defender. The inside foot then follows, and the guard moves along a plane that is parallel to the line of scrimmage.

He then moves outward and widens his base to contact the force with what had been his outside shoulder. A hammer block on the right side is made with the right shoulder. The head of the guard should ideally be positioned slightly behind the force defender. This head positioning makes the defender run around the hammer block to make the play. By the time he is able to run around the block, the ballcarrier has hit the crease of the alley.

The kick-out block technique off of the short pull is very different from the hammer pull. As described in the previous paragraph, for the first four to five steps, the hammer-blocking guard pulls on the same track as the wall-blocking guard. The kick-out technique pulling guard departs from this path on his second step. Obtaining depth and tracking on a vertical charge toward the line of scrimmage are key coaching points of the wall and the hammer blocks.

The kick-out blocker doesn't gain significant depth off the line of scrimmage when pulling. His angle is near that of a long trapper. He keeps his shoulders facing the sideline, as he moves to kick-out the hard-charging force. On contact with the force defender, the kick-out, sweep-pulling technique is identical to that of the trap-pulling contact. If the kick-out blocker is sweep pulling to the right, he should contact the force defender with his right shoulder. If the kick-out blocker is sweep pulling to the left, he should contact the force defender with his left shoulder.

The long-sweep pull starts out like a long trap. It normally is used as a wall-blocking technique. The initial step is a flat step off of a push with the outside foot. The guard's shoulders face a plane parallel to the line of scrimmage, as he passes between the quarterback and the center. The split of the guard should be wide enough to allow him to clear the center, as he makes his third step.

A tight split alters the timing of the pull, as well as presents a potential threat for causing a fumble. Guards who take too tight a split may hit the ball on the handshake opening of the long-trap technique. They sometimes cause a fumble, because they hit the ball before the quarterback can properly seat the ball. Once the guard clears the center on his third step, he crosses over and gains depth. The crossover is sometimes called the "Heisman pull," because the movement resembles the Heisman trophy pose. Depth is gained to approximately two yards behind the line of scrimmage.

• *Trap pull.* The trap pull is one of two basic types of pulling techniques. The other type is the sweep pull. The term "trap pull" is normally used to describe a trap pull from the offside to the onside. However, a trap-pull technique can also refer to an onside-trap pull known as a G-block.

A trap-pulling lineman pushes off hard on his push foot. When pulling to trap across the ball, the offensive lineman can use his down hand to help push with his outside foot. This pushing action forces the trapper's hips to open in what is called the pivot stage of the trap pull. During the pivot, the trapper should jerk his inside elbow backward so that his lead hand opens to the path he is about to take.

The opening of the hand to the trapping path is called the handshake move, because the finish of the move results in the lead hand being in the position of a handshake being offered. The length of the trap influences the depth to which the lead shoulder should be opened. For a longer trap, the inside elbow should jet backward in a manner closer to a sweep-pull technique. Jetting the elbow further back opens the shoulder to a greater degree, thereby resulting in the trapper being in a position to better track flat down the line of scrimmage. To track sharper into the line of scrimmage on a short trap, the lineman should offer a sharper handshake (i.e., pointing his fingers into the line of scrimmage).

The track of the inside foot off of the initial pivot-push starting sequence should be on the same angle as the point of the handshake. The footwork of any trap is the pivot-push. The blocker uses the handshake to facilitate the opening of the hips and the pivot. The inside foot plants near the desired track, as the outside foot pivots to turn the backside knee inside. The outside foot then pushes hard against the turf to propel the trapper on the track. The outside foot pivots, and then pushes to track the blocker on his trapping angle.

While offensive guards most commonly function as trappers, tight ends and tackles also trap. Guards run long and short traps. Tackles run only long traps. Tight ends normally trap off of a formation shift and motion across the center—an action that makes them primarily a short trapper. The length of a trap is significant, because it determines the angle of the trapper's track to the defender. Short trappers run short angles off a sharp handshake move. Long trappers run a flatter angle. In fact, long trappers should run their track on a parallel plane to the line of scrimmage. A long trapper should run on his flat track, until he clears the center. As he passes the playside leg of the center, the trapper should immediately begin angling inward to kick-out the defender.

Trap-pulling involves a two-fold cardinal rule: "pull left—hit left; pull right—hit right." While several extended coaching points can be included in coaching the trapper, the cardinal rule explains trapping in a clear and concise way to players of all competitive levels. The rule has a straightforward meaning to offensive linemen. When pulling to the right, the trap-pulling lineman must contact the targeted defender with his right shoulder. When pulling to the left, the trap-pulling lineman must contact the targeted defender with his left shoulder. If a lineman adheres to the trap rule when he pulls, he is guaranteed to be on the correct trapping path. He will always be on the kick-out angle.

Unfortunately, a number of coaches "over-coach" the trapper. These coaches often require the trapper to read the action of the defender. If the defender closes down the line of scrimmage to stuff the trapper, the pulling lineman can simply convert his trap technique to a log technique and seal the defender inside. The ballcarrier is trained to read the log and skip off the butt of the log-blocking lineman.

The term "over-coach" is not necessarily a derogative reference with regard to this coaching technique. It simply refers to the degree of extended teaching that can be attempted in coaching the trap. Many offensive coaches believe that "over-coaching" the trap is as an integral part of the scheme. For an offensive system such as the wing-T, the trap must be a series that cannot be stopped. Accordingly, the wing-T offensive line coach is well-advised to spend as much time as possible coaching the various elements of the trap pull.

On the other hand, some offensive line coaches feel that the over-coaching of the trap leads to poor trap angles by the blocker. In this situation, the blocker becomes tentative and gets caught between the sharp trap angle and the rounded finish of the log block. These coaches feel that the problem of a defensive lineman closing down and spilling the trap can be eliminated, if the trap block is called at the proper time, thereby setting the defense up during its most vulnerable alignment and game situation.

Keep in mind that the trap is an opportunistic type of play. It is most successful when used on passing downs—when the defense least expects it. Traps can keep the dominant defensive lineman honest as the offense takes advantage of his aggressiveness. Traps can hurt the penetrating front that is supported by linebackers from a deep alignment. G-blocks are highly effective against defensive ends who are outside conscious. Positioning a wingback near a defensive end enhances the G-block's effectiveness, because the defensive end becomes extremely alert to the threat of the wingback blocking down on him.

The G-block is simply an outside trap by the playside guard. The trapping guard doesn't cross the center, as on other traps. The G-blocking technique is a true mirror technique of the normal trapping guard's technique: the blocker's pivot is to the outside; his outside hand makes the handshake move; and he pushes off the inside foot to track inside-out to the defensive end. The G-blocking guard always kicks out the first man on or outside the tight end. The defensive end may be set up by a rip move of the tight end to the inside, or a combination of a rip move to the inside by the tight end and a down-block influence by the wingback.

Offensive linemen don't use a down-block influence move. It is a move used exclusively by a wingback. On a down-block influence, the wingback baits the defensive end by driving toward his outside shoulder—faking a down block—and then planting off the inside foot to angle outside to kick-out the strong safety.

• *Waggle/bootleg pull.* The terms waggle and bootleg are essentially synonymous terms for a type of play-pass (i.e., a pass executed off the fake of a run). The waggle/bootleg involves one or two linemen pulling opposite the flow of the backfield.

A play-pass action, the waggle/bootleg is an excellent play and an important part of any offensive attack, from the full house-T formation to the one-back, spread scheme. On the waggle/bootleg action, the playside is the side opposite the side to where the running backs flow. On the waggle/bootleg pull, the playside guard should short-sweep pull to gain two to three yards depth and should immediately focus his line of sight on a triangular area, slicing through the outside hip of the near tackle. By throwing his eyes to the tackle's hip, the guard can immediately recognize the action of the man on the tackle. The quick recognition of the defender's reaction enables the guard to take the proper path to log block the defender.

The backside guard should pull flat past the center and gain depth on his third step. The backside guard should also look through the triangle. If he recognizes an upfield charge by the defensive end, the guard should flatten out and trap block the defensive end. On a trap block, the pulling lineman should block with the shoulder corresponding to the direction of his pull. When pulling to the left, the right guard should trap block, using his left shoulder to make contact with the defender. This block is designed to drive the defender outward and allow the quarterback to duck under, in the seam between the log of the playside guard and the trap of the backside guard.

• *Horn pull.* An alternative to a drive block against the inside-shaded defensive tackle is the guard-horn block. The horn block should be used with off-tackle plays in which the guard is drive blocking the linebacker in the 30 front. Normally, this block is a read block, since the guard makes a pre-snap read of whether he should pull around the horn, instead of drive blocking the linebacker.

The basis for converting the drive block into a horn pull is the presence of a 4i technique defensive tackle. A 4i defensive tackle—particularly a gap 4i technique tackle—blocks the guard's path to the playside number of the linebacker. When he reads an off-tackle play, the linebacker can easily scrape over the top, as the defensive tackle occupies two blockers—the guard and tackle.

Some coaches feel that the outside-zone block combination is a better scheme for dealing with the 4i technique in a 30 front. However, a combination block—such as the outside zone—involves precise

execution by two players working as one. The horn pull, while a combination in theory, involves only the tackle caving down the 4i technique, while the guard simply uses his tag technique to step around the horn and seal the linebacker. The drive block by the tackle and the horn pull by the guard are a much simpler and easier-to-execute scheme than the outside zone.

An important coaching point for the guard to remember, when horn blocking, is to keep his shoulders parallel, as he steps back to read the flow of the linebacker. He can use the tag-block technique of stepping back with his inside foot, and then driving off the tackle's hip.

The guard may also execute the horn block by simply stepping laterally off the line with his outside foot and reading the linebacker's flow. With either technique, the most important coaching point for the guard is to keep his eyes on the linebacker.

If the defensive scheme puts the tackle in a 4 technique and plays games—sometimes sparking him inside and other times sparking him outside, the horn pull can be used as a simple countermeasure to the confusion that could be caused by the stunts. To counter the games, without using a zone-blocking scheme, the guard may simply step to read the linebacker, as the offensive tackle latches on to the defender, no matter which direction he stunts.

If the 4 technique tackle stunts inside, the guard should read the linebacker scraping over the top and pulls around the horn to junction him. If the 4 technique tackle stunts outside, the offensive tackle pins him and the guard reads the linebacker filling inside the tackle's stunt. When the guard reads the linebacker hanging inside to fill the "B" gap, he should simply drive off his outside foot and block the linebacker with a proper run-blocking demeanor.

• *Quick screen pull.* The quick-screen pull is executed by the playside tackle. Sometimes called a "running pull," the quick-screen pull is used to kick-out a cornerback who is attempting to cover the wide receiver. The quick screen, also known as the slip screen, involves the wide receiver driving off the line for two steps and then planting his feet to circle around behind the line of scrimmage to catch the ball on the run. Since the pass is a screen, the other offensive linemen should also be using a screen-blocking technique against the other defenders. However, the playside tackle's block is the key block that springs the wide receiver on the play. While his teammates fan out to block their assigned defenders, the offensive tackle should sprint to a point approximately two yards in front of the line of scrimmage.

The tackle can visualize this pull as a type of extended fan block. He should pull neither too flat nor too sharply upfield. He must make contact with the cornerback with a tight fit. Ironically, while his block is a key block, it isn't the tackle's responsibility to make him get into position to contact the cornerback. It is the wide receiver's responsibility to bring the cornerback to the offensive tackle. The offensive tackle needs only to get his body under control, just as he comes to within four yards of the receiver. Because the pass is a screen pass, the tackle does not need to be concerned with being downfield illegally or being flagged for interference. The tackle may legally block the cornerback past the line of scrimmage, as the ball is thrown, while the ball is in the air.

The other four offensive linemen basically perform a type of fan pull toward their assigned defenders, as the ball is released. Some coaches run this play as a double-screen, with both tackles pulling to the widest cornerback. Other coaches run this play in the nature of a kick-off return-blocking scheme, thereby giving the interior linemen a numbered defender to block outward in the same manner as a kick-off return blocker.

- *Reverse spin pull.* An extremely deceptive pulling technique for the reverse, the reverse spin pull resembles more of a ballet move than a block. The reverse spin pull is normally executed by one or both of the guards. It seems to be most effective when the guards fake a block to one direction and then reverse spin to the opposite direction. The reverse spin pull calls for the guard to fake a zone block for three steps to the side of the initial fake. If running the reverse to the left, the guard should fake his zone block to the right for three steps. He should then plant on his right foot and cross over with his left foot.

When he zones to the right, he should zone block hard on an overly flat angle. This action allows him to turn his shoulders nearly perpendicular to the line of scrimmage as he faces the right sideline. By overemphasizing the set to reach and turning his shoulders, the guard can quickly cross over with his left foot (or bucket step with his right foot) to spin around and begin pulling in the opposite direction.

Ideally, the lead guard of the reverse will pull around the end and log any defender who redirects his pursuit as he recognizes the reverse. The backside guard will pull around the wall block and hammer block the cornerback, who—by the time play develops—should be coming off his man or should be out of his zone to provide late run support. The reverse spin pull can be a game-breaking technique when used with a timely reverse off of a common sweep series.

Pass-Blocking:

Effective pass protection begins with a thorough knowledge of the fundamentals involved and a mastery of the various techniques attendant to sound pass-protection blocking. As such, your offensive linemen must not only be well-trained in the various skills, they must also know when to apply a specific technique. A protection technique can be categorized as a dropback-protection technique, a play-pass technique, or a sprint-out/dash-pass technique. A list of the individual dropback pass-protection techniques includes the following:

- Hard post
- Soft post
- Soft kick
- Jump 'em
- Kick slide

The offensive lineman's selection of a particular technique is directly related to the defensive alignment of his opponent. As with any football position, the proper technique begins with the proper stance. As noted previously, some coaches prefer that their offensive linemen use a three-point stance when pass blocking; others prefer that a two-point stance be utilized.

The stance is the first phase of any type of block. The second phase of the pass block is the set-up. The set-up is defined as the snap up or the kick-out to the prescribed depth of the pass set. The key to executing the proper set-up is the quickness in making the move. The set-up has to be made as quickly as possible. The outcome of an entire pass-protection scheme is usually determined by the speed at which each offensive lineman makes his first move in setting up for the block.

For the pass-blocking offensive lineman, the main purpose of the set-up is to establish a cushion between himself and the pass rusher. The appropriate depth of the cushion—the proper amount of the separation—between the pass rusher and the pass protector is dependent upon the technique of the defender and the particular offensive line position. For example, an offensive tackle may kick out to gain a separation of three to four feet against an angled defensive end who is aligned to his outside. A center, on the other hand, punches with his up hand on the snap to gain a maximum of 12 to 18 inches of separation against a nose tackle. Setting to gain depth is also necessary for an offensive lineman to be able to read the pass rush, whether the scheme is either a man-protection or an area-protection scheme.

An offensive lineman is often required to master several types of pass sets. The one characteristic of every type of pass set is the inside-out relationship of the pass protector. An offensive lineman must set to protect the inside-out relationship. Simply setting to an inside-out relationship doesn't guarantee that the offensive lineman will effectively protect the quarterback. It does, however, put the offensive lineman in the most suitable position for accomplishing his objective. Among the factors that relate to a blocker snapping up into a proper pass-blocking demeanor include the following coaching points:

- Keeping his shoulders square
- Setting his base to a staggered relationship to the blocker's base—with the outside foot pointing to the crotch of the defender
- Keeping most of his weight balanced, with a slight emphasis on his inside foot

- Keeping his backside low and his knees bent
- Keeping his elbows inside his body's frame
- Keeping his hands up, with his thumbs pointing up
- Keeping his chin tucked and his head back
- Keeping his chest out
- Keeping his feet slightly wider than shoulder-width apart

On all pass-set moves, the pass protector snaps up and gets his eyes on the target. Most coaches teach their offensive linemen to target the breast plates of the defender. The pass protector should snap up and use the heels of his hands to punch the defender in the chest. The blow should be made in an upward motion, as the blocker drives his hands up through the defender's breast plates in a low-to-high plane. The blocker's goal in punching the defender is to stop the defender's charge, so that the defender has to restart and redirect his pass rush to another lane.

- *Hard post*. For an offensive guard who is facing an inside-shaded defender, the desired pass set against an inside-shaded defender is the hard post. The hard post is used against a 2i technique defender, a 1 technique defender, and an onset-offset nose tackle aligned to his side. The main feature of the hard-post move is a sharp lateral-jab step to the inside. The guard should push off his outside foot to throw his body inside to seal the "A" gap off from penetration. The primary objective of a hard-post set is to get to an inside-out or a head-up leverage position on the defender. The blocker should push off his outside foot and plant his inside foot to point at the toes of the defender's inside foot. As the guard hard-post sets inside, he should punch the defender in the breast plates, while keeping the proper pass-

blocking demeanor. His outside foot should also slide inside, so that the blocker doesn't overextend his base as he sets the hard post. It is important that both feet shuffle along the turf, as the blocker shuffles inside. The guard should keep his feet in close contact to the turf, as he sets inside. Both steps should be quick, hard jab steps.

If the guard is uncovered and is helping the center, according to the area rule against an offset/onset nose tackle aligned to his side, the guard should hard post but keep his outside arm free. He should use his inside arm to drive to the near breastplate of the nose tackle. Striking the nose tackle's breastplate stops his charge through the "A" gap and allows the center to punch and slide to a head-up position on the nose tackle.

It is especially important that the guard punch upward into the nose tackle's breast plate, when using only his inside arm. By striking the nose tackle in the chest with a low-to-high block, the guard forces the defender's shoulders upward and creates a better target surface for the center. Striking the nose tackle in the near breast plate also helps the guard to keep his shoulders square. An area-protection scheme requires that the guards keep their shoulders square when helping the center. Keeping their shoulders square is important for the guards, if they are to pick up an inside-twist game between one of the inside linebackers and the nose tackle.

A tackle or a tight end should also use a hard-post move, if his assignment is to block an inside shaded defender. The tackle must be particularly alert to the possibility of the guard "talking." If a dog blitz from an eagle front shows inside the "A" gap, the guard should hard post to take the linebacker, after making an "alert" call. The tackle should always keep his eyes inside, when the guard is facing a 3 technique. If an inside linebacker shows in the near "A" gap, the guard should slide inside and take the linebacker. By keeping his eyes to the inside, the tackle can visually pick up this stunt at the last second, without the guard having to make the call.

If the linebacker subsequently backs out on the snap, the guard should use the "jump 'em" technique to grab the 3 technique. The tackle can easily recognize the guard jumping the 3 technique and quickly kick out to help on the edge with no harm done to the basic integrity of the protection scheme.

The center should hard-post set when he is applying his man blocking rule against an even front. Against a front that is characterized by having a backside 1 technique or a stack alignment, the hard-post technique by the center can secure the backside "A" gap. Against a front that is characterized by a middle linebacker, the center can hard post to the near lineman to help the guard. When the center hard posts to help the guard, he should keep his eyes on the middle linebacker. If the linebacker over the center delays and dogs straight ahead, the center should simply push off the hard-post set and slide a half-step to pick up the dog stunt.

If the middle linebacker loops around behind the near defensive lineman, the center and the guard can either switch assignments or remain locked in. If the lock-in scheme is used to pick up the twisting stunts, the center should remember to set slightly behind the guard's inside foot.

By setting behind the guard's near foot, the center can simply slide behind the guard to pick up a twisting-dog stunt. When the offensive linemen slide with the twist stunts and remain locked in, the offensive lineman who is locked in on the

linebacker should use the soft kick to set slightly off the line of scrimmage.

If two offensive linemen are pass blocking, according to an area-protection scheme, they should switch assignments on the middle twist. In an area-protection scheme, the center should use the hard-post technique when helping the guard. The hard post of the center builds a shoulder-to-shoulder wall, as he and the guard set shoulder-to-shoulder. If the center sees the middle linebacker looping, he should yell "switch, switch," as he physically pushes the guard outward with his outside arm. Pushing the guard and yelling "switch" help the guard recognize the stunt and cue him to push off the penetrating defensive lineman and pick up the middle linebacker, dogging through the "B" gap.

• *Soft post.* The second pass-set technique is the soft post. The main move of the center versus a nose tackle—the soft-post technique—requires the offensive lineman to simply jab step his inside foot, without moving hard to the inside. An offensive lineman should use the soft-post move, when a defender is aligned head-up on him. When pass blocking a 2 technique, the guard should soft post by quickly picking up his inside foot.

Picking up the foot helps the guard to snap up and punch his hands to the 2 technique's breastplates. The soft-post technique also helps rein in the guard's natural tendency to attack the 2 technique. A pass protector should never move forward into a defender; he should only move side-to-side or back. Upon picking up his foot, the guard should immediately put his foot down. The soft-post, inside step is made in the manner of a boot stomping on a scurrying insect. It is a quick, forceful step in one spot.

As with every pass-set technique, the pass protector should establish an inside-out, staggered relationship to the pass rusher. He should soft post, with his foot slightly inside of the defender's inside foot and set to the proper pass-blocking demeanor. A defender using a head-up technique may have the option of rushing to either side. Accordingly, the pass protector should be ready for a pass-rushing move to either side.

The soft post is used by a center against a head-up nose tackle. The center should use a one-two punch combination, as he soft posts with the foot corresponding to his up hand. A center using a four-point stance should deliver a one-two punch with his off-hand, followed by his ball-hand, as he soft posts with the foot corresponding to his off-hand. Against a head-up nose tackle, a right-handed center should soft post with his left foot; a left-handed center should soft post with his right foot.

The center, the guards, the tackles, and the tight ends all use the soft-post move, when dropback-pass protecting against a head-up technique. The snap-up and punch to the breastplates are vital factors in getting into the proper pass-blocking demeanor when using a soft-post move. It is also very important that the blocker should keep his chin tucked, his head back, and his back flat, when making the soft-post move.

• *Soft kick.* The third pass-set technique is the soft kick. The soft kick is used against a tight outside-shaded technique, such as a regularly aligned 3 technique, 5 technique, or 9 technique. To soft kick, the blocker should push off his inside foot to take a short-jab step with his outside foot. A coaching point that should be emphasized, in this instance, is that an offensive guard should not jump outside, when he soft kicks. Basically, he should pick up his outside foot and return it to nearly the same spot on the turf.

For a guard, the soft kick is essentially the mirror technique of the soft post, except that the soft kick will result in a small degree of lateral movement, as the kick foot slides approximately four inches outside. Unlike when he uses a soft-post technique, the blocker should allow his back foot to slide with the kick foot. For example, when a guard soft posts against a 3 technique, his outside foot should kick and jab, while his inside foot should slide to reestablish the good base for a proper pass-blocking position. If his inside foot doesn't slide with his kick foot, the blocker's base will get too wide, causing him to lose his power leverage.

Punching the outside hand is an important coaching point involving the proper execution of the soft post. The heel of the outside hand should be driven through the outside breastplate of the outside shade. Punching the hand to the defender's near breastplate gives the pass rusher free leverage with the outside half of his body, since no resistance is applied. He can easily escape around the short edge of the pass set, if the blocker doesn't reach to punch through his outside breastplate. By punching through the outside breastplate, the blocker actually pulls the inside half of his body outside and squares up on the defender. A lazy inside foot and inside arm are common flaws of the undisciplined lineman's soft-kick technique. Teaching the "outside-hand-to-the-breastplate" coaching point forestalls the problem of a pass rusher getting off against the short edge.

While an offensive guard doesn't move much laterally on the soft kick, the offensive tackle should soft kick outside to gain more leverage on an outside shade. Since the tackle is further from the ball, he should soft kick one step off the ball, as he widens by approximately two feet. The offensive tackle should soft kick with a proper pass-blocking demeanor—slightly inside-out of the defender.

After kicking to set in the proper demeanor, the tackle should initially keep his shoulders square. His outside foot should be slightly staggered behind the inside. His hips may be opened slightly to facilitate a quick pivot to the outside, should the defender attempt a quick speed rush around the edge. If the pass rusher attempts to speed rush, the offensive tackle may quickly punch and open his stance to wall the pass rusher from the pocket.

• *Jump 'em.* The fourth pass-set technique is the jump 'em set. The jump 'em technique is a change-up technique for the soft-kick set. Most often used as a quick-pass protection, dash protection, or play-pass protection, the jump 'em technique is a quick jump to the outside into the proper pass-blocking demeanor. On the snap of the ball, the blocker using the jump 'em technique should literally jump out to the side—landing in the proper pass-blocking demeanor to the defender. Not only should the jump 'em technique blocker hop into the proper demeanor, he should simultaneously punch both hands into the breastplates of the defender. From that position, the blocker should work to maintain a snug, inside-out relationship, while stalemating the pass rusher.

• *Kick slide.* The kick slide is the fifth pass-set technique. The kick slide is used by an offensive tackle, when he is presented with a wide pass rusher who is pointing in to the backfield. The kick slide gives an offensive tackle added depth on the pass set. To kick slide, the tackle should push hard off his inside foot—an easy task since most of the weight of the two-point stance should be on the lineman's inside foot. The hard push off the inside foot should get the tackle moving backward and outward to intercept the angle of the wide pass rusher. Even though the kick-sliding tackle is moving outside on the snap, he shouldn't turn his shoulders. Although his path is diagonal, his shoulders and hips should remain facing forward.

Once an offensive tackle kick slides, he can then shuffle backward to intercept the path of pass rusher. The kick slide puts the offensive tackle into a position that may appear to make him vulnerable to an underneath move, but this vulnerability is deceiving. Most offensive tackles would be happy to see a wide rusher attempt to cross his face and slip under the pass set. If an offensive tackle keeps his shoulders square, a defender cannot beat him to the inside. Once the inside pass rusher closes, the offensive tackle can punch the defender, knock him off balance, and pin him down inside.

If the pass rusher doesn't take the bait inside, he must attempt to get around the long corner. When an offensive tackle kick slides, the pass rusher must go deeper upfield, before he can attempt to make a move on the blocker. Because of the kick slide, the pass rusher has to take two extra steps to speed rush around the edge.

The kick slide is a technique sometimes used by offensive guards in dropback passing schemes which call for a fan pass protection. In such a scheme, the guard will have to kick slide versus a 50 front structure.

Normally, a kick slider should punch first with his outside arm. As when punching from a soft kick technique, an offensive tackle should make sure that he punches his outside hand to the outside breastplate of the defender. Failing to punch the outside hand to the outside breastplate of the defender will give the pass rusher free leverage with the outside half of his body and make the corner short.

☐ *Coaching the Center*

The center is one of the most important positions on the offensive line, if not the entire football team. In his positional role, he has a number of critical responsibilities, including snapping the ball, blocking, and potentially making the line (blocking) calls.

Center's Stance:

It is essential that the center assumes a balanced stance. Centers typically use two types of stances: the three-point stance and the four-point stance (both of which were previously described in this chapter). In reality, many coaches prefer the four-point stance, which allows the center to be quicker and more explosive. He still snaps the ball with only one hand, while his other hand is in an advantageous position to begin the block. The four-point stance involves the following considerations:

- Position his feet slightly more than shoulder-width apart.
- Place his hips slightly higher than his back.
- Bow his neck.
- Put his toes parallel to the line of scrimmage.
- Angle his heels.
- Do not assume too wide a stance, which can make it relatively difficult to get out of his stance to block quickly.

The three-point stance is frequently used in pass blocking situations. In this stance, the center's off-hand is just inside his knee. On the other hand, if you have a smaller center (size-wise) or simply prefer quickness in your center, a four-point stance may be your best choice.

Gripping the Ball:

Photo 9-10

Teach your centers to grip the ball properly. This involves the following:

- Spread the fingers of his off-hand.
- Place the ball under the corresponding eye of his snapping hand, only an inch or so to the side of his nose. A right-handed center puts the ball under his right eye, while a left-handed center positions the ball under his left eye.
- Grasp the ball, using a quarterback's grasp. His four fingers, however, should not be on the laces of the ball.
- Place his thumb on the laces, with his hand over the forward third of the ball.
- Wrap his hand around the forward third of the ball, without covering the point of it.
- Roll his wrist outward to force the ball to tilt slightly, with the nose up.
- Keep the wrist locked in this position throughout the snapping motion, which will cause the ball to have a natural rotation as it is snapped. The nose of the ball will turn left with a right-handed center, and to the right with a left-handed center.

Snapping the Ball:

The center starts every play by snapping the ball to the quarterback, who will be either directly behind him or in the shotgun position, aligned approximately three to five yards back.

- Direct snap:

Photo 9-11

- Never raise his hips as he snaps the ball, which could compromise his ability to block.
- Hold his head up.
- As he snaps the ball, move forward into his block.
- Snap the ball back in a straight line. The ball should not swing up in a pendulum-like motion.
- Snap the ball quickly and hard to the palm of the quarterback's right hand (for a right-handed quarterback).
- Flex the wrist as the ball is snapped.

- Shotgun snap:

Photo 9-12

- Instead of merely lifting the ball to the quarterback's hands, as in a direct snap, be aware that, in this instance, he has to send the ball via an accurate backward pass.
- Prior to the snap, square the feet with the line of scrimmage and position his feet shoulder-width apart.
- Either snap the ball without looking, or, at the last instant, lower his head to look between his legs at the quarterback, prior to snapping the ball.
- When snapping the ball, keep the snapping arm straight and locked throughout the snap.
- Find that spot where his arm hits the inside of his leg, when he is snapping the ball properly, and try to hit that spot every time.
- Shoot his non-snapping arm forward, as he delivers the snap.

Blocking:

The center should develop the ability to effectively execute his blocking responsibilities on either a running or passing play. For example, he will often be expected to block the nose guard or a defensive tackle on a running play. In addition, like his teammates on the offensive line, he will be expected to help protect the quarterback on a pass play.

Making Line Calls:

The center may give verbal and nonverbal commands to call the team's blocking scheme on a particular play. These decisions are made before each snap after the center surveys the defense. For example, the center may change the blocking assignments for the offensive line if he determines that the defense has an advantage.

☐ *Blocking on the Goal Line*

Once an offensive unit penetrates its opponent's 10-yard line—especially inside the five-yard line, it may be faced with a defensive scheme that is characterized by an interior line charge and aggressive play from the secondary. The closer the ball gets to a defensive unit's goal line, the more aggressive the defensive play, particularly from the secondary. With less area to cover, the secondary will be able to play underneath the receiver (i.e., between the receiver and the quarterback). Most defensive secondary personnel are aware that the end line of the end zone functions as an extra defender.

Goal-line blocking presents a unique problem for offensive linemen because the defensive line will concentrate on penetrating into the backfield. Defensive-line defenders on the goal line will normally get in a "nose-to-the-turf" stance, with their elbows bent. They will typically key the ball and charge through their assigned gap on the snap of the football. Perimeter defenders (i.e., strong safeties and cornerbacks) will contain by charging up the field.

To block goal-line defenders, offensive linemen should utilize their own goal-line stance. When facing a definite goal-line charge by the defensive front, offensive linemen should consider using a four-point stance. A good four-point offensive goal line stance is a characterized by the following components:

- The weight is forward.
- The hands are slightly forward of the shoulder.
- The elbows are bent.
- The feet are balanced under the hips.
- The heels are slightly off the turf.
- The head and neck are bowed.

Against a penetrating style of defense, the landmarks of the various blocks are slightly exaggerated. The set-to-drive landmark is approximately four inches below the normal blocking plane. The set-to-reach landmark is extended to the far elbow of the defender. When setting to reach, the blocker should attempt to get his facemask through the far elbow of the defender. The blocker can exaggerate his set-to-reach step, because the nature of the goal line defense is a penetrating nature.

As a rule, penetrating defensive linemen do not attempt to fight across the face of angle blockers. Therefore, under normal circumstances against a goal-line front, offensive linemen should not worry about the defender playing underneath an exaggerated set to reach.

Because a full line slant can open up running lanes between the ends, few defensive coaches run a full line slant from a goal-line look. While some defensive coaches slant their front on the goal line, in reality, the probability of a full goal-line front slant is decreased, as the ball moves closer to the goal line. If the scouting report shows a probability of a full line slant, the offensive linemen should be taught not to extend to the set to reach landmark.

Against a slanting front, the offensive line should keep a normal set to reach landmark and should aim to the opposite breastplate of the defender.

If the blocker gets to the far elbow on his set to reach, he is in a position to "get around" on the defender and to work his shoulders upfield in a cutoff technique. When reaching a penetrating defender, it is important for the blocker to get his backside shoulder across the defender's face and to work his frontside shoulder upfield. Getting the shoulders square and scrambling into a vertical blocking position are key factors in the success of a cutoff or a reach block against a penetrating defender.

☐ *Offensive Line Drills*

Select drills that are appropriate to your team's needs and circumstances. The right drills for your offensive line can significantly advance its skill level.

<u>Four Corners Drill:</u>

This drill is designed to help warm up the offensive line, as well as develop its footwork and agility. Four cones are required to conduct the drill, which involves the following steps:

- Set four cones in a square, five yards apart from each other.
- Have one player at a time start the drill in a three-point stance, behind a cone.
- Have each player begin the drill by exploding out of his stance and then sprinting through the first cone.
- Then, have that player shuffle (while maintaining a proper pass protection technique) to the next cone, kick slide to the next cone, and finish with a carioca step through the last cone.

* Perform the drill at full speed and emphasize proper footwork.

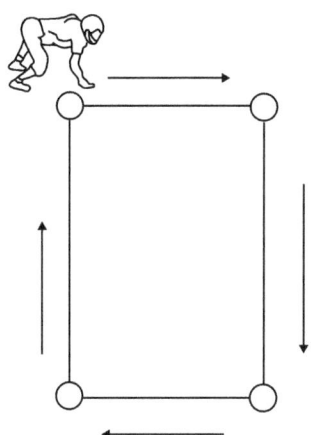

Figure 9-13

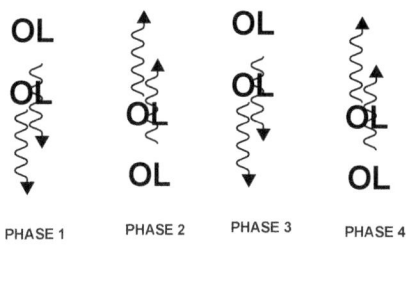

Figure 9-14

Inside Hand Leverage Drill:

This drill is designed to help develop an offensive lineman's ability to regain leverage and to execute proper hand positioning against a defender who uses his hands. No equipment is required. Performing the drill involves the following steps:

- Pair the players up and assign them to run block approximately two feet apart.
- Have one player act as an offensive lineman and the other as a defender.
- Have the offensive lineman establish the proper hand positioning to the defender's chest and drive him backward for a few steps.
- After he has taken a couple of steps, have the defender gain hand position against his teammate.
- Then, have the defender and offensive player switch roles.
- Repeat the drill.

* Have both players keep their shoulders low and their backs flat during the drill.

Squeeze Drill:

This drill is designed to teach the blocker on outside-zone or toss plays how to squeeze back into the defender and to get his hips past him to help prevent him from pursuing to the ball. No equipment is necessary to conduct this drill. Performing the drill involves the following steps:

- Pair up the players, facing the sideline, leaning into each other.
- On your command, have both players work to get their inside hip past their teammate, by ripping their inside arm into the other player, while driving their inside foot downfield.
- Be aware that this competitive exercise involves one player being the right-side blocker and the other serving as the left-side blocker.

* Teach your players to avoid a false step and use their foot quickness to drive downfield with their inside foot. The emphasis should be on having the players maintain proper leverage.

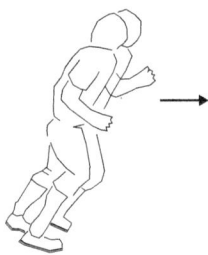

Figure 9-15

Pass Block Drill:

This drill is designed to teach an offensive lineman to move out of his stance and into the proper pass blocking position. No equipment is required to conduct the drill. Performing the drill involves the following steps:

- Pair off the players and have them face each other.
- Have one player initially serve as the pass protector and the other as the defender.
- Have the pass protector assume a three-point stance.
- Have the defensive player stand in front of the pass protector, with his hands held over his head.
- On your command, have the pass protector move his head up, get into the proper pass block position, and punch the defender's chest.
- Inform the defender that his objective, in this drill, is to provide resistance against the pass protector.
- Simultaneously, have the pass protector try to move his head and chest upward through the hands (resistance) of the defender.
- Do not allow the defender to respond to the offensive lineman's hand contact—this drill is to help your offensive line learn proper technique.
- Be sure that the pass protector is aware that his objective in this drill is to set and punch the defender before the defender can stop him.

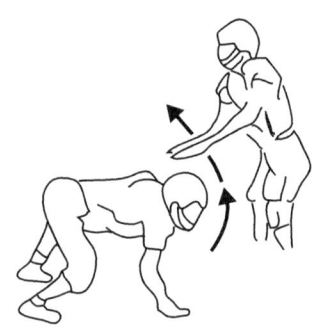

Figure 9-16

DEFENSE

Defensive Linemen

A good defensive team has defensive linemen who attack the line of scrimmage and give a 100 percent effort on every play. A defensive lineman should know how to assume a proper stance, align correctly, defend the run, rush the passer, defeat common blocking schemes, and stunt.

☐ *The Proper Stance*

Stance refers to the "ready" position, which the player assumes prior to the snap. Coaching this aspect tends to be influenced by one of two general philosophies regarding the stance. One line of coaching thought places considerable emphasis on the stance, with some coaches even calling it the single most important factor that determines how well the player will handle his assignment.

The primary point on which the two coaching philosophies differ is the interpretation of the relative importance of the technique of the pre-snap stance. Mechanical considerations (e.g., which foot is back, which hand is down) are typically major points of concern to those coaches who believe in rigid stance requirements. Others believe that it is more important for a player to be comfortable in a given stance.

When deciding which philosophy you should adopt, keep in mind that it is vital that a player's stance allows him to move efficiently and quickly. The mechanics of a defensive lineman's stance are not nearly as important as his ability to move from his stance. When coaching defensive linemen, you should not "over-coach" the stance at the expense of the player's ability. In other words, coaching points involving the stance, such as which foot is up (i.e., staggered forward) or which hand is down, should not interfere with a defensive lineman's focus to anchor the line of scrimmage and pursue to the ballcarrier.

The general rule of thumb when coaching the stance to defensive linemen is relatively straightforward: the younger and more inexperienced the athlete, the more attention you should give to coaching the stance. In turn, experienced, higher-level players should not be "over-coached" on the parameters of a "good" stance.

The parameters of a proper stance are somewhat dependent upon the philosophy of your defensive scheme. If it is a scheme that calls for the defensive lineman to penetrate quickly on the snap of the ball and read on the run, the defensive lineman should demonstrate a stance that has the following characteristics:

- The feet closely set, with a sprinter's stagger. The player bunches up (i.e., aligns his back foot as close as possible to his front foot), so that he gains ground across the line of scrimmage on the first step.
- The buttocks high in the air, with his nose tilted downward
- The eyes looking up at the screws of the offensive lineman's headgear, with the ball kept in his peripheral vision
- The up-hand placed on his up-knee, so that he can push downward with his hand on takeoff
- Ready and able to move quickly as the ball is snapped

On the other hand, if the scheme is a read scheme that calls for the defensive lineman to first read the blocker's action and then to react to the scheme, the defensive lineman should have a stance that has the following features:

- The feet set shoulder-width apart, with a slight toe-to-heel stagger
- The buttocks level with his back, with his weight shifted onto his hips
- The eyes intensely focused on the screws of the offensive lineman's helmet
- The up-hand open and typically hanging loose, with his up-arm slightly flexed outside of his up-knee
- Although he should be hypersensitive to his opponent's movement, a reading defensive lineman should operate with a slower, more controlled approach.

An important point to remember is that, regardless of whether he is playing an attack philosophy or a read philosophy, a defensive lineman often assumes a stance that is tailored to the circumstances at a particular moment in the

game. For example, read-scheme defensive linemen may be assigned to an attack stance in passing situations. By the same token, both attack-scheme and read-scheme defensive linemen may shift their weight forward to their hands or backward to their hips, depending upon the down-and-distance situation or the time factor in the game.

The following factors are among the ways that a four-point stance is inherently different from a basic three-point stance:

- A four-point stance is more compact; the player's hands are closer to his toes.
- His elbows are bent and slightly pronated (i.e., turned outward) to help him get lower.
- His hips and backside are positioned at a much higher plane than normal.
- His neck is bowed, but his body is tilted downward, so that he cannot see much more than the feet of the offensive linemen and the movement of the ball.

A player may tailor his stance to allow him to gain an edge from a specific position. For example, the defensive lineman who is aligned at the nose tackle position uses a more compact stance than a defender aligned at the defensive end position. A nose tackle faces a triple threat on every snap (i.e., the possibility of being blocked from head-on, from one side, or from both sides). In addition to encountering double-team and occasionally triple-team blocks, a nose tackle has to be able to play zone blocks, as well as angle blocks from either side. Consequently, a nose tackle should use a stance that enables him to attack a blocker coming from either side, as well as from directly in front of him.

Defensive ends may use an elongated stance, with a slight point to the inside. By cocking his body to the inside, a defensive end shortens the corner, thereby giving himself a more direct path to the quarterback. Defensive ends may also point straight upfield in their stance. When pointing straight ahead (somewhat as a nose tackle might), a defensive end should keep his outside foot staggered behind the inside foot, which enables him to immediately gain width by stepping to the outside with his back foot upon recognition of pass. The outside-foot-back stagger also gives the defensive end an advantage against the threat of a double-team sealing him to the inside. He can use his outside foot to gain more leverage, as he defeats the block of the lead blocker (i.e., the blocker from the outside of a double-team).

As a general rule, the closer to the ball that the defensive lineman aligns, the less pronounced the stagger of his feet should be. For example, a nose tackle should keep his feet on an even plane, while a wide defensive end should use a heel-to-toe stagger. All factors considered, defensive linemen should not normally position their feet in a stagger that is greater than heel-to-toe.

In some instances, however, defensive linemen can adjust the normal positioning of their feet. For example, a defensive end may slightly elongate his stance when the offense is in an obvious passing situation. Whenever a defensive lineman's primary responsibility is linked to gaining a vertical push, he may elongate his stance and increase the stagger of his feet. Defensive linemen who are playing in the gap between two offensive linemen may also stretch out in a longer stance. The point to be emphasized, however, is that anytime that a defensive lineman exaggerates the stagger of his feet, he should keep his feet closer together. The general rule is: the greater the stagger, the less distance the feet should be set apart.

Another factor to consider regarding a defender's stance is whether a defensive lineman is to play on the defensive right or the defensive left. Traditionally, a defensive lineman who lines up to the right of the football will put his left hand down and his left foot back, while a defensive lineman who takes a position to the left of the football will put his right hand down and his right foot back. If you adhere to this philosophy of coaching defensive linemen, you should attempt to position your defensive linemen to the side of the ball that is opposite their dominant hand. In other words, a right-handed athlete should be assigned to play on the defensive left, while a left-handed athlete should be assigned to play on the defensive right. You should keep in mind that, depending upon the circumstances, it may be appropriate to instruct a defensive lineman to play his position with his outside hand down and his outside foot back. In these instances, you should emphasize the proper footwork techniques.

One final point is that the stance of the player is the starting point of the defensive assignment. A stance must help a player meet his objective after the snap. Coaches should tend to be more liberal about a player's stance, as long as it doesn't result in a waste of movement (e.g., false step, hitch step). Keep in mind that a technical flaw in a player's stance shouldn't necessarily be corrected in all instances. The primary factor in evaluating a stance should be the level of success it produces. If a player is operating from what his coach perceives to be a mechanically imperfect stance, and the player is highly effective, that mechanically imperfect stance is empirically flawless.

Nevertheless, under normal circumstances, the ideal defensive lineman's stance should reflect several characteristics, including the following:

- The defender's weight is centered on the hips.
- His back is flat.
- His knee is in line with the corresponding toe (i.e., the right knee is in line with the right toe, and the left knee is in line with the left toe).
- His off-hand is positioned so that his open palm can quickly be punched into the blocker.

☐ *Aligning Correctly*

Alignment refers to the specific location of a defender within the confines of the defensive line, with regard to a particular offensive landmark. Accurately specifying where a defender should line up enables you, as his coach, to designate which gap he is expected to control. Gap control involves a defender getting in the proper gap, achieving a level of penetration, and applying leverage on the blocker. Among the offensive landmarks that are commonly employed are the following:

- The A gap (i.e., the gap between the center and the guard). The A gap is further defined by whether it's on the strongside or the weakside of the offensive formation.
- The B gap (i.e., the gap between the guard and the tackle). The B gap is also defined by whether it's on the strongside or the weakside of the offensive formation.
- The C gap (i.e., the gap between the tackle and the tight end). The C gap is also defined by whether it's on the strongside or the weakside of the offensive formation.
- The D gap (i.e., the area extending from outside of the tight end to the sideline). The D gap is also defined by whether it's on the strongside or the weakside of the offensive formation.

In general, the four gaps are specified in the same manner on each side of the ball. On occasion, gaps are numbered, instead of lettered (i.e., 1 gap, 2 gap, 3 gap, 4 gap). A few coaches label the gaps consecutively from right to left or from left to right. Despite the substantial number of innovative defensive coaches in the game, the generic identification of gaps by consecutively lettering A to D on each side of the ball is still the most common terminology used (Figure 9-17).

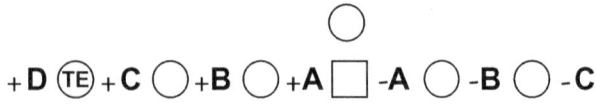

NOTE: THIS FORMATION IS STRONG LEFT.

Figure 9-17

Another popular way of handling defensive line terminology involves giving defensive coaches common ground to discuss the various details of defensive line play. This approach is designed to provide a basis to clearly identify the position of a defensive lineman along the line of scrimmage. In this concept of alignment terminology, the defensive lineman plays a numbered technique. Each numbered technique identifies a specific alignment against a particular offensive lineman. As illustrated in Figure 9-18, the possible alignments are assigned a number. Each numerical technique corresponds to one of the following alignments:

- Head-up on the blocker
- Shaded to the inside of a blocker
- Shaded to the outside of a blocker
- In the gap between two blockers

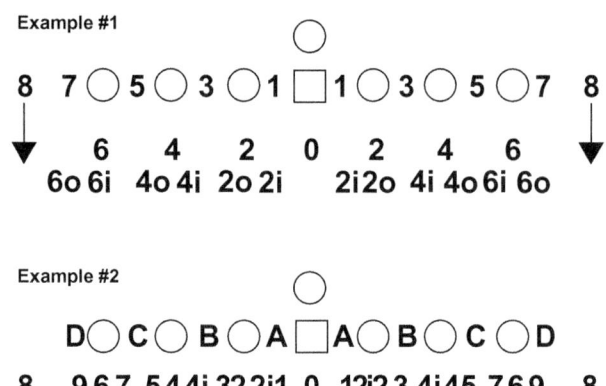

Figure 9-18

In the generic alignment numbering system (example #1) illustrated in Figure 9-18, an even-numbered technique corresponds to a head-up technique. Inside and outside shades are designated by assigning either an "i" (for inside) or an "o" (for outside). The second example of a generic alignment numbering system shown in Figure 9-18 is similar to the first example. This approach also adheres to a system in which an even-numbered technique corresponds to a head-up technique. In this system, outside shades are odd-numbered techniques. The 7 technique is the one exception to this rule. In this system, the 7 technique is the only inside shade technique identified by an odd number. The remaining inside shades are specified by even numbers, accompanied by the letter "i."

To differentiate between a head-up technique and an inside shade technique, the letter "i" is used to specify when the even-numbered technique is an inside shade—and not a head-up alignment. For example, the inside shade alignment on the offensive guard is called a 2i technique, while an outside shade alignment on the offensive tackle is called a 4i technique.

Another problematic aspect of the classical (generic) numbering system occurs when you attempt to identify a gap technique. With one exception, no identifying number for a gap alignment exists in the classical system. To identify the particular gap in which the defender is to align, you should either assign the gap a letter designation or add the word "gap" after the technique number. For example, in the latter option, when a defender aligns in the gap between the guard and tackle, he aligns in a 4 gap. You could also accurately describe that particular gap alignment as a 3 gap. The designation of a defender aligned in the guard-tackle gap as either a 4 gap or a 3 gap is a matter of preference and a matter of what name fits your system best.

In a similar vein, a defender who aligns in the gap between the tackle and the tight end may be designated by one of two names. In the classical number system, the defender aligned in the tackle–tight end gap may be accurately named a 5 gap or a 7 gap. Again, the choice of which term is best is one of personal preference. Somewhat ironically, the classical numbering system provides a name for the defender who is aligned in the center-guard gap (the only gap alignment number in the entire classical numbering system). This defender is called a 1 technique.

Due to the inherent problems (i.e., inconsistencies) in the classical (generic) technique numbering system, a few alternative numbering concepts have been developed. For example, several of the numbering concepts currently in use eliminate the inconsistency of the system regarding where the technique is numbered over the tight end position. In this regard, the most common revision of the classical (generic) numbering of the techniques over the tight end results in a more consistent theme within the numbering concept.

As illustrated in Figure 9-19, this particular approach to numbering assigns the inside alignment on each offensive player an even number. For example, the inside shade on the offensive guard remains a 2i technique, while the inside shade on the offensive tackle remains a 4i technique. The inside shade on the tight end, however, is assigned the number 6i, instead of the number 7.

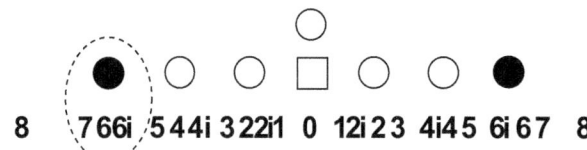

Figure 9-19

Detailed Alignment Specifications:

Every technique numbering system is structured to include the three basic alignments—inside, head up, and outside. The two shade alignments are the inside and outside alignments. In most numbering systems, a player is shaded when he aligns to one side of the blocker. If the defensive player aligns inside (i.e., between the ball and the blocker), the defender is playing an inside shade. On the other hand, if the defender aligns outside (i.e., the defender is positioned so that the blocker is between him and the ball), the defender is playing an outside shade. Inside shades have been traditionally referred to as "inside-eye" alignments, while outside shades have been called "outside-eye" alignments.

The origination of the "eye" terminology comes from the approach that the defensive player should match one of his eyes to one of the blocker's eyes. For example, a 5-technique tackle plays an outside-eye alignment. Therefore, the defensive player who is playing the 5-technique position aligns so that his inside eye is directly in front of the offensive tackle's outside eye. As might be imagined, a wide range of discrepancy is possible with regard to individual interpretations of exactly what is an inside-eye or outside-eye alignment.

A much more acceptable method for accurately aligning defensive linemen in a consistent shade involves having the defender position his foot on a plane cutting through the blocker's stance. Three such planes exist. One plane splits the stance into two even parts. Referred to as the midline plane, this plane splits the crotch of the blocker. The second plane—called the inside plane—runs parallel to the instep of the blocker's inside foot. The third plane—christened the outside plane—runs parallel to the instep of the blocker's outside foot. Figure 9-20 shows the stance of an offensive player and the three dissecting planes of the blocker's stance.

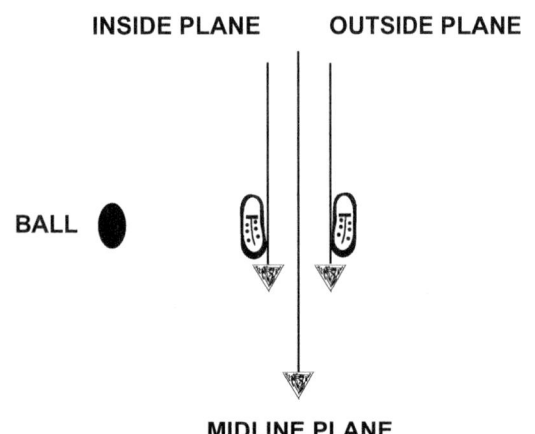

Figure 9-20

To realize the full advantage of identifying the three planes that cut through the offensive lineman's stance, the defender must specify one of his feet as his "leverage foot," while designating the other foot as his "anchor foot." Given the fact that the defender must keep "leverage" in his gap, the leverage foot is the foot that he must keep free in his gap responsibility. Consequently, the defender's gapside foot is his leverage foot. Conversely, the defender's opposite foot is his anchor foot. Proper positioning of the anchor foot guarantees that the defensive lineman will align in the precise location desired—as a shade, a crotch, or a shadow technique.

- The 2i, 2, 4i, 4, and 7 techniques use the foot furthest from the ball as the anchor foot.
- The 0, 3, 5, and 9 techniques use the foot closest to the ball as the anchor foot.
- The 1 technique aligns in the A gap and has no designated anchor foot.

Outside Techniques (3, 5, and 9 Techniques):

When a defensive lineman assumes his stance, he places his anchor foot on one of the three intersecting planes of the offensive lineman's stance. The outside defender (i.e., the 3 technique, the 5 technique, or the 9 technique) uses his inside foot as his anchor foot. If an outside technique places his anchor foot on the inside plane of the blocker's stance, he is aligning in a shade alignment (Figure 9-21).

The shade alignment is the tightest alignment variation of any numbered technique. A tight alignment is an alignment that is as close as possible to head-up on the blocker, without actually being head up. For example, a 3-technique defender aligns on the guard and has B-gap responsibility. Like all outside techniques, his anchor foot is his foot closest to the ball. The 3 technique's leverage foot is the foot closest to the B gap. By placing his anchor foot on the inside plane, the 3 technique aligns in the tightest possible 3-technique alignment (the shade 3-technique alignment). On the other hand, if a 3-technique defender were to place his foot directly in front of the guard's inside foot, his alignment would no longer fall under the definition of a 3 technique. At that point, he would then be a 2 technique.

When an outside technique places his anchor foot on the midline plane, his anchor foot points directly at the offensive lineman's middle. Accordingly, this alignment is called a half-man alignment (Figure 9-22). The half-man alignment is typically used for any odd-numbered technique. Likewise, the usual alignment for the even-numbered "i" techniques (e.g., 2i and 4i techniques) is also the half-man alignment.

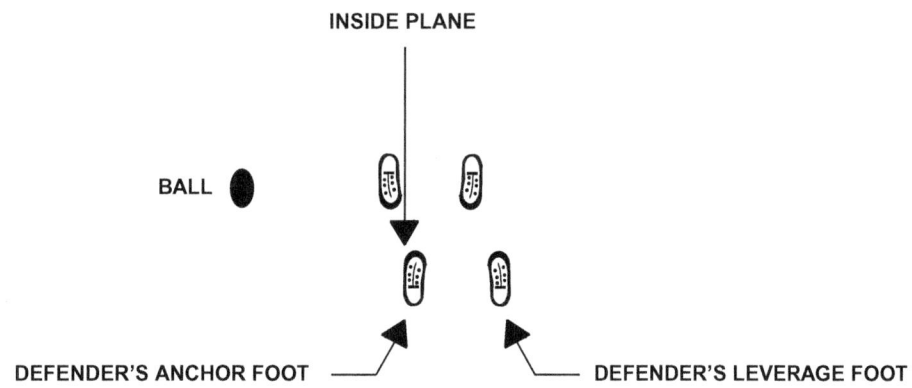

Figure 9-21

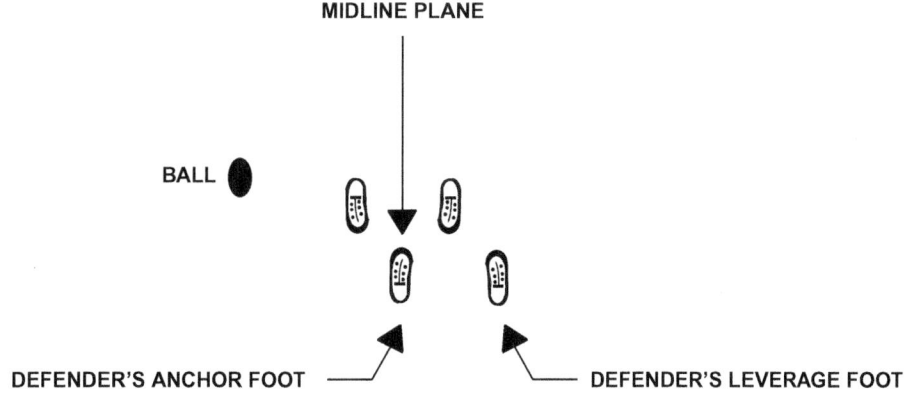

Figure 9-22

When an outside technique places his anchor foot on the outside plane, he aligns in a shadow alignment (Figure 9-23). A shadow alignment is also known as a "loose" alignment. In a shadow alignment, the outside-technique lineman plays from his widest alignment. Should the defensive lineman move out wider than an outside technique, the defensive tackle's alignment would be classified as a gap-technique alignment. The shadow alignment is a good adjustment for the outside technique to assume versus foot-to-foot (i.e., very tight) offensive line splits, and also in pass-rushing situations, regardless of the offensive line splits.

Inside Techniques (2, 4, and 7 Techniques)

The inside-technique defender uses his outside foot as his anchor foot. If an inside-technique defender places his anchor foot on the outside plane of the blocker's stance, he is in a shade alignment (Figure 9-24). For example, a 2i-technique defender assumes a shade 2i alignment, when he places his outside foot on the outside plane of the guard's stance. Likewise, a 4i-technique defender takes on a shade 4i alignment, when he places his outside foot on the outside plane of the tackle's stance. Similarly, a 7-technique defender is positioned in a shade 7-technique alignment, when he places his outside foot on the outside plane of the tight end's stance.

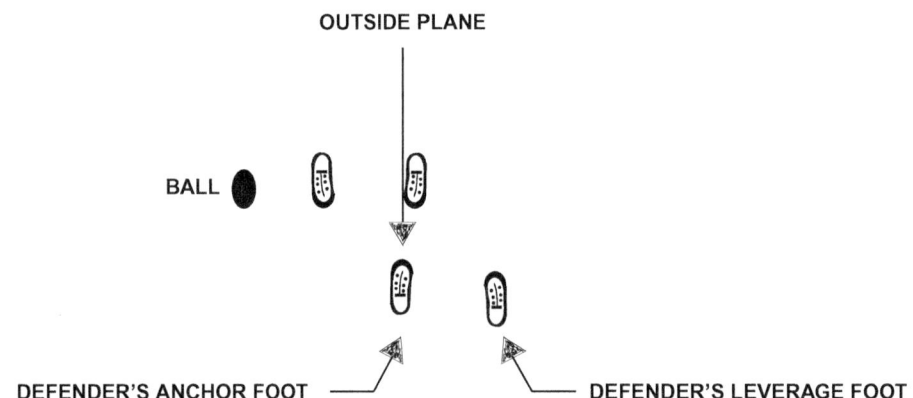

Figure 9-23

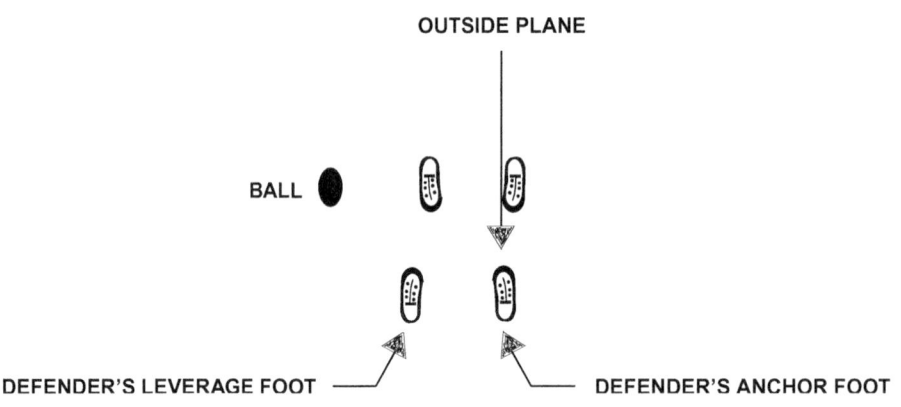

Figure 9-24

When an inside technique places his anchor foot on the midline plane, his anchor foot points directly at the offensive lineman's midsection. This alignment is the half-man alignment of the inside technique (Figure 9-25). Remember, the crotch alignment is the standard alignment for the inside techniques.

The shadow alignment (Figure 9-26) of an inside-technique defender is the tightest available alignment to the ball. For example, a shadow 4i defender is closer to the B gap than he is to the offensive tackle. The inside-technique defender aligns in a shadow alignment, when he feels that the gap closest to his leverage foot is too wide for the offensive lineman to control. The shadow alignment allows the inside-technique defender to beat the blocker by blitzing through the gap. The shadow alignment should never be used when the offensive line splits are relatively narrow.

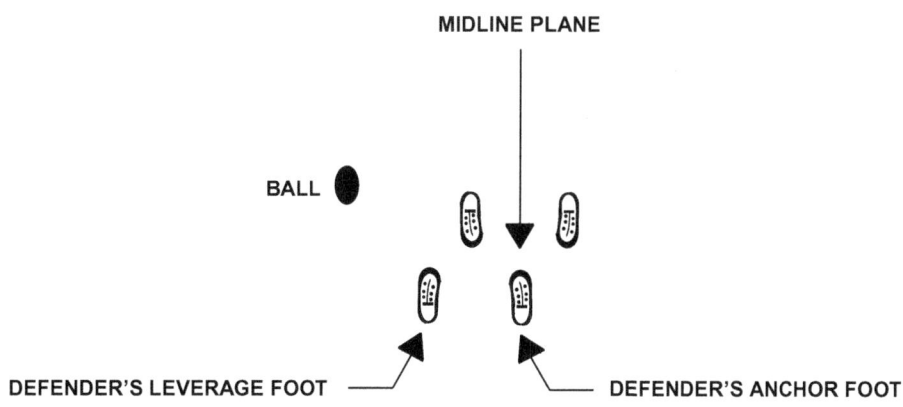

Figure 9-25

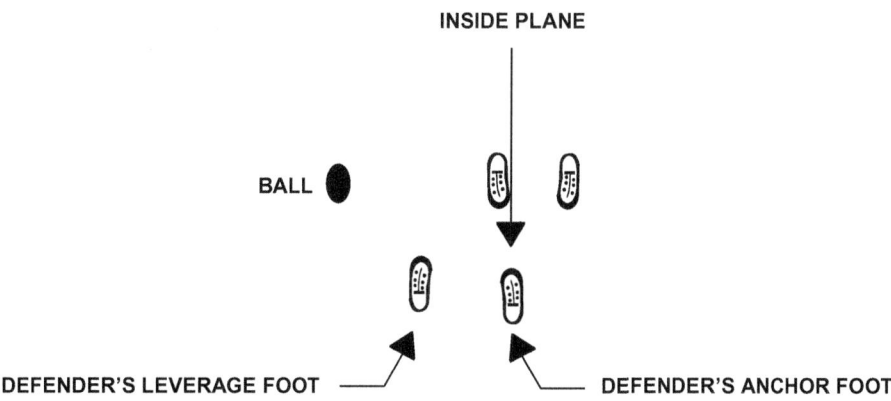

Figure 9-26

Head-up Technique (Shade and Shadow):

The head-up 0-technique nose tackle doesn't have the luxury of an "inside" or "outside" reference foot. However, if a nose tackle assumes a shade alignment or a crotch alignment, he must offset his alignment to one side of the ball. Once the nose tackle offsets to one side, he then establishes an "inside" foot and an "outside" foot. The offset nose tackle's inside foot is his anchor foot, while his outside foot is his leverage foot.

The center's inside plane naturally corresponds to the inside anchor foot of the offset nose tackle. These facts established, the shade 0 technique aligns with his inside foot on the outside plane of the center. Figure 9-27 provides an overview of the foot positioning points for the three basic types of alignments (shade, half-man, and shadow) for both outside and inside techniques.

☐ *Defending the Run*

The most important rule of defensive line play versus the run is that a lineman can never leave his gap until he can guarantee that the ball is not going to be run there. Beyond this basic principle, a team's philosophy of defensive line play against the run depends on the coach's preferences.

An Attack Philosophy:

Several significant advantages exist for a defensive lineman in an attack scheme. An attack philosophy of defensive line play is utilized in both the seven- and eight-man-front schemes. An attack philosophy (i.e., read-on-the-run philosophy) has several distinct advantages over a read philosophy (i.e., read-then-run philosophy). The perceived advantages of an attack technique over a read technique are:

Outside Techniques:
- A shade 0 technique puts his inside foot on the inside of the center.
- A shade 3 technique puts his inside foot on the inside plane of the guard.
- A shade 5 technique puts his inside foot on the inside plane of the tackle.
- A shade 9 technique puts his inside foot on the inside plane of the tight end or third man.
- A crotch 0 technique puts his inside foot on the midline plane of the center.
- A crotch 3 technique puts his inside foot on the midline plane of the guard.
- A crotch 5 technique puts his inside foot on the midline plane of the tackle.
- A crotch 9 technique puts his inside foot on the midline plane of the tight end or the third man.
- A shadow 0 technique puts his inside foot on the outside plane of the center.
- A shadow 3 technique puts his inside foot on the outside plane of the guard.
- A shadow 5 technique puts his inside foot on the outside plane of the tackle.
- A shadow 9 technique puts his inside foot on the outside plane of the tight end or the third man.

Inside Techniques:
- A shade 2i technique puts his outside foot on the outside plane of the guard.
- A shade 4i technique puts his outside foot on the outside plane of the tackle.
- A shade 7 technique puts his outside foot on the outside plane of the tight end or the third man.
- A crotch 2i technique puts his outside foot on the midline plane of the guard.
- A crotch 4i technique puts his outside foot on the midline plane of the tackle.
- A crotch 7 technique puts his outside foot on the midline plane of the tight end or the third man.
- A shadow 2i technique puts his outside foot on the inside plane of the guard.
- A shadow 4i technique puts his outside foot on the inside plane of the tackle.
- A shadow 7 technique puts his outside foot on the inside plane of the tight end or the third man.

Figure 9-27

- An attack technique forces the offensive linemen to defend against penetration. One likely result of this scenario is tentative play along the offensive line, as each offensive lineman tends to be overly concerned about "stopping" the defender's penetration instead of focusing on controlling the defender. Any time an offensive lineman focuses on "defending" or "stopping," that offensive lineman is essentially defeated.

- An attack technique forces the offensive line coach to double-team at the point of attack. When coaching the offensive line, all factors considered, neutralization is better than penetration, because neutralization implies that a stalemate has occurred. Instead, an offensive line coach should view a stalemate as a situation that is synonymous with failure. The point to remember is that under most circumstances, the offensive line must try to create a new line of scrimmage, gain a push along the front, and use its leverage to create seams for the running back. A stalemated offensive lineman can accomplish none of these objectives. Consequently, the most basic strategy in gaining an offensive edge at the point of attack versus an attack-style defensive lineman is the double-team strategy, but the defense gains a numerical advantage in its pursuits when the double-team is forced at the point of attack.

- An attack technique tends to break down the offensive line's scheme. Versus an attacking defensive line, the offensive line coach must design his game plan according to his opponent's defensive philosophy. An entirely new dimension is added to a team's offensive preparation when its opponent's defensive philosophy is an attack scheme on the defensive line.

- An attack technique frees the defensive line to disrupt the blocking scheme. By charging upfield on the snap, a defensive lineman becomes the aggressor. Most defensive coaches agree that movement is one of the keys to success on the offensive line. If this is correct, then movement should be the pre-snap objective of the defensive lineman. Each defensive lineman should remember to gear his reactions to a high level of sensitivity and to get in the gap. This approach forces the offensive lineman to adjust to the defender's attacking technique.

Along the offensive and defensive lines, the player who forces his opponent to make an adjustment has the advantage. The defensive lineman who attacks the line of scrimmage on the snap of the ball gains the upper hand.

- An attack technique maximizes the talent and the skills of every athlete. In some instances, an attack scheme can enable an undersized defensive lineman to succeed at the line of scrimmage. A defensive lineman playing within an attack scheme can overcome mismatches of strength, quickness, and size—all because of the jump he gets by keying the ball and attacking a specific area or gap, rather than waiting for the offensive lineman to cue him to anchor and control the blocker.

- Waiting to read the blocking scheme and slide horizontally upon establishing control of the blocker is a skill that few young athletes can physically accomplish. On the other hand, attacking to establish a new line of scrimmage and break down the offensive scheme is a skill that most can accomplish.

- While an attack technique may limit the ability of some defenders to physically focus on the peripheral action, well-coached, disciplined defensive linemen tend to be aware of it. This includes reacting to peripheral threats, such as traps and angle blocks.
- An attack style of defense is designed to let a defensive lineman play. He doesn't need a defensive call to rush the passer. He doesn't require a defensive call to tell him to attack, instead of read; he attacks on every snap of the ball. An attack style puts the game into the hands of the athlete. In the process, the defender is given the opportunity to concentrate on the physical dimension of line play.

A Read Philosophy:

When comparing an attack versus a read philosophy of defensive play, keep in mind that there are merits to a read philosophy, including the following:

- The read scheme gives a defensive lineman a greater degree of leverage in horizontal control. An attack philosophy, on the other hand, can create seams in the front as the defensive linemen charge upfield on the snap.
- The read scheme provides a defensive lineman with an increased level of pursuit to the ballcarrier, whereas an attack philosophy causes the defender to change his pursuit angle, if the ball does not immediately hit in his area.
- The read scheme frees the linebackers. An attack philosophy, on the other hand, puts more pressure on the linebackers to stop the interior traps and hard dives and requires them to fill their gap assignments immediately.
- The read scheme provides an opportunity for the defensive lineman control the opposing blocker. An attack philosophy—because of its emphasis on the defender's vertical push—may compromise the potential effect that a defensive lineman's level of strength actually has on a play.
- The read scheme allows the defensive lineman to use his peripheral vision. On the other hand, an attack scheme may have a negative impact on the effect of a defender's peripheral vision, because the defensive lineman's ability to react is compromised to a degree by his vertical charge on the snap.

Control Schemes:

- One-gap control. In both the eight- and seven-man-front schemes, an attack philosophy is conducive to "one-gap" control. One-gap control is an important concept in coaching defensive line play. A lineman who is playing in a one-gap control scheme can pursue moving upfield at the snap. This feature refers to the fact that a one-gap control player can possess and utilize his quick reactions and be assigned to attack the line of scrimmage.
- Two-gap control. The read technique is the only suitable style of play for the two-gap philosophy. The two-gap control player, as the phrase implies, is responsible for the control and anchoring of two gaps instead of just one. This is a pure two-gap assignment only in the moments before the ball is snapped. Once the ball is snapped and the point of attack is recognized, the two-gap player becomes a one-gap player. The defender makes such a transformation by correctly reading the blocking scheme or blocking key.

Defeating Blockers:

• *Throwing-the-hands technique.* If a rule was passed to limit a coach's instruction of defensive line play to a single word, that coach could still teach correctly, if the chosen word was "hands." Hands are the key to successful line play. While the feet, legs, hips, and shoulders each have an essential role, they're not as critical as the defender's hands.

The importance of the proper use of the defender's hands is more easily understood once the movement of an attacking lineman is broken down and analyzed. If the motion of the attacking defensive lineman is examined, it can be seen that the hands lead the body. The faster the hands are thrown into the opponent, the more momentum he will generate. When the defender's hands are violently thrown into the body of the blocker, the defender's hips snap forward, leveraging the power in his lower body.

Although most young football players don't possess the upper-body strength to maximize the throwing-the-hands technique, teaching this technique fosters skill development. When a defensive lineman throws his hands, his forearms and shoulders naturally follow. The throwing-the-hands technique can be easily modified for the shoulder-strike delivery technique. To modify the "hands" technique, the defender simply has to throw his hands so that the front of his hands faces the defender on contact. Rolling the hands in this manner forces the defender's elbow outward, so that his forearm and shoulder can be used as an attack surface.

Athletes at the more competitive levels of play should be coached to concentrate on using their hands to gain separation from a blocker. To gain separation, a defender must first gain control through the proper placement of his hands. Hand placement involves two factors—"how" and "where." "How" refers to how the defender uses his hands when making contact with a blocker's body. "Where" refers to where on a blocker's body the defender places his hands. The defensive lineman should be trained to use his hands in a manner that controls the blocker. Ideally, a defensive lineman will use his hands to slow the blocker.

The defensive lineman should throw his hands so that he strikes his opponent's blocking surface with the heels of his hands. Much consideration has been given to the placement of the thumbs when contact is made. It appears that most coaches believe that the positioning of the thumbs should be left to personal preference.

Some coaches teach the "thumbs-up" method, in which the fingers are slightly flexed and loosely bent, so that the defensive lineman can grab cloth. This type of hand positioning is called a "chuck" grasp—a dual reference to the clamp-like look and the quick-throwing motion of the same name. The defensive lineman uses his chuck grasp to control a blocker and feel the pressure, so that he may move the blocker away from his angle of pursuit and sprint to the ballcarrier.

Some athletes prefer to roll their thumbs inward or downward on contact. The major negative factor involved in doing so is that such an action causes the defender's elbows to point outward. This position offers little power to the defensive lineman, since his elbows are out of line with his main thrust of force. To maximize his power, an experienced defensive lineman should keep his elbows inside the frame of his upper body, exactly as his elbows should be when he is bench pressing. This position enables a defensive lineman to increase his power by keeping the force moving in a direct line. A major coaching point to emphasize in this regard is that a defensive lineman should prevent his thumbs from rolling inward or downward on contact. Throwing the hands and engaging with the blocker with the thumbs pointing upward not only helps a defensive lineman to keep his elbows in, it also increases his ability to exert power.

Where the hands are placed is primarily dependent upon the relative height of the blocking surface (i.e., the blocker's shoulders). If the blocker comes off the ball in a relatively high posture, the plane of the blocking surface is consequently high (possibly above the shoulders of the defensive lineman). If the blocker comes off the ball in a scrambling, ultra-low posture, the blocking surface is relatively low (probably well below the defensive lineman's knees). The defender's hands should be thrown to a common plane—the plane at which a blocker carries his shoulders when conducting a normal base block.

If the blocker comes off the ball with a high blocking surface above the common plane, the defensive lineman has a good shot at making contact into the blocker's numbers and lifting the blocker's shoulders. On the other hand, if the blocker comes off the ball below the common plane to attack the knees of the defensive lineman, the defender can adjust the angle of his hands so that he strikes the blocker on his shoulder pads and pushes the blocker into the ground.

It is important that a defender be coached to keep his eyes focused on the screws. He cannot afford to peer through a blocker's headgear to look for the ball. He should have a twofold primary objective—defeat the blocker and stay on his feet. Failing to maintain a focus on the screws often results in the defensive player getting cut down by a low blocker. Focusing on the screws of the blocker is an essential factor in the defensive lineman being able to defeat a scramble blocker and stay on his feet.

• *Forearm-and-shoulder blow-delivery technique.* The forearm and shoulder are not separate blow-delivery mechanisms. They are both part of a single technique. The forearm-and-shoulder blow is an excellent technique against any block. When a defensive lineman is delivering a forearm-and-shoulder blow, his elbow is allowed to fly outward. Because his elbow points outward on contact, his thumb points upward, with his palm facing the blocker. The defensive lineman can also make a fist with his contact-delivery hand, as he strikes the chest of the blocker with the front of his hand and the outside of his arm. The relatively compact physical characteristics of the forearm-and-shoulder blow increase the speed of the defender's arm and shoulder in striking the blocker.

The hand and the arm provide a lift to the blow delivery. When this technique is employed, the defender's shoulder can stop the blocker. The forearm-and-shoulder technique is actually a misnomer. It should more accurately be described as the shoulder-and-forearm technique.

If aligned in a gap technique in a goal-line situation, the defensive lineman should use both shoulders to deliver contact. He should penetrate the gap in a low charge, while delivering an uplifting force with each shoulder. This action prevents him from being knocked off course to one side and ensures that he can push a point through the line of scrimmage and disrupt the continuity of the offensive scrimmage line. The gap charge is the only time that a defensive lineman should use both to deliver contact. Normally, a defensive lineman should make a forearm-and-shoulder

contact with the shoulder that is furthest from his responsible gap and closest to the player on which he is aligned. So, if a defensive lineman aligned on the guard is responsible for the B gap, he should use his inside shoulder against the guard. Likewise, if the defensive lineman aligned on the tackle is responsible for the same B gap, he should use his outside shoulder against the tackle.

When a forearm-and-shoulder contact-delivery technique is done from a shade alignment, the defensive lineman should visualize throwing his forearm—instead of his hands—into the blocker. No motion is wasted as the defender's forearm and fist lead his shoulder into the blocker's chest. The defensive lineman's off-hand immediately follows his active forearm in contacting the blocker. Defensive linemen should be taught to use their off-hand to strike the blocker in a manner that is similar to the throwing-the-hands technique.

The defensive lineman should use the heel of his hand to strike the blocker inside the plane of the blocker's upper body. Using the chuck grasp, the defensive lineman should grab cloth and do one of two things. The first option is to pull the blocker's shoulder down. This action turns the blocker's shoulders and twists him so that he loses his blocking surface. The defensive lineman should then quickly release off the blocker and go to the football.

The second option is to jam and extend the chuck hand so that the blocker's shoulder twists backward. This action also causes the blocker to lose his square blocking surface. Jamming the blocker's shoulder backward enables the defensive lineman to bring his blow-delivery shoulder across the face of the blocker and clear the blocker. Through regular repetition in practice, the defensive lineman should develop a better feel for which option he needs to execute. He should eventually be able to make this decision instantaneously, and then use his off-hand to pull or push the blocker's shoulder and escape to tackle the ballcarrier.

☐ *Rushing the Passer*

To play the pass, a defensive lineman should be aware of the following coaching points for pass-rush techniques. As a pass rusher, a defensive lineman should:

- Have a plan—An effective pass rusher predetermines his move. Pre-snap planning of the move can make a pass rusher more successful.
- Maintain a consistent stance—Prior to the snap of the ball, a defensive lineman should crowd the ball and take a good stance, but he shouldn't tip his stance and alert the offensive lineman about where he is going or what move he is going to make.
- Pass rush from a shade alignment—Such an alignment enables a defensive lineman to attack only half the man (his opponent). Forcing an offensive lineman to commit to one side is often the initial step in making a good move. A shade alignment not only allows the defensive lineman to squeeze through a hole, but also forces an offensive lineman to commit to one side.
- Learn to feel the depth of the quarterback's drop—This can determine the type of pass-rushing technique to use. For example, a short quarterback drop would suggest using a quicker pass-rush move (e.g., grab and rip).
- Keep in mind the precept "same hand, same foot"—The primary key to finishing all pass-rushing moves is to have the defensive lineman adhere to the "same hand, same foot" precept, which states that the defensive

lineman should use the same foot as his primary hand to finish a move. For example, when extending his right hand over to perform a swim technique, the defensive lineman should swing his right foot across to gain upfield position on the blocker.

- Use the hands with sharp movements—A pass rusher should use his hands in sharp movements to defeat the offensive lineman.

- Use a counter move when caught (i.e., when the original move did not work)—A defensive lineman should have a counter move to every base pass-rushing move. For example, the counter move for the rip is the re-rip or swim.

- Spin the blocker when being carried past the quarterback—A pass rusher should never "give up" on his pass rush and allow himself to be carried past the quarterback.

- Keep his weight and momentum going forward toward the quarterback—Above all else, a pass rusher should keep his feet moving and avoid dancing.

- Run through the sack—A pass rusher shouldn't jump or leave his feet to sack the quarterback.

Pass-Rush Techniques:

As a rule, defensive linemen have seven proven pass-rushing techniques at their disposal. On the other hand, most coaches feel that their players need to master only a few (i.e., one to three) of these techniques.

- *The rip technique.* The rip technique is sometimes referred to as speed rush—particularly when it is used by a defensive end. The rip technique involves a defensive lineman dipping the shoulder that is nearest the blocker as he powers past him. The move is initiated by the defender as he uses the hand that is opposite the blocker to pull his near arm forward. The pass rusher should execute such a pull in an explosive, snatching manner. Grabbing and pulling the blocker's near arm enables the rusher to gain an upfield advantage with his outside shoulder. The pass rusher should then rip his leverage arm (i.e., the arm closest to the blocker) upward in the manner of an uppercut to the armpit of the pass blocker, though in reality this uppercut should be directed to a point outside the plane of the blocker's body. Such an uppercut punch is designed to drive the pass blocker's leverage arm upward and force him to turn his shoulders—an action that figuratively opens the gate to the quarterback. (Note: One point that should be strongly emphasized to the pass rusher is that the only time he should raise either hand is when the quarterback has released the ball, and the ball is in the defender's path.)

The action of the defender dipping his leverage shoulder also gives the pass protector less blocking surface to contact. The lateral arm (i.e., the arm furthest from the defender's path) really has no available frontal surface to contact. In this instance, the blocker is forced to try to "hip steer" the pass rusher with his lateral arm. The hip-steering technique—a technique that involves the pass protector putting his off-hand on the hip of the speed rusher—is effective on the edge of the line of scrimmage, but not in the interior. The rip technique is suitable for either a defensive tackle or a defensive end and can be made either to the inside or outside of the blocker.

- *The swim technique.* The swim technique begins exactly the same way as a rip technique, with a swift slap and grab of the blocker's near shoulder with the defender's offside hand (i.e., the hand opposite the blocker). The offside-hand slap-and-

grab aspect of a swim technique is slightly different from the offside-hand slap-and-grab employed in a rip technique. Whereas the rip-technique slap-and-grab is made using a sideways motion (i.e., across the body), in the manner of a roundhouse punch, the offside-hand slap-and-grab of the swim technique is performed with a pulling motion.

When initiating the swim technique, the pass rusher should snap the off-hand downward and grab the blocker on his shoulder—slightly behind the point of the shoulder. Grabbing the blocker's jersey in this manner enables the pass rusher to pull the near shoulder of the blocker downward. By doing so, the pass rusher gives himself clearance to punch his onside hand (i.e., the hand nearest the blocker) over the depressed (i.e., pulled down) shoulder of the pass protector. A key coaching point regarding this technique is to use the word "punch" to describe the action of the defender's onside hand swinging over the top of the pass protector's depressed shoulder. The word traditionally used to describe this action is "swim" (the name given to the technique).

When learning the swim technique, players should be taught to move their onside hand and onside foot as one body part. Defenders should be encouraged to remember the "same hand, same foot" rule. As the defender's onside hand punches over the depressed shoulder of the pass protector, his onside foot drives to a point near the heel of the blocker's near leg. The defender's objective when driving his foot to the heel of the blocker is to simultaneously get his hip past the blocker's hip. Once the pass rusher's hip has cleared the hip of the blocker, the pass protector cannot recover. The pass rusher can add a final touch to the move by using his onside hand to push off the pass protector's back, after he punches his onside hand over and clears the blocker.

The swim move is best used by a taller defensive player on the edge who possesses long limbs and exceptional upper-body strength. It is also an excellent pass-rush move against top-heavy, overly aggressive pass sets.

• *The bull technique.* The primary objective of a bull rusher is to elevate the blocker's shoulders and force him back on his heels. Once a defensive lineman reads the high hat and becomes a pass rusher, he should strike the blocker with the heels of his hands. The heels of the rusher's hands should be positioned with the thumbs up, just below the top of the numbers. The defender should then push the blocker's shoulders back to cause the blocker's weight to shift backward. This type of rush is best when used against a shallow quarterback drop (i.e., a three- or five-step drop). A bull rush is also effective against a blocker who has set too high, has his weight on his heels, or is floating (i.e., drifting) off of the line of scrimmage.

• *The club technique.* As one of the more physical pass-rushing techniques, the club technique is excellent when used by a defensive lineman who possesses both extraordinary upper-body strength and the quick hands of a boxer. When executing a club technique, the pass rusher should sell a vertical push to one side of the blocker. Once the blocker shifts his weight and commits to stopping the rusher's upfield penetration, the pass rusher should then drive his opposite hand into the chest or shoulder of the blocker. The pass rusher's clubbing action is designed to force the blocker toward the direction of his weight shift and to use his own momentum against him. After knocking the blocker off balance with his club hand, the pass rusher should then finish the move by ripping past the blocker with his opposite arm.

Like the rip technique, the club technique can be used to beat the blocker either to the inside or to the outside. It is also frequently used by defensive linemen to set up counter moves.

• *The spin technique.* An effective technique for defensive linemen at any level, the spin technique offers several advantages, including—depending on the circumstances—providing an opportunity for a quicker, less-physical pass rusher to dominate a bigger, stronger offensive lineman. More than any other technique, however, the spin technique enables a defensive lineman to use his shoulder. To execute a spin move, the pass rusher drives upfield to a point immediately outside the near shoulder of the blocker. The offensive lineman will usually respond by leaning into the pass rusher to maximize his weight advantage.

At the point where the pass rusher feels the pass protector shifting his weight into the block, the pass rusher should plant his foot nearest the blocker. As he plants his near foot, the pass rusher should take advantage of the momentum of his onside shoulder by using his onside hand and arm to shove the blocker in the direction of the pass rusher's momentum. While shoving the blocker with his onside arm, the pass rusher should sharply swing his offside elbow rearward. Swinging the elbow opens the pass rusher's shoulders and hips so that he can drop step around to hook the back of the blocker's leg. The pass rusher has thus pinned the pass protector. The pass rusher should then complete his spin and work to regain an appropriate degree of leverage on track to the quarterback's passing arm and shoulder. The spin technique is very effective for the defensive end and can be used by the tackle against an offensive guard who employs a wide set.

• *The shake-and-bake technique.* The shake-and-back technique is a great pass-rushing method for a defensive lineman who is quicker and faster than his opponent. The shake-and-bake technique essentially involves a situation in which a defender "pretends" to be doing one thing and then does another. The pass rusher simply uses his best move(s) to fake-out the pass protector and pressure the quarterback. As such, the shake-and-bake technique is best used from the edge, where the pass rusher has a lot of room in which to operate. The shake-and-back move is also an excellent change-up technique for a quick defensive end to use on an obvious passing down. It should be executed as close to the blocker as possible.

• *The push-pull technique.* A complementary technique to the bull technique, the push-pull technique is a fundamentally simple move that can be most effectively used by a pass rusher who is able to maintain a relatively low center of gravity. An effective bull technique is designed to enable a pass rusher to stun and lift the pass protector. After stunning the blocker, the pass rusher finishes his bull technique with an explosively strong bench press. Using his chuck grasp to grab the blocker just below the top of the numbers, the pass rusher quickly pulls the off-balance pass protector toward him, releases him, and clears the blocker.

The push-pull technique is a very effective complement to the bull technique that can be utilized in the interior line. It is an especially appropriate technique for use at the lower levels of competition, where young offensive linemen frequently tip their weight forward when pass blocking. The push-pull technique uses the pass blocker's tendency to overextend against him.

- ▸ Is there a specific characteristic of the opponent's approach to blocking that can be better attacked through a stunt?
- How much emphasis within the game plan should be placed on stunts? Again, the emphasis on stunts is usually related to the match-up of the team's opponent versus the defensive unit. A mismatch usually indicates that stunts should be a part of a team's defensive package. The irony of this consideration is that a mismatch can be either in a team's favor or in its opponent's favor.

    When your team is seriously outmatched in size, strength, and ability, the defensive coach should consider an extensive stunt package. However, a stunt package is even more likely to be devastating to an opponent who is overmatched by a team's defensive personnel. Additional considerations that should be addressed when deciding how much emphasis should be placed on a stunt package within a team's game plan are the element of surprise and the opponent's offensive system. If a defensive coach adds an element of surprise by tailoring his team's system to meet a specific purpose, the emphasis on the stunt package that week should probably be increased.

- How much variation is needed within a defensive stunt package? The number of stunts and the relative emphasis on the teaching of the various stunt combinations are directly related to a coach's decision regarding the amount of variation needed within the team's defensive stunt package. Generally speaking, the offensive system that a team is facing should also be a primary consideration in the makeup of a defensive team's stunt package. For example, an offensive team that utilizes a wide range of formation concepts dictates that the nature of a team's stunt package be relatively limited. Against such an offense, the stunt package should be confined to stunts that allow the call to be run without checking off. Including multiple check-offs and automatics in a team's defensive system will undermine the defense's aggressiveness.

On occasion, a defensive lineman may be asked to stunt a gap—either alone or in tandem with a teammate. As such, when defensive linemen stunt, they should:

- Know the gap they are stunting.
- Get out of their stance quickly.
- Drive through the outside/inside shoulder of the man they are stunting. Never loop or be blocked wide to that side. Use the rip or swim technique.
- Get one yard into the backfield and read the play.
- Stay in control.
- Do not penetrate too deep into the backfield.
- Never get deeper than the ballcarrier.
- Protect their gap.
- Pursue the ballcarrier.

☐ *Defensive Line Drills*

<u>Get-off Drill:</u>

This drill is designed to develop the ability of a defensive lineman to take a "big" first step. One football is required to conduct the drill. Performing the drill involves the following steps:

- Have the players form two or more lines facing you.
- Put the defensive linemen who play on the defensive left on the left line, and vice versa for those who play on the defensive right.

☐ *Sacking the Quarterback*

Ideally, the defensive lineman should always use a draping technique when sacking the quarterback. In other words, whenever possible, the pass rusher should bring both of his arms down on the shoulders of the quarterback as he makes contact. A pass rusher should use his outside arm to hook the elbow of the quarterback's passing arm as the quarterback cocks his arm in the throwing movement. By draping his arms downward on the passer, the defender is able to prevent the last-second release of the ball by the quarterback.

The draping sack technique also helps a pass rusher finish sacking an agile quarterback who is attempting to duck under him. By being under control and by draping the quarterback, the defender is able to avert an up-and-under "duck" move by the quarterback. The draping technique prevents the defender's forward momentum from carrying him past the quarterback, if he steps up to duck under the pass rusher. The pass rusher should always rush toward the passer's back shoulder, with the intention of sacking him from the outside-in. If possible, the defender should chop downward with his outside arm on the quarterback's passing arm, trying to create a fumble and hopefully a turnover.

☐ *Stunting*

Defensive line games—particularly those geared toward providing a pass rush—are best when used as a change-up and as an additional factor to create a great jet pass-rush technique. One of the responsibilities when coaching defensive linemen is to develop stunts that take advantage of offensive schemes and individual player technique weaknesses demonstrated by the opponent. The primary key to unlocking the code to recognizing and exploiting these weaknesses involves intensive film study and practice separation. An excellent approach for teaching and implementing effective stunts involves the following steps:

- *Talk*—The purpose of the stunt, the key coaching points of the stunt, and the contingencies that may affect the execution of the stunt should be explained to the players during a chalk talk.
- *Air*—The aforementioned considerations should be more thoroughly discussed and explained during a walkthrough on the field, using defensive linemen to simulate the pass blockers.
- *Bags*—The stunts should be performed (practiced) in a slow, controlled manner under the direction of the defensive line coach, with primary emphasis on the major coaching points attendant to the stunt. Defensive linemen should be used to simulate pass blockers.
- *Control*—The stunts should be run at a faster pace against offensive linemen who demonstrate a predetermined, specific pass-protection scheme. The emphasis should be placed on the sharpness of the stunting technique.

When deciding what stunt packages should be included in your defensive scheme, consider three factors:

- How many stunts does the team need? Stunts should never be included in a team's defensive scheme just for the sake of having them. Each stunt should have a specific purpose and address a specific need. The number of stunts that is needed is related to two factors:
  - ▸ How good—or bad—is your team's base defensive production against the run or pass?

- Kneel down between the two lines, call out cadence, and initiate the drill by moving the ball.
- On the ball's movement, have the first defensive lineman in each line sprint 5 to 10 yards ahead, making sure that each player pushes off his front foot and takes a big first step, as he explodes from his stance.

* If you prefer, have all of the defensive linemen perform the drill simultaneously (i.e., all of them line up and face you at once). You could also mix up the count before you move the ball.

Figure 9-28

Throw the Hands Drill:

This drill is designed to develop the ability of a defensive lineman to perform a throwing-the-hands technique. A football, hand shields, and two form-tackling dummies are required to conduct the drill. Performing the drill involves the following steps:

- Have the players form two lines.
- Have a teammate, holding a hand shield just above his knees, stand in front of each defensive lineman at the front of the line.
- Kneel between the players, call out cadence, and then move the ball.
- On the movement of the ball, have each player in front of each line drive out of his stance and throw his hands into the hand shield.

- Have the defensive lineman strike the shield with the heels of his hands, trying to drive the shield upward.
- Have the defensive lineman drive the shield-holder backward for two to three steps, and then release, before sprinting to the stand-up tackling dummy, upon which he executes a form tackle.

* Emphasize the explosive punch of the hands.

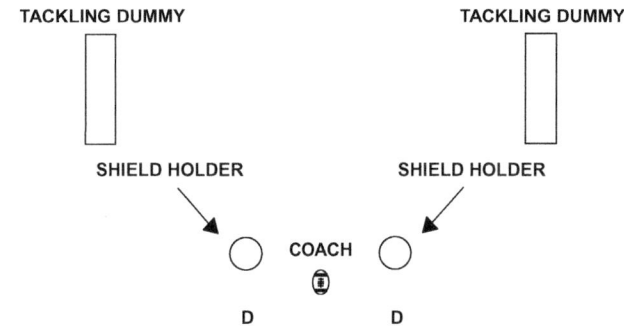

Figure 9-29

Takeoff/Pursuit Drill:

This drill is designed to develop the ability of defensive linemen to get off on ball movement, while using a strong base, penetrating the backfield, and chasing the ballcarrier at the proper angle. A football and a lined field are required to conduct the drill. Performing the drill involves the following steps:

- Have four or five defensive linemen crowd a football, four yards from a yard line.
- Simulating a quarterback, bark out signals.
- When you subsequently snap (move) the ball, have the defensive linemen burst out of their stance and explode (forward) to the yard line.
- Once the defensive linemen get to the yard line, give them a directional signal either to the right or left, and have them then sprint five yards in that direction.

* Make sure the defensive linemen utilize the proper angle of pursuit to the ball.

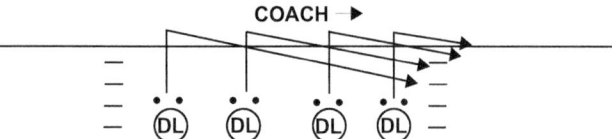

Figure 9-30

Indicator Drill:

This drill is designed to develop the ability of defensive linemen to spot what the quarterback's indicators are and to determine what his intentions are when he throws the football. Two footballs are required to conduct the drill, which involves the following:

- Position the defensive linemen (i.e., the pass rushers) in their respective positions in a line along the front.
- Simulating a quarterback, call out cadence, and subsequently snap (move) the ball.
- On the movement of the ball, have the defensive linemen rush the quarterback at three-quarter speed.
- When the quarterback's indicators (i.e., his hands, his front arm, the ball) reveal that he is going to throw the ball, have the defensive linemen immediately (not before) get their hands up and try to knock it down.

* Use pump fakes to test the discipline of the defensive linemen.

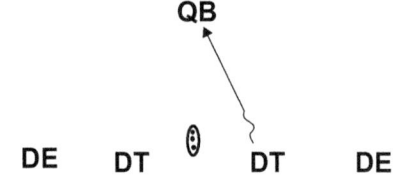

Figure 9-31

Linebackers

On many teams, linebackers serve as the quarterback of the defense. Not only do they tend to have a good sense for the flow of the action, they also have a nose for the football. In other words, they are able to recognize plays quickly, make the proper reaction, and adjust according to the situation. A linebacker ideally has the quickness of a defensive back and the power of a defensive lineman. As a rule, linebackers must be able to:

- Diagnose running plays, provide strong support to the defensive line, and control their areas of responsibility.
- Recognize and quickly take the proper angle of pursuit against outside plays (sweeps, options, etc.). Inside linebackers pursue from inside to outside, keeping the ballcarrier on their outside shoulder (the shoulder on the side of the direction in which they are going). Outside linebackers should pursue straight down the line of scrimmage or give ground slightly once the ball has gotten outside of them.
- Blitz (immediately attack an offensive area on the snap of the ball).
- Play zone pass defense (covering a specific area of the field—flats, curls, middle).
- Play man-to-man pass defense (covering a particular offensive receiver). In this area of responsibility, a linebacker can either approach his duties cautiously (covering an offensive receiver when he does not have deep help) or aggressively (taking away the passes in the area from the line of scrimmage to 18 yards deep, knowing that deep help is available).
- Recognize the offensive formation and make adjustments to unanticipated situations.

The ability of each linebacker usually determines the defensive alignment. If all linebackers are of equal ability, it is generally most advantageous to simply align them according to sides (left and right). However, if the linebackers are more or less capable in certain areas, it may be necessary to align them in various positions, according to the placement of the football (i.e., shortside vs. wideside) or the type of offensive formations being used (i.e., weakside vs. strongside). Most commonly, two of the linebackers align to the strongside, while the others align to the weakside. The strongside is determined by the side of the field in which the offense has the most room to maneuver or the strength of the formation.

Coaching linebackers entails having athletes who play the position master several skills and techniques, including assuming the proper stance, moving purposely, shedding blockers, tackling, pursuing to the ball, playing pass defense (both zone and man-to-man), blitzing, and rushing the passer.

☐ *Assuming the Proper Stance*

Photo 9-13

When in the contact zone (i.e., close proximity to blockers, receivers, and/or ballcarriers), it is necessary for a linebacker to be in good hitting position. While the appropriate position for each player may vary slightly due to differences in body builds, a list of general guidelines concerning what constitutes a proper stance should include the following:

- His feet should be at least shoulder width apart or slightly wider.
- His toes should be pointed straight forward.
- The weight of his body should be on the toes and balls of his feet, but his heels should not be off the ground.
- His knees should be bent and positioned slightly beyond his feet.
- His legs should be tense (muscles contracted) and ready for sudden movement.
- He should bend forward at the waist so that his head and chest are positioned slightly beyond his knees.
- His hands should be positioned slightly outside the knee joint, with his palms facing inward and parallel to his leg.
- His neck should be bulled (i.e., tented), with his eyes looking up at the target.
- His upper body should be relaxed in order to facilitate ease of movement but should become tense immediately before contact.

When moving in the contact area, whether it is forward, backward, laterally, or on an angle, a linebacker should try to stay very close to the recommended hitting position. For example, his arms should move freely. Having a proper stance becomes more important the closer he is to the offensive players. Linebackers must be able to move efficiently (i.e., not waste motion or effort) in all directions and not raise or lower themselves anymore than necessary while moving. All linebackers should strive to be smooth and fluid.

The type of movement utilized by a linebacker may depend on your defensive scheme. As a rule, linebackers move laterally, forward, and backward.

• *Lateral movement.* When moving laterally, the linebacker should not raise or lower himself from his initial stance. He should maintain his shoulders relatively parallel (or "square") to the line of scrimmage. The direction in which he moves laterally is dictated by a key or the ball.

One of the most basic lateral movements is the slide or shuffle. This maneuver is the easiest movement from which to change direction, because a player's feet never cross. On occasion, it may be necessary to slide once. A systematic analysis of lateral movement shows that the linebacker should lean in the direction he wants to go, slide his back foot (the one opposite the direction that he wants to go) in the direction of the body lean, and then slide the lead foot in the direction that he is going. It is very important to note that he should not hop or cross his feet. This movement must be a quick move, with his feet remaining as close to the ground as possible. His elbows should be kept close to his body. Any upper-body motion should be minimized. If play dictates, he should continue to slide in this same manner.If sliding is not fast enough, it may then become necessary for him to run laterally. To run in this manner, he should keep his shoulders square and allow his arms to swing naturally. Again, he should lead with his back foot (the one opposite the direction he wants to go), but, this time, he should cross over with the other foot (e.g., if he is going to his left, it is right over, left out). When moving laterally, a linebacker should adhere to the following factors:

- He should turn his shoulders to run only as a last resort.
- He should not waste motion or become overextended.

- He should employ his opposite hand in an opposite-foot-movement pattern. As his left foot goes forward, his right hand shoots upward to shoulder height and left hand moves backward toward his hip, and vice versa.
- He should bend slightly, flexed (bent) at the waist, with his head tilted slightly downward and his eyes directed straight ahead.
- He should try to move as smoothly and fluidly as possible (no wasted motion).
- Finally, he should concentrate on moving his feet as fast as possible.

• *Backward movement.* When the linebacker is moving backward, he should employ the following techniques:

- He should pump arms similar to the way he does when he's moving forward, employing the opposite hand with an opposite-foot-movement pattern.
- He should push off the ball of one foot and paw back with the other foot.
- His upper body should be relaxed, his elbows in, and all movements smooth and fluid.
- Finally, he should keep his knees flexed (bent) and lean forward in order to be in a position to be able to change directions quickly.

☐ *Shedding Blockers*

In playing off blockers, it is important for a linebacker to do only what is required to make a play. His primary objective should be to make tackles, not initiate unnecessary contact. It is important to stay square; move swiftly after contact; react to the blocker's pressure; control the blocker; and come off the block at an angle to meet the ballcarrier (most of the time laterally). In order to neutralize a blocker charging above the waist, a linebacker should:

- Stay square with the blocker, not commit to a side.
- Take a short step, and keep a pad level that ensures the eyes are below the facemask of the blocker. The defender should get underneath (apply vertical leverage) the blocker. His hands should be driven underneath the shoulder pads of the blocker. Upon contact, he should lower his hip and backside so that his feet are underneath him.
- Not wind up or waste motion, but instead create maximum momentum with a minimum amount of wasted effort.
- Not get overextended, but rather maintain a balanced position.
- Strain upward and into the pressure of the blocker, while accelerating his feet upon contact in short, choppy steps.
- Work to get his head up (his back should arch).
- Make an all-out effort to get rid of the blocker. Do not stay blocked. Come off the block laterally and quickly.

A number of additional factors should also be emphasized regarding the effort of a linebacker to shed blockers, including the following:

- He should prevent the blocker from getting a position between himself and the ballcarrier.
- He should never spin away from the blocker.
- He should strain into the pressure of the block, give ground, keep his shoulders square, and take a proper pursuit angle if a blocker has managed to position himself between the defender and the ballcarrier.
- He should not go around the block through the "back door" (i.e., the "so-called" easy way).

If a blocker comes down from the outside or out from the inside (at an angle), a linebacker should stay square and deliver a blow with his forearm and shoulder. He should not wind up, but, instead, make sure that he is in a good defensive position. His lower arm should be flexed (bent) slightly and his elbow driven out from his body. His shoulder and forearm should be underneath the blocker. As always, he should strain into the pressure of the blocker, accelerate his feet, stay square, and be ready to give a step and instinctively come off the block at the proper angle.

When a blocker attacks him below his waist, a linebacker should:

- Concentrate on the blocker, while watching the ballcarrier out of his periphery.
- React to the blocker's head, slide in the direction of his head, and strive to maintain his position.
- Use his hands to stop the offensive man's charge. His hands should be directed in the area of the offensive player's shoulder pads.
- Flex (bend) his knees, push with his hands, and give with his feet to clear the offensive man's charge.
- Keep his shoulders square and make his second move before the offensive man's charge.
- If necessary, give ground to keep his shoulders square. He should not go around behind the blocker, if the offensive man has good position. He should keep moving in the direction that the offensive man is trying to go.
- Be prepared. A good linebacker has the ability to slide and coil at the same time, in order to be able to initiate proper contact.

☐ *Tackling*

An intense desire to excel, being in the proper body position, and having appropriate balance are essential factors in the ability of a linebacker to consistently demonstrate proper tackling techniques. An overview of the recommended fundamentals involved in sound tackling is detailed in Chapter 8.

Pursuit:

It is essential that linebackers approach ballcarriers at the proper angles. Using good judgment and taking the proper angle of pursuit can help to overcome the comparative speed advantage, which is enjoyed by most offensive backs. When pursuing a ballcarrier, some important points for a linebacker to remember are:

- If he is an inside defender, he should try to keep everything on his outside shoulder until the action comes to his side. He should pursue in a lateral direction until the ballcarrier has turned upfield and then pursue from an inside position.
- When a ballcarrier goes away from him, he should maintain a position slightly to the inside, so that he can guard against a cutback.
- He should attempt to make the ballcarrier continue to run laterally. He should not create a seam so that a back can run upfield.
- He should take a steeper angle of pursuit (from the line of scrimmage) in order to save a touchdown, when the ballcarrier is farther away.
- When playing the quarterback against the option, his pursuit should be at least at a flat angle to intersect the ballcarrier's path, once the quarterback has pitched the ball. If the ball is pitched well out in front of the quarterback, it will be necessary for him to take a steeper angle (from the line of scrimmage) to meet the ballcarrier.
- If he is an outside defender (e.g., playing a flat zone), he should attack flare and screen passes from an outside position, attempting to force the ballcarrier into the middle of the field.
- He should converge on plays to his inside from an outside-in angle (maintain a "fence" when aligned on the outside).

☐ *Playing Pass Defense*

Zone:

Defenders playing zone pass defense position themselves at a relative distance to each other, so that they can cover the areas of the field into which a quarterback might want to throw the ball. When playing zone pass defense, the linebacker's primary concern is guarding an area of the field between the defensive secondary and the line of scrimmage and reacting to the look of the quarterback. A linebacker playing zone must also be aware of the positions of potential receivers who might be a threat to his area of responsibility. The recommended techniques for a linebacker playing zone pass defense are:

- As soon as he recognizes a pass play, he should call it out and start moving to his area of responsibility as fast as possible. Assuming a proper depth initially gives him an opportunity to come under better body control when the ball is about to be thrown.
- Most of the time he should turn and run laterally, looking over his shoulder at the quarterback.
- As he is going to his zone area, he should glance for receivers who might be coming into

his area, but should never turn completely away from the ball. He should know where receivers are yet still be able to react if the quarterback throws quickly into his area.

- He should position himself between the ball and a potential receiver in his zone. Once he has gotten within about three yards of the receiver, he should settle down (stop in a basic hitting position) where he can see both the receiver and the quarterback (match up with the receiver). He should be turned at approximately a 45-degree angle toward the outside, aligned three yards in front of the receiver and three yards to his inside. Have him concentrate on the ball but watch the receiver out of his periphery, being ready to react to any throw at an angle that would allow him to intercept it. If the receiver breaks to the inside behind him, he should pivot back to face the ball and react to it.

- If no receiver is in his zone (12 to 15 yards deep), he should square his shoulders to the line of scrimmage and be ready to backpedal. While running backward, his weight should be on the balls of his feet, his arms should move as if running, and his elbows should be close to his sides. As he is retreating, he should scan for receivers.

- He should react to all "looks" of the quarterback in his area. When the quarterback looks, he should turn his shoulders and sprint at an angle to cover the receiver.

- If he attempts to intercept the pass, he should try to catch the ball at its highest point, lock it into his hands, and head toward the opponent's goal line.

- All of the linebackers should communicate with each other. They should tell the adjacent linebacker if a receiver is crossing into his area.

- If a receiver crosses a linebacker's path, he should be disrupted, but the linebacker should not get overextended or ever go out of his way to hit a receiver. The linebacker should not lose his position in attempting to disrupt a receiver.

- Once the ball is thrown, all linebackers should be running at full speed toward the ball, until it is either intercepted or batted to the ground.

Man-to-Man:

Defenders playing man-to-man pass coverage should concentrate on the eligible receivers and cover them wherever they might run. Two types of man-to-man pass coverage techniques can be used. A linebacker can play reckless man-to-man coverage, when he has help in the deep secondary. Reckless techniques are used to take away the underneath passes (from the line of scrimmage to a depth of about 18 yards). He can also utilize cautious man-to-man techniques, which are employed when the linebacker does not have help in the deep zones and must protect those areas.

When playing cautious man-to-man pass defense, the linebacker should do the following:

- Align himself approximately one yard inside the offensive receiver at a depth of about four yards with his inside foot forward.

- Concentrate on the receiver.

- Begin to run backward, leading with his front foot, as the receiver comes forward.

- Try to maintain a distance of two to three yards between himself and the receiver and a position one yard to the receiver's inside. As the

receiver gets closer to him, he should begin to run laterally in order to maintain his position.

- Break parallel to the receiver's changes of directions, and then gradually get closer to the receiver as the ball is thrown.
- Guard against deep passes.
- Turn his back to the ball in pursuit if the receiver has gotten beyond him, concentrating on the receiver, especially his hands, and then turn toward the quarterback to look for the ball when the receiver's hands come up.

When playing reckless man-to-man with two defensive backs helping in deep outside zone, the linebacker should:

- Align in the same manner as when playing cautious man-to-man pass defense.
- Concentrate on the receiver.
- Not let the receiver go inside, jamming him if he tries to get inside position.
- Wait (i.e., does not move), if the receiver releases to the outside, until the receiver reaches his outside shoulder and then turn and jam him with his hands. He should also let the receiver get slightly ahead, so that he can cover the underneath passes.
- Chase the receiver, staying to the inside and slightly behind him.
- Play all pass cuts of the receiver from underneath (the side closest to the ball), concentrate on the receiver's hands, and go for the interception when the receiver reaches for the ball.

☐ *Blitzing*

Blitzing can be effective to change the normal pattern of linebacker play. When blitzing, the linebacker attacks an offensive area on the snap of the ball. Blitzing is used in an attempt to change the tempo of play, to create a long-yardage situation for the offense, to break the continuity of an offensive drive, and to rush the passer—especially if certain blitzes take advantage of an offense's pass-blocking scheme. It is also possible to disrupt blocking assignments or stop certain running plays by blitzing. When blitzing, the linebacker should:

- Not alarm the offense by altering his stance or starting too soon.
- Go immediately on the snap of the ball.
- Attempt to penetrate across the line of scrimmage.
- Notice the offensive linemen and the action of the ball and adjust as the offensive linemen are moving (inside linebackers should follow pulling guards, etc.).
- Stay under control.
- React to the pressure of blocks, as if he were playing normally.
- Use his hands when rushing the passer.
- Try to get the offensive man turned one way and then go in the opposite direction.
- Don't dive (leave his feet) to make a tackle, except as his last resort.
- Use his hands when playing lead blockers in the open field, where the ballcarrier has plenty of running room.
- Try to make the blocker miss or give ground in order to save a touchdown.
- Not become impatient or attempt to make every tackle for a loss of yardage.
- Give ground around piles of blockers and defenders in order to allow plays for a two- or three-yard gain, instead of creating potential big plays.

☐ *Rushing the Passer*

The ability to rush a passer is predominately innate, but several general coaching points for a linebacker exist, including the following:

- Get a great jump on the football. Anticipate; know the situation; study the stance of the opponents.
- Get on a corner if possible.
- Get the offensive player into an awkward body position. Cause him to move either laterally or forward. Get the blocker turned or overextended.
- Outside linebackers should establish a speed rush, while inside linebackers should develop a bull rush.
- Do not get hooked up with the blocker. Strive to keep his hands off of him by slapping, pushing, etc. Use quick fakes, and then move upfield.
- Operate with his elbows close to his body; his hands should be positioned inside the hands of his opponent.
- Have a sense of timing. Know when his opponent is off balance, and when to push or pull and accelerate by the defender.
- Use the arm-under or over techniques, whichever one is appropriate, depending upon his height. Develop a counter move off of his best move (e.g., immediately follow an arm-under move with a "club" maneuver).
- Keep moving upfield, maintain constant pressure on the quarterback.
- Get his hands up, when the quarterback is ready to throw the ball. Have a sense of timing, know when to raise his hands. Do not leave his feet until the ball is released.
- Maintain a relative position to his teammates, who are also rushing. Develop a feel for one another during a dropback pass.
- Recognize the blocking direction and react to the pressure of the block.
- Take care of the immediate problems first.
- Learn to concentrate on blockers, while seeing the ballcarrier out of his periphery.
- Don't waste motion and effort.
- Have a sense of timing and know when to exert himself.
- Avoid being a "robot" or afraid to take a chance in order to make things happen.

☐ *Linebacker Drills*

Stance Run Drill:

This drill is designed to develop the ability of linebackers to maintain a good defensive stance, while running in different directions. No equipment is necessary to conduct this drill. Performing the drill involves the following steps:

- Have the linebackers spread out in one or more lines facing you.
- Have the linebackers assume a proper defensive stance.
- Then, have them run in the direction to which you point, while maintaining a good hitting position, until you call out for them to stop. At that point, have them resume being in a proper defensive stance.
- Have them run in a variety of directions and vary the sequence of the directions.

* Stress the importance of the linebackers being in the proper alignment and stance.

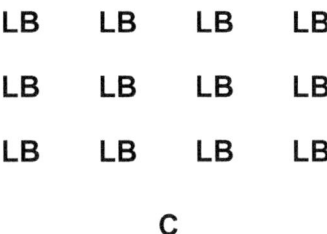

Figure 9-32

React-to-Block Drill:

This drill is designed to develop the ability of a linebacker to deliver contact, to react to blockers at different angles, and to come off blocks properly. No equipment is necessary to conduct this drill. Performing the drill involves the following steps:

- Align three offensive blockers alongside each other, with about one and one-half yards between each player.
- Position a ballcarrier about five yards behind the middle blocker, with the linebacker aligned across from the middle blocker, facing him.
- Point to one of the blockers, which is a signal to the designated player to block the linebacker above the waist.
- Have the linebacker react by squaring up on the blocker and engaging with contact.
- After contact, have both players recover to the starting position as quickly as possible.
- Then, point to another blocker to continue the drill.
- To conclude the drill, raise your hand to one side, which is a signal to the ballcarrier to go in that direction, while the blocker on that side follows suit.
- Finally, have the linebacker play off the block and then either touch or tackle the ballcarrier.

* Emphasize the need for the linebacker to execute proper fundamentals and techniques.

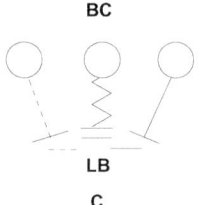

Figure 9-33

Terminal Mirror Drill:

This drill is designed to develop the ability of a linebacker to be in the proper position, relative to a receiver in his zone. A football is needed to conduct this drill. Performing it involves the following steps:

- Position a receiver at an angle 20 yards from you.
- Position the linebacker between the receiver and you so that he can see both of them.
- Signal to the receiver whether the ball will be thrown on his break or on your look. Then, throw the ball to him.
- Have the linebacker react to the first movement of either you or the receiver.
- Have the linebacker move to try to make an interception.
- If the ball is caught by the linebacker, have him shout a predetermined verbal signal (e.g., "bingo") and then sprint at full speed toward you, at which point, he should hand the ball to you.

* Stress the need for the linebacker to "look" the ball into his hands.

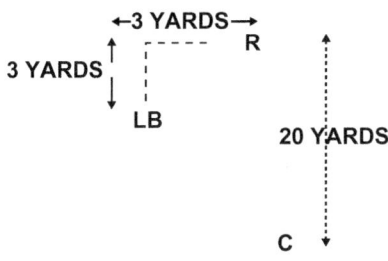

Figure 9-34

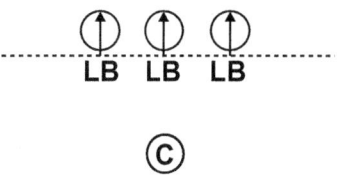

Figure 9-35

Lock, Lift, and Spin Drill:

This drill is designed to develop the ability of a linebacker to use leverage to shed a blocker and to practice performing the spin technique. No equipment is required to conduct the drill. Performing the drill involves the following steps:

- Divide the linebackers into two groups, with one group acting as offensive blockers and the other group serving as pass rushers.
- Next, have the players pair up and line up, facing opposite directions on a yardage line, next to each other hip-to-hip.
- On your command, have the linebacker, who dips his underarm and uses leverage, engage the blocker in an attempt to dislodge him off the yardage line.
- Simultaneously, have the blocker use his hands and body in an attempt to prevent being moved across the yardage line by the backer.
- After a predetermined number of repetitions, have the players switch roles.

* Emphasize the importance of having the linebackers adhere to the proper techniques for applying leverage.

Defensive Backs

As a rule, defensive backs (collectively referred to as the secondary) are the last line of defense for a team. You want your defensive backs to be athletic, fast, and focused.

In other words, your defensive backs need to be able to move quickly and aggressively to the ball. They also need to be able to handle the physical demands of their role (e.g., shed blocks, tackle, cover receivers, etc.), as well as endure both disappointment and success.

Sound defensive back play involves being in the right place, at the right time, and doing the right thing. In order for that scenario to occur, your secondary players must be fundamentally sound. They need to understand spacing and positioning. They also need to be wherever and whenever they should be during the game. Finally, they should have a firm grasp of the basic principles of playing in the secondary.

As their coach, there are certain aspects of play that you want your team's defensive backs to master, including assuming their stance; aligning properly, recognizing the play; moving purposely; defending the run; playing pass defense; and shedding blocks.

☐ *Assuming the Stance*

Photo 9-14

Similar to every other position on a football team (offense or defense), effective play starts with having a good stance. A good stance for a defensive back involves the following factors:

- He must be very balanced with no sideways lean.
- He needs to be able to move in any direction.
- His base should be relatively narrow.
- He should have a slight forward lean, with his chin in front of his toes.
- His knees should be slightly flexed.
- His head should be up.
- His shoulders should be parallel to the line of scrimmage.
- His arms should be relaxed and held at almost 90 degrees to his elbow.
- His hands should be relaxed.
- His hips should be slightly sunk.
- Most (i.e., 85 percent) of his weight should be on the ball of one foot.

☐ *Aligning Properly*

Where a defensive back is positioned prior to the snap is largely dependent on what type of defensive scheme your team is employing. The coverage call, defensive formation, down and distance, hash mark, and the opponent's field position may determine his positioning.

☐ *Recognizing the Play*

In general, a defensive back recognizes the play (run or pass) by either looking at his keys (e.g., what a particular offensive player does once the ball is snapped) or considering the flow of the offense, particularly in light of any predetermined tendencies the opponent's offense may have. Being able to recognize a play relatively quickly (i.e., run or pass) can provide a defensive back with a competitive edge to successfully defend the play.

☐ *Moving Purposely*

Photo 9-15

On every down, movement is the key for effective play by defensive backs. They must be able to move in, run backward, or change directions at any time. In other words, defensive backs need to be able to recognize where they should be on any given play and then get there as quickly as possible.

On a pass play, it is absolutely essential that a defensive back is able to perform four movement-related tasks, including backpedal, break out of his back pedal, track the ball in the air, and finish his coverage.

• *Backpedaling.* To young athletes, the concept of running backward is somewhat foreign. Backpedaling may not be a natural movement for most of your players, but it is a key part of cushion man-to-man and zone pass coverage.

Like most skills and techniques in football, the ability to backpedal can be practiced, as follows:

- Push off the inside half of his front foot, while simultaneously reaching back with his back foot.
- Maintain rounded shoulders and having his chest over his toes.
- Drive his elbows back in normal running style to help generate momentum.
- Move his hips (not his shoulders). Visualize being pulled by a rope.

As such, backpedaling involves a four-phase progression: control, speed, zone-turn, and turn and run. Depending on the receiver's route, the defensive back will go through at least one of these phases. In some situations, going from a hitch route to a post route, for example, he may go through all four phases.

The control phase entails keying the route and deciphering what the information means. In this phase, the defensive back is trying to decide if the play is a run or a pass. If it is a pass, is it a running pass or a hot pass (i.e., a three-step drop and throw)? Most passing teams indicate what they're going to do on the first three steps the quarterback takes.

If the quarterback, after receiving the snap, starts his drop sequence and looks immediately to the flat to throw the ball, the play involves a hot route. If the defensive back can read the situation on the quarterback's first step, he should be able to react and respond appropriately based on that one step.

On most secondary techniques, defensive backs are asked to key the quarterback. Subsequently, they leave him, them play the receiver (first), and finally the ball (next).

The second phase of the progression is the speed aspect. Speed backpedaling is utilized when the situation involves a dropback pass. In this set of circumstances, defensive backs are required to defend against passes of intermediate or larger depth. In this scenario, defensive backs are often expected to hold their backpedal as long as they can. It should be noted that as their speed increases, their pad level should stay the same.

The next stage is the zone-turn phase. Just as the stance for a defensive back can vary, the amount of cushion that exists between himself and the receiver can also vary. On the other hand, once a receiver breaks a defensive back's cushion, the defensive back must open his hips and turn. If he does not get his hips open, the receiver will run by him. In reality, each secondary player can have a different cushion. Regardless of the length of his cushion, a defensive back will not be in a zone-turn very long.

The final stage of the backpedal is the turn-and-run phase. If and when a receiver has eaten up the cushion between him and the defensive back, the defensive back has to turn and run with the receiver. In the process, he needs to stay on the receiver's upfield shoulder, protecting the goal line. Furthermore, his eyes should be on the receiver, as opposed to looking back at the quarterback.

• *Breaking.* At some point in the play, the defensive back will have to stop going backward. In that situation, the defensive back will quickly "break" to the receiver, who is typically about six yards from him. His alignment before he breaks will be based on several factors, including the split of the receiver, the type of passes he will have to defend, and from where help may be coming. Ideally, the defensive back should wind up on either the inside armpit or the outside armpit of the receiver, depending on the inside or outside technique that the defensive back is playing.

The quick change-of-direction involved in a break entails two quick steps—a plant and a jab. To stop, the defensive back has to get his plant foot down, directly under his backside. Then, he performs a jab stab, which is a six-inch step in the direction he is going. To get going again, he repeats the process.

• *Tracking the ball in the air.* Using his eyes properly is a key skill for a defensive back. A defensive back must develop the ability to know where the ball is and to anticipate and react to it.

• *Finishing his coverage.* Once the ball is in the air, the defensive back must do his job in coverage. An overview of coverage responsibilities is detailed in Chapter 12.

☐ *Establishing a Cushion*

As his coach, you face the issue of determining how far you want a defensive back in man coverage to be off a receiver to keep him from getting beat. He still must be able to break back to the football. As a rule, a defensive back establishes a cushion of at least six yards (i.e., 12 to 14 steps) for the receiver's typical break point, plus a buffer for himself between himself and the receiver.

One of the key considerations with regard to the amount of the cushion is the speed of the defensive back. At some point, he will have to open his hips. If he has average speed, you want him two yards past the receiver's six-yard break point. If he has good speed, he can reduce the separation point by 1.5 yards. On the other hand, if he can really open up and run, and you want him to really squeeze the receiver, he can play off the receiver at one yard.

☐ *The Basic Assignment of a Defensive Back*

In youth football, a defensive back, ideally, has a "pass-first" mentality. In other words, he should assume that the play is going to be a pass. Once he reads that the play is a running play, he should put himself in position to either make the tackle or force the ballcarrier to alter his route so that one of his defensive teammates can make the play.

In essence, a defensive back has two core assignments: defend the run and play pass defense. To a degree, how a defensive back carries out those assignments can be affected by such factors as his role in his team's defensive scheme, the opponent's offensive system, and his personal skillset.

Defending Against the Run:

In general, defensive backs are expected to help defend against the run in specific situations. They are given four primary roles:

- Primary force: to constrict and contain the play; to serve as the first defensive back in the run rotation

- Secondary force: to defend the play-action pass; to tackle the playside breakthrough
- Cutback: to defend play-action; to prevent a long gain on a cutback run
- Backside contain: to defend against throwbacks, reverses, etc. (i.e., play-action); to stop a big play; to prevent a touchdown run

Playing Pass Defense:

The responsibilities that a defensive back has for pass coverage can vary according to your defensive scheme. The better he understands and fulfills his role, the better the team is going to be. Regardless of the scheme, certain attributes characterize a defensive back who is able to successfully play pass defense, including the following:

- He knows and does his job.
- He is mentally tough.
- He knows and understands his team's defensive calls.
- He is able to recognize his opponent's offensive formations.
- He aligns properly on every play.
- He is able to read his keys and react appropriately.
- His body is always in the proper position to make the play.
- He knows how and when to break on the receiver.
- He never takes an inside fake.
- He plays the ball, not the man.
- He does not overreact to the short-arm action of the quarterback.
- He plays one play at a time—never looking back or ahead.
- He has great vision (eyes).
- He has exceptional movement skills.
- He has a compelling desire to do his best.

☐ *Shedding Blocks*

Similar to their defensive teammates, defensive backs often find themselves in situations in which they must shed one or more blockers. Ideally, their first strategy should be to try to avoid the blocker(s) altogether. If that doesn't work, they should square up to the blocker(s) and get rid of them as soon as possible. Their focus needs to be stopping the ballcarrier. If the blocker comes at them high, they should get under him and jam him while he is shuffling. If he comes at them low, they should keep their feet moving, jam down on his shoulders, and push him to the ground.

☐ *Defensive Back Drills*

Run-Pass Reaction Drill:

This drill is designed to develop the proper fundamentals and techniques involved in backpedaling and reacting to a run or a pass. Several footballs are needed to conduct this drill, which involves the following steps:

- Align a defensive back in the proper pre-snap stance on a selected yard line.
- Position yourself with a football five yards in front of the defensive back.
- Have the other defensive backs stand in a line adjacent to the drill area.
- Execute one of two signals—either tuck the ball under your arm (indicating a run) or raise the ball over your head (indicating a pass).

- Have the defensive back read your signal. If it is a running play, he should sprint to and break down one yard in front of you. If you signal a pass, he should begin to backpedal and wait for it.
- Once the defensive back has backpedaled 8 to 12 yards, throw him a pass to either his left or right.
- Once the ball has been thrown, have the defensive back try to make the interception, and then sprint upfield past the coach.
- Continue the drill until all of the defensive backs have had a sufficient number of reps.

* Make sure that the defensive backs assume the proper stance, backpedal correctly, watch the quarterback (you), closely read the play, and try to intercept the ball at its highest point.

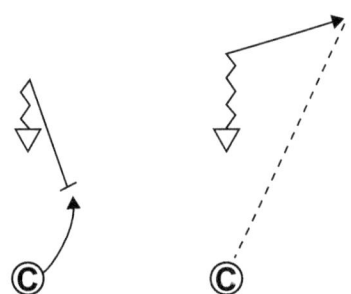

Figure 9-36

Cushion Drill:

This drill is designed to develop the fundamentals and techniques involved in cushioning a receiver. No equipment is needed to conduct the drill. Performing the drill involves the following steps:

- Position a row of wide receivers perpendicular to a selected line of scrimmage.
- Align a defensive back in his normal position across from the first wide receiver.
- Have the other defensive backs stand adjacent to the drill area.
- Position yourself around the drill area.
- On your command, have the first receiver run at one-half to three-quarter speed straight down the field. Simultaneously, have the defensive back backpedal, keeping a designated cushion of two yards vertically and one yard horizontally on either the inside or the outside of the receiver. If the wide receiver breaks the designated cushion, the defensive back should turn out of his backpedal and run with him.
- Continue the drill until all of the defensive backs have executed a sufficient number of repetitions, both to the inside and the outside of the receiver.

* Try to view the drill from various angles to ensure that the defensive backs are maintaining the proper vertical and horizontal cushion.

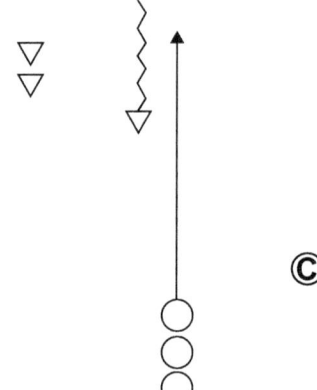

Figure 9-37

Stem-and-Break Drill:

This drill is designed to develop the proper fundamentals and techniques involved in a defensive back maintaining vertical and horizontal leverage on a receiver, when the defensive back is in man-to-man coverage. Four cones and a football are needed to conduct the drill. Performing the drill involves the following steps:

- Place four cones one yard apart on a selected line of scrimmage.
- Align a defensive back five yards behind and facing the cone on his far right.
- Assume a position on the opposite side of the cones, facing the defensive back. Remain stationary throughout the drill.
- Have the other defensive backs stand adjacent to the drill area.
- On your cadence and snap count, have the defensive back begin his backpedal.
- At some predetermined point during the backpedal, move the football laterally, pointing it in the direction of the second cone. The defensive back reacts to the movements of the ball and stems back at a 45-degree angle to the second cone.
- Once the defensive back is positioned behind the second cone, have him again go into his backpedal. He should then look for and react to your lateral ball movement by stemming to the third cone.
- After he has stemmed from the backpedal in front of the third cone, have the defensive back plant his outside foot and break back upfield at a 45-degree angle, catching the pass that you have thrown.
- Continue the drill until all of the defensive backs have had a sufficient number of repetitions, moving both to the left and the right.

* Make sure that the defensive backs execute the stem correctly, keeping their shoulders square to the line of scrimmage as they gain width and depth stepping laterally.

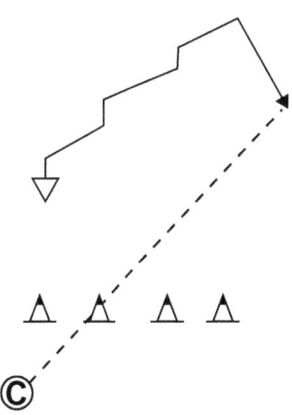

Figure 9-38

Build-Up Drill:

This drill is designed to develop the proper fundamentals of covering a receiver and making an interception. Several footballs are needed to conduct the drill. Performing the drill involves the following steps:

- Assume a position in the proper play relationship to the first wide receiver.
- On your cadence and snap count, have the receiver run a predetermined pass route. Concurrently, you should take a designated pass drop and throw him a pass.
- Have the defensive back cushion the receiver, and then react to and either intercept or deflect the ball.
- Continue the drill until all of the defensive backs have executed a sufficient number of repetitions, both to the left and right and from various positions on the field.

* Make sure that the defensive backs get a good plant and take the proper angle, as they react to the receiver's cuts.

FLAG FOOTBALL

A number of the skills and techniques that are essential in tackle football (running, passing, receiving, moving, etc.) translate to flag football. The key for flag football coaches is to know the rules of the sport (refer to Appendix C) and then work on developing those skills and techniques with their players. Teaching those skills should reflect the players' skill level, age, motor abilities, and aptitude for learning.

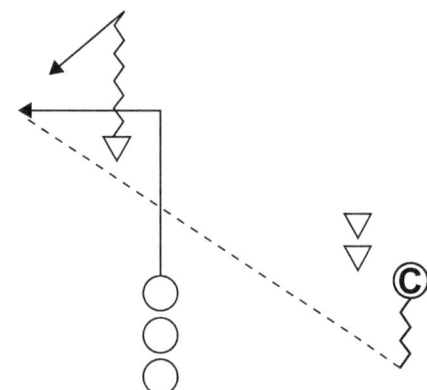

Figure 9-39

SECTION IV

PUTTING IT ALL TOGETHER FOR SUCCESS

CHAPTER 10

HOW TO DEVELOP A TRUE TEAM

A true youth football team is more than just a group of players. It is a band of young athletes who love the fun of the sport and are committed to achieve a common goal. They understand where the team is going, what's involved in getting there, and why its important for them to work together.

Having a true team rarely just happens. It takes planning and concerted effort on your part. At the beginning of the season, you will have a group of players assigned to you. While you may refer to them as your "team," they are not a team yet. At that point in time, they are a group of children who want to enjoy the sport and all that it offers and who refer to you as "Coach."

THE DIFFERENCES BETWEEN A GROUP AND A TEAM

Many people use the words "group" and "team" interchangeably. In reality, they are not the same. In fact, distinct differences exist between the two. Members of a team work together and share in the outcome of their efforts, while individuals who are part of a group tend to be more independent of each other.

Team members realize that working together is the way to achieve a goal. Group members, in contrast, may be preoccupied with their own task, knowing or understanding relatively little about what other individuals who are part of the group are expected to do.

A team almost always outperforms a group. A team outshines the combined expectations of its individual members. In other words, a team can have a synergistic effect (i.e., one plus one can equal a lot more than two). In the process, your ability as the coach to impact the outcome is increased. What might previously have been difficult becomes much easier. Furthermore, what might have been relatively impossible becomes possible.

STRATEGIES FOR BUILDING A TRUE TEAM

As everyone knows, there is no "I" in the word "team." Getting everyone to work together, however, takes a lot more than a pep talk. It takes action on your part. Someone is almost always the catalyst for brining a team together. For your team, that someone is you. The following steps can be helpful to develop the kind of self-identity, chemistry, culture, and spirit that leads to having a true team (as well as a more rewarding experience for everyone involved in your program):

- ☐ Develop a clear vision and mission of what you want to achieve as the team's coach. Articulate both to your players and their parents.
- ☐ Work with your players to create a vision and a mission for the team and the program.
- ☐ Establish a team culture. Encourage your players to think in terms of group success, rather than individual accomplishments. Put the focus on "we," as opposed to "I."
- ☐ Strive to have your players invest in the process. For example, make sure your players know their role and why they should work together to be their collective best.
- ☐ Make your players part of the decision-making process (e.g., create team rules).
- ☐ Ensure that your players are aware that each of their teammates has something to offer the program. Everyone's efforts (including the non-starters) should be valued.
- ☐ Establish team goals and values.
- ☐ Set roles (e.g., offense or defense) and expectations for each player.
- ☐ Build respect and trust on the team. Gain the players' respect with your passion, knowledge, and ability to get everyone focused on playing their position and working together.
- ☐ Teach your players how to confront and handle disagreements in a constructive way.
- ☐ Treat every player as a unique individual. Each one has something to contribute and is one of your coaching "priorities"—no more, no less.
- ☐ Set an appropriate example by modeling the essence of "team" in everything you do (e.g., encourage effort; give positive feedback; encourage players to support one another; apply all team rules equally and fairly).

CREATING A GREAT TEAM CULTURE

People are at the heart of a true team. When human beings are involved, the situation will entail human dynamics. Even at their relatively young age, the behavior of your players will tend to be driven by certain factors. Arguably, one of the most important of those factors is your team's culture.

A team's culture creates the norms of acceptable behavior. Either explicitly or implicitly, these norms convey what is allowed and what is not to your players. These norms can have an impact on your athletes with regard to how to act, communicate, cooperate, and manage problems. The culture of your team can affect every facet of your program.

Culture can have real implications concerning how a team functions. Is the atmosphere relaxed or stressful? Collaborative or every person for themselves? Supportive or uncaring?

With regard to building the culture you want your team to have, you need to have a systematic plan for making that culture a reality. One way or another, your team will have a culture. As the team's coach, you need to decide if this culture will occur by default or by design.

If you want to develop your team's culture by design, there are certain factors you need to keep in mind. First, a team's culture is built one choice at a time. Many of those choices will be yours to make. For example, how will you treat your players? What expectations will you have for your players and your program? What rules will you establish? What leadership style will govern the way you coach? What specific behaviors do you want your players to live by? And so forth.

You also need to be aware of the fact that your beliefs, values, opinions, likes, and dislikes can have a significant impact on the culture of your team You need to be the example that your players want to follow. In addition, you need to coach in a way that elicits the trust and respect of your players. You need to foster a one-for-all, all-for-one team atmosphere.

CREATING GREAT TEAM CHEMISTRY

A true team is more than just a collection of skilled players. More often than not, it is also a team with great chemistry. Arguably, team chemistry is a term that reflects an environment in which players stick together in pursuit of the goals of the program.

Athletes on teams with great chemistry tend to have good relationships with each other. These players exhibit a level of togetherness that reflects a "team-first" attitude. They pull for the team rather than focus on individual success.

Team chemistry is the "X" factor that results in a group of players becoming a cohesive unit. It is the glue that helps bind players together. Lack of team chemistry is a common reason for teams not reaching their potential or having fun.

Building and sustaining team chemistry is always a challenge. In fact, building team chemistry is a process that can take time, as well as a systematic effort. Fortunately, there are a number of steps that coaches can take to strengthen team chemistry, including the following:

- ☐ Clearly explain all team rules, including their rationale and how they fit into the philosophy of the coach.
- ☐ Keep the channels of communication with the players open.
- ☐ Prohibit negativity from one player or group of players toward others.
- ☐ Always display an enthusiastic, fun, and encouraging style of coaching.
- ☐ Base your approach to coaching, as well as your overall program, on values (e.g., sportsmanship, teamwork, cooperation, respect, trust, etc).
- ☐ Emphasize team goals, objectives, and accomplishments, rather than individuality.
- ☐ Periodically arrange for team outings away from the game itself.
- ☐ Focus on fun.

OVERCOMING THE FACTORS THAT CAN HINDER TEAM TOGETHERNESS

Building a true team is a process. It will not happen overnight. It is not something that comes naturally. It is a learned experience, which requires work. Coaches need to work at it with the same commitment they have for developing their on-field skills. More often than not, however, coaches will have to manage factors that may disrupt a team's spirit of togetherness. Among the more common issues are the following:

☐ *Competition Among Teammates*

A certain amount of competition can help spur players to do their best. Unhealthy competition, on the other hand, can break teams apart.

☐ *Dissatisfaction About Playing Time*

Two of the most fundamental issues affecting team cohesion are playing time and which players are chosen to be starters. The best approach for addressing these issues is for coaches to establish a relationship of trust with their players, as well as with the parents of their players. By their words and actions, coaches must demonstrate that they care about the players. Coaches must also clarify each player's role on the team, as well as the expected amount of playing time that each player can expect to have.

☐ *Conflicts Between Players and Coach or Players and Other Players*

Conflicts are often a natural part of the process for building a true team. More often than not, they stem from either miscommunication or misunderstanding of team rules, norms, roles, and goals. There are a number of steps that coaches can take to effectively manage conflicts. For example, coaches can review their teams' communication process to learn if and where a breakdown occurred. Whenever a conflict arises, it should be dealt with directly, honestly, and immediately. If at all feasible, a win-win resolution should be the desired outcome.

☐ *Conflict Between the Parents of Players and the Coach*

On occasion, the parents of some players in any youth sport may not understand their role (i.e., to support the players, coaches, and program). When that situation occurs, disagreements can arise that can be disruptive to the team's sense of unity. Prevent or minimize these occurrences by communicating the team's purpose, goals, and approach to parents or others who might assist with the program. In addition, consider a code of conduct so that all who support the team are reminded of how they are expected to behave. Behavior that detracts from the fun of the sport or is counterproductive to the well-being of the team should not be tolerated.

☐ *Cliques*

Another potential barrier to team togetherness can happen when a few players band together to form a clique. At a minimum, cliques can limit the ability of players to get to know each other. Even worse, cliques can lead to frustration, tension, and alienation. Coaches have several options when dealing with cliques, such as intentionally giving teammates a variety of opportunities to get to know each other better, assigning older players to mentor younger ones, mixing players up for drills or warm-ups, etc.

☐ *Lack of Understanding of Team Rules, Roles, and Expectations*

In almost every endeavor in life, including youth football, misunderstandings will occur. The relevant issue is what can be done to prevent or minimize them from happening. The nature of misunderstandings can range from minor to serious and the more consequential the level of confusion, the more severe the situation. The key for coaches is to make their team rules, roles, and expectations crystal clear from the beginning of the season and then periodically review them.

☐ *Counterproductive Communication*

Verbal styles are called patterns for a reason, they happen regularly and without much forethought. When coaches employ dysfunctional communication patterns (e.g., using put-downs, sarcasm, and patronizing comments; repeating the same message over and over in the same way, without adapting to the needs of the listener; overusing hyperbole, providing irrelevant and distracting messages; etc.), a variety of program-related factors can be affected, including team unity. Coaches must not allow themselves (or their players) to fall into any of these patterns.

☐ *Staff Disagreements*

As a rule, most coaching staffs are going to have their share of occasional differences concerning the program—different philosophical approaches, different styles of working with kids, different ways of handling matters, etc. Many athletes can sense these differences of opinion among the coaching staff, which can then subsequently lead to an array of problems, particularly if the players start to choose sides. Coaches need to set the example for teamwork. At a minimum, they need to work out their disagreements in a reasonable, rational manner.

☐ *A Culture of "Me-First"*

Nothing will destroy team unity more than an atmosphere of individualism. One of the most important jobs of a coach who wants to build a true team is to get everyone to put team goals in front of their own.

COACHING NOTES

☐ Create a team environment in which every player strives to help accomplish the team's goals and objectives.

☐ Work to gain the respect and trust of your players. Set the example.

☐ Continue to improve your communication skills. Be a good listener.

☐ Give your team the encouragement it needs to do its best. Remember that motivation can come in a variety of forms.

☐ Make sure your players know what is expected of them, on and off the field. Make your expectations clear and realistic.

☐ Employ team-building exercises. Select activities (from the many that are available) that can help unify the team.

☐ Enforce your rules and make every player your top priority.

CHAPTER 11

HOW TO DEVELOP AN OFFENSIVE SYSTEM

When designing your team's offensive system, several factors need to be considered. Arguably, none is more important than remembering that every situation is unique. What may work well for another team may not be the best alternative for your team.

First of all, you need to take your players into account. How skilled are they? How teachable are they? For example, you may have a relatively athletic quarterback, in which case you may want to design and implement a system that takes advantage of his ability to run the ball. The basic key is for you to develop an offense that takes advantage of the skillset of your players.

Another fundamental matter is: how complex is the system you're considering to employ? How well does your staff know this system? Is it relatively easy to teach? Not only must you have a thorough grasp of the potential strengths and weaknesses of the system, you should be able to anticipate possible problems before they arise. The system you devise must be adaptable to different situations.

Ideally, it is important for you to keep in mind that you want to have an offense that is compatible with the three main reasons your young athletes are participating in your program—to have fun, to play with their buddies, and to get involved in a sport they love. For example, while installing a north-south run-oriented offense may give your team its best chance to win, consider its fit with the needs and interests of your players. Never ever forget why you're coaching and why your kids are playing.

Philosophical Base

When designing your offense, you should establish a vision of what you want it to accomplish. For example, you can decide whether you want your team to have a strong and effective running game. On the other hand, you may want your team to pass more often or feature a balanced approach. Either way, as the head coach, the decision is yours. Keep in mind that there is no single "right" answer. The key is to make the best decision possible, after consideration of the factors you deem important.

OFFENSIVE BASICS

Regardless of what offensive system you design or what plays you decide to have your team run as part of that system, there are certain elements that tend to be common to most systems, including numbering systems, line splits, huddle procedure, cadence, formations, and motion.

Numbering Systems

Most teams utilize a numbering system to help simplify your offense. As a rule, the numbering system is composed of two digits. The first digit indicates the ballcarrier, while the second designates the hole to run through. The numbers are typically preceded by some sort of formation call (e.g., full house). A descriptive term can be added to the digits (e.g., trap, boot, etc.) which signals the blocking rules for both the offensive line and the backs. For example, in the play call "full house 44 counter," the offense is in the full house formation and the 4 back gets the ball and runs through the 4 hole.

Two examples of numbering systems are illustrated in Figures 11-1 and 11-2. Figure 11-1 depicts an odd-even system, which numbers the hole where the play will go. Figure 11-2 shows a system in which the holes are numbered 1-9, starting in one direction.

Figure 11-1

Figure 11-2

Line Splits

Line splits are the distances between offensive linemen. Advantages and disadvantages exist concerning how much distance you put between your linemen. On one hand, relatively wide splits will spread out the defense. On the other hand, they can also make your team more vulnerable to a defender who may be slanting or blitzing into a gap on the line.

In turn, smaller splits can make it easier to protect gaps that may exist. They will also make it more difficult for your team to execute inside running plays, given that the small splits tend to bunch the defense.

In fact, your team's line splits can be affected by several factors. Obviously, one key element is the type of offense (e.g., plays) your team prefers to employ. Another is the tendencies and capabilities of your opponent's defense. What kind of pressure on the quarterback do they normally bring? Do they stunt a lot? What kind of speed do they have on the perimeter. Figure 11-3 illustrates a fairly common line split.

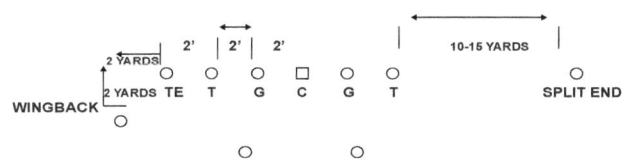

Figure 11-3

Huddle Procedure

Prior to each play, the offensive players gather together behind the line of scrimmage (LOS) to learn what play the quarterback will call for the upcoming down. It is the center's responsibility to align the huddle properly—approximately five yards directly behind the ball. As a rule, two main types of huddles are utilized—circular (the players form up in a circle) and typewriter (the players line up in two rows facing the LOS and the quarterback). An example of a typewriter huddle is shown in Figure 11-4.

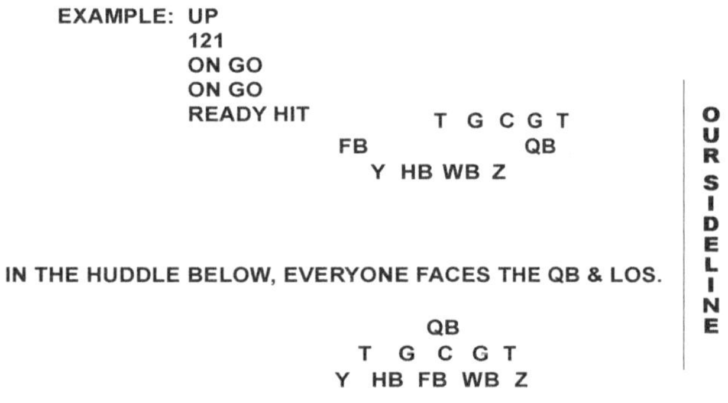

```
EXAMPLE:  UP
          121
          ON GO
          ON GO
          READY HIT          T G C G T             O
                        FB             QB          U
                             Y HB WB Z             R
                                                   S
                                                   I
IN THE HUDDLE BELOW, EVERYONE FACES THE QB & LOS.  D
                                                   E
                             QB                    L
                         T G C G T                 I
                        Y  HB FB  WB Z             N
                                                   E
```

Figure 11-4

When the center wants the huddle to form up, he raises his hand and yells, "huddle." Everyone hustles to the huddle. Once the quarterback enters the huddle, no one else speaks.

The quarterback (QB) enters the huddle on the side closest to his sideline, which allows him to look at the coach or notice a sub entering the game. At that point, the QB steps in to the huddle and calls "up." Everyone snaps to attention and looks at the QB. The QB then calls the formation and play once, along with the snap count. The QB repeats the snap count and says, "Ready, break" (or whatever word you feel is appropriate). The team mirrors the QB by simultaneously calling "break" and clapping their hands. Everyone then hustles to the LOS.

No-Huddle Procedure

One of the creative ways that coaches use to gain a competitive advantage is to run plays without huddling. The underlying goal is to get the offense moving quickly, ideally minimizing the ability of the defense to respond with the proper alignment and adjustments to what the offense is doing. Not only can a no-huddle offense change the tempo to fit its strategy, it can help dictate match-ups by not enabling the defense to substitute particular players based on what personnel the offense has on the field.

In contrast to offensive teams that huddle, teams that utilize a no-huddle system employ a variety of techniques for communicating what play the QB should call from the LOS, including hand signals, cards, wristbands, verbal cues, etc. Whatever method you decide to adopt, you need to make certain that it is both simple for your players to understand and easy to signal into them. The technique you employ also has to be sufficiently disguised so your opponent won't be able to decipher it.

Cadence

Cadence is the vocal rhythm used by the quarterback when calling out plays at the line of scrimmage. Cadences can be either rhythmic (adhering to a specific tempo) or non-rhythmic (adhering to a specific speech). Rhythmic cadences tend to be easiest to practice and use. The potential downside of rhythmic cadences is that they can result in a quarterback becoming predictable, which can enable the defense to anticipate his snap count and get off of the LOS more quickly than the offense. In contrast, non-rhythmic cadences can be used to help throw off the timing of the defense, including helping to draw them offsides.

Whatever cadence procedures you choose for your team's offense, you need to ensure that its timing allows for different types of motion. It should also have a level of flow that facilitates a proper takeoff. An example of a typical cadence might involve the following:

> Huddle: QB says, "On go"
> LOS*: QB says*, "Even set, (pause), blue, (pause), set go"

* In this instance, the QB will call odd or even set, depending on the defense he sees. Odd means a defender over the center (C); even means no man over the (C). The color refers to the type of motion used on the play, if any. The center snaps the ball on the "G" sound of go.

Formations

In football, the formation details how the players on offense (or the defense) are positioned on the field prior to the snap of the ball. Depending on the strategy being utilized, a number of variations (on both sides of the ball) are possible. The offensive formation must include at least seven players on the LOS (within one yard).

Figures 11-5 through 11-13 illustrate the possible alignment of the backfield (only) in nine basic formations. In reality, multiple alignments are possible from each of these basic formations. Figures 11-14 through 11-19 show the alignment of the receivers in six different receiver sets, including wide receivers, tight ends, and backs.

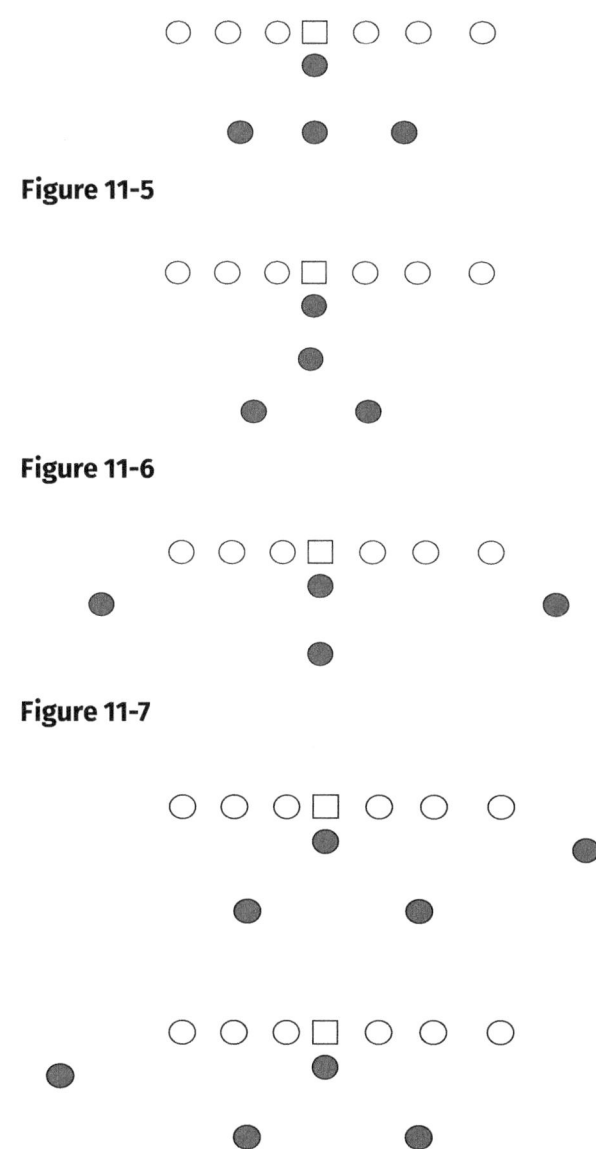

Figure 11-5

Figure 11-6

Figure 11-7

Figure 11-8

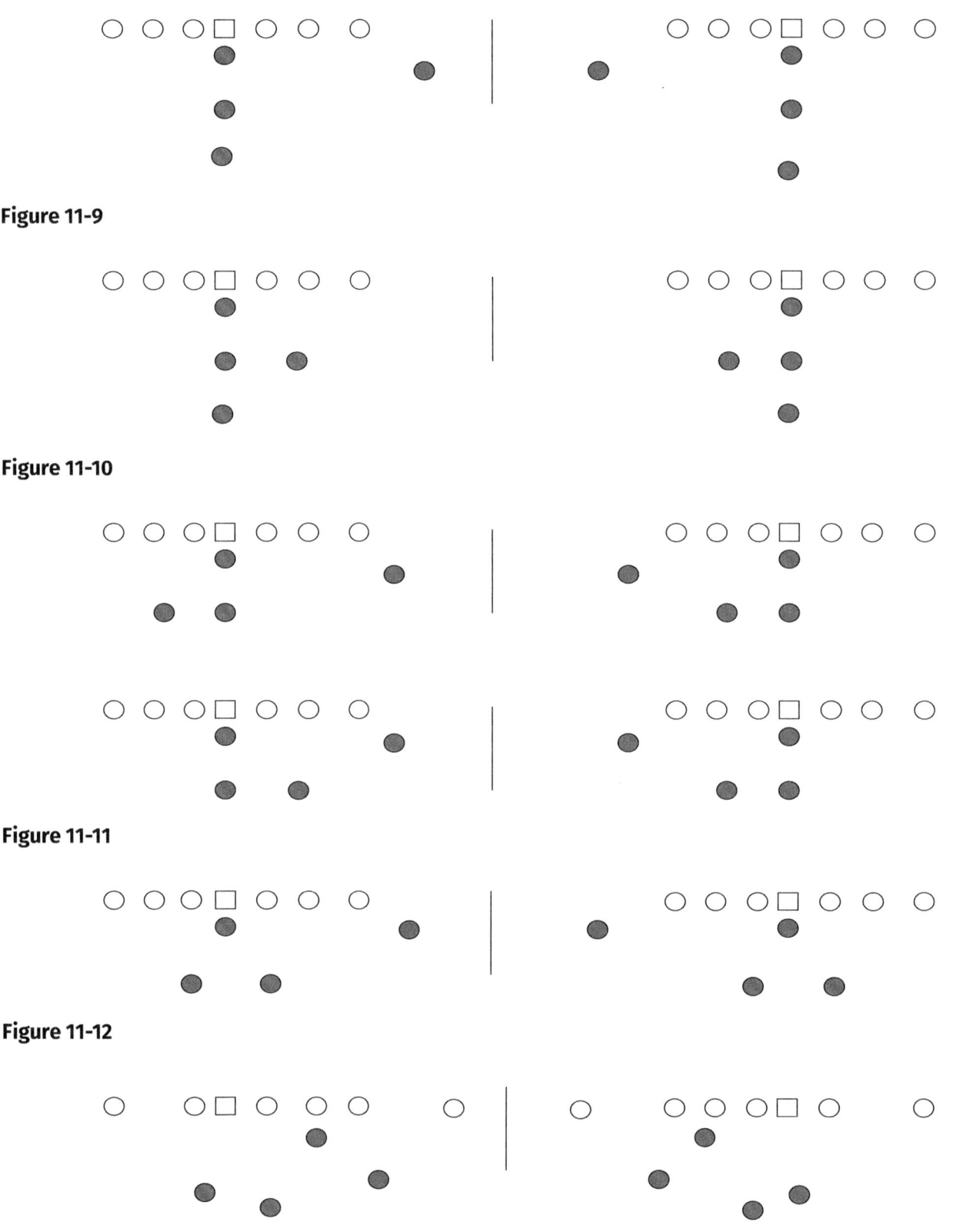

Figure 11-9

Figure 11-10

Figure 11-11

Figure 11-12

Figure 11-13

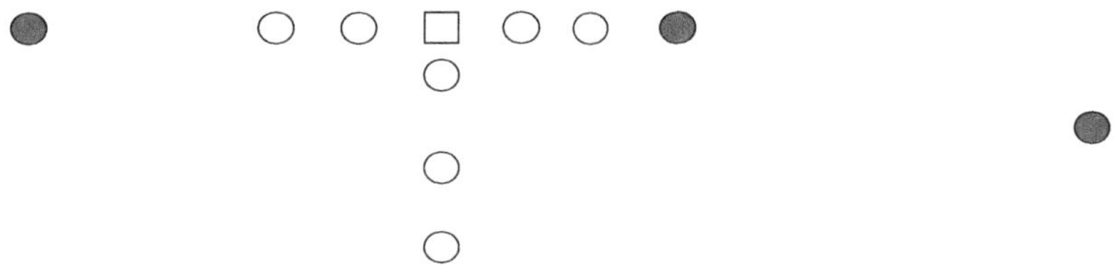

Figure 11-14

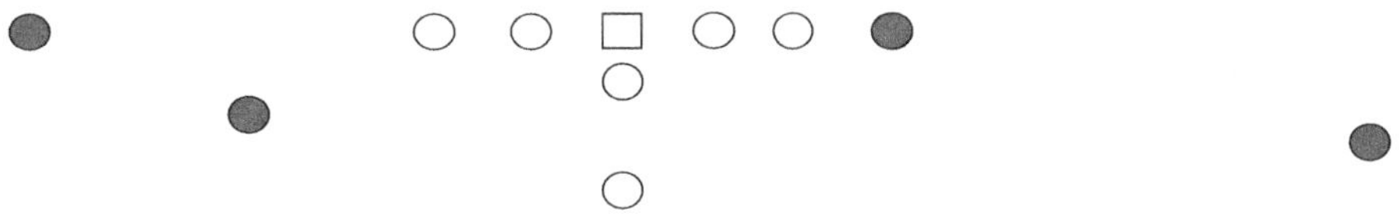

Figure 11-15

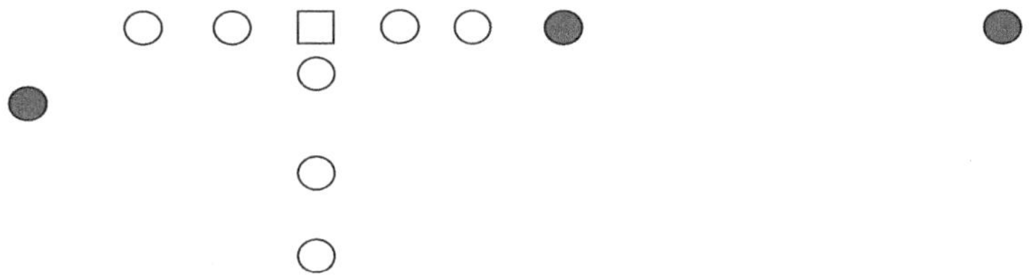

Figure 11-16

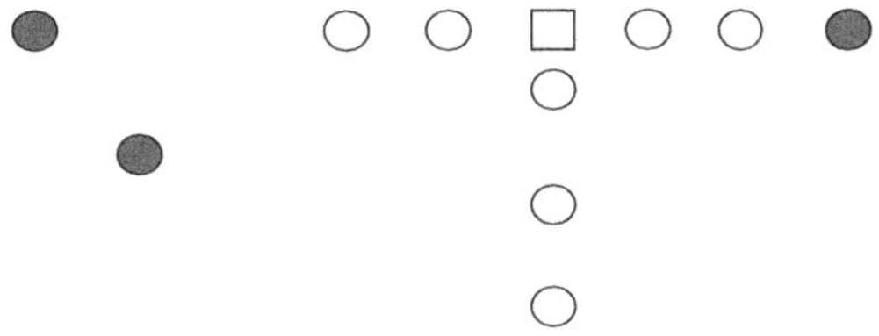

Figure 11-17

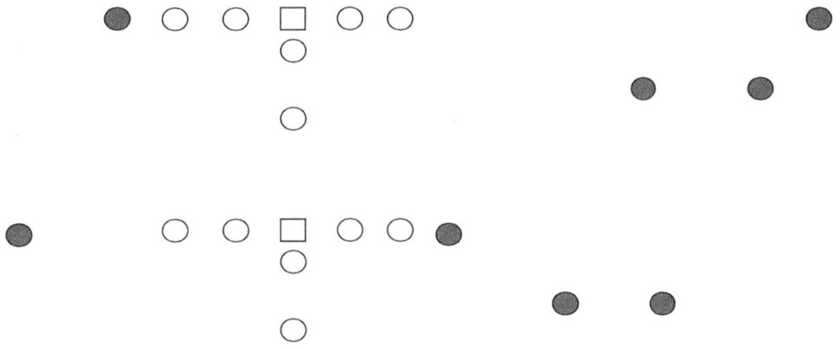

Figure 11-18

Figure 11-19

Motion

Motion is the movement of a running back during the snap of the play. Motion is utilized to change formations and confuse the defense. The terminology used to signify motion generally varies from team to team, but the types of motion are similar.

The most important factor to remember concerning motion is that the back cannot be moving forward at the time the ball is snapped. Furthermore, only one player can be in motion at once. If two players are moving at the same time, they must reset their stance, along with their teammates, before the snap. This situation would be considered a shift, not motion. Motion can begin after a shift, as long as the entire team is set for at least a second.

Systems

What makes an offense effective? In general, an effective offense has the ability to efficiently penetrate multiple parts of the field. Furthermore, a good offense has the ability to do something so well that the defense has to adjust what its scheme calls for it to do to stop it. Subsequently, a good offense can achieve even greater success against an adjusting defense.

It's important to keep in mind that an offensive system is properly identified by its underlying philosophy and base concepts, as opposed to the plays it entails. An offensive system has two basic elements—a running component and a passing component. In fact, there have been a lot of offensive systems developed over the years—some more successful than others, depending on the circumstances. Each of these strategic approaches has its advantages, as well as disadvantages. Among the more well-known and widely adopted offensive systems are the following:

☐ *Flexbone*. The flexbone is predominantly a running formation drawn from the wishbone formation. It features a quarterback under center, with a fullback positioned directly behind the QB and two relatively smaller running backs aligned behind the LOS on each side of the offensive line (also referred to as slotbacks). The underlying philosophy for the flexbone offense is the triple option play.

Advantages:

- Allows teams with undersized players to compete with teams that may have greater athletic ability.
- Prohibits the defense from keying on just one player.
- Utilizes simplified blocking schemes that require little to no adaption to various defenses.
- Forces the defense to play balanced or risk being caught with not enough defenders on one side.
- Compels the defense to account for four immediate vertical threats in the passing game.
- Does not make the offense rely on specialization with the positions it uses.

Disadvantages:

- Requires more than one (preferably 3-5) running backs to play the B back.
- Ideally, needs more than one quarterback who has the skills and ability to run the option.
- Takes time and patience to install and perfect. Initially, it can lead to multiple turnovers.
- Can lead to a certain amount of frustration at frequently calling the same play.

☐ *I Offense.* Featuring one of the most common offensive formations in football, the I offense entails a quarterback under center and two backs inline behind the QB. While a number of variations to this alignment exist (e.g., big I, power I, jumbo, stack I, three-wide I, tight I, and offset I), this offensive system emphasizes the running game. The fullback (the back closest to the QB) fills a blocking (as opposed to a receiving or rushing) role. The tailback (the back furthest from the QB), on the other hand, is the ballcarrier. Starting from six to eight yards behind the LOS in an upright position, the tailback surveys the defense and runs into any weak points he may find.

Advantages:

- Can incorporate plays from any other system including the wing-T, the veer, the bunch, or the spread.
- Can easily be adapted to any type of personnel.
- Can be extremely effective against certain defensive schemes (e.g., the 3-3-5).
- Can be expanded or contracted to include more or fewer running backs.
- Can offer fully developed sequential play packages.
- Employs an enormous amount of real misdirection.

Disadvantages:

- Because defenses often stack the box against the I, it can result in the offense having to block nine defenders.
- Requires the offense to be a cut above on the offensive line. The I requires the offense to push defenders back, which can be challenging.
- Not only does it limit passing concepts within the current "spread-em-out" philosophy, it also restricts multiple run schemes.

☐ *Option.* A run-based offense that can be run from any formation, this system emphasizes option running plays. A relatively wide variety of option offenses (which carry an array of different labels and entail an assortment of different techniques—double, triple, lead, counter) are employed at various levels of football. This system relies on timing, deception, and the ability to make split-second decisions under pressure.

Advantages:

- Can be very effective in managing the clock.
- Can help keep your defense fresh.
- Can be a viable alternative offense for teams lacking exceptional athleticism.
- Uses an option package as a change of pace.
- Can force the defense into upfield charges and undisciplined pursuit.

Disadvantages:

- Can be limiting for a team that needs to score quickly.
- Can be high-risk (possibility of turnovers) and high-reward (putting the offense in positions to score).

☐ *Pass-first.* Underlying philosophy is to throw the ball short to people who can score. Features a pass-first, fast-paced, primarily spread-based system of offense. The system is designed out of the shotgun formation, with four wide receivers and one running back. Its relatively simple run game is designed to complement the system's pass-first philosophy.

Advantages:

- Limits the ability of the defense to substitute players and adjust their scheme.
- Can lead to mental mistakes by the defense.
- By forcing the defensive line to widen (because of the wide splits by the offensive line), opens up the passing lanes for the QB to throw through, without having the ball knocked down or intercepted.
- Enables the offense to score quickly (and often).
- Gets the ball to people in space who can score and lets them make moves with the ball in their hands to create plays and gain yardage.
- To a degree, gives teams a chance to be successful, without having to be athletically superior.

Disadvantages:

- Places undue demands on your defense given the fact that they will tend to be on the field more than they otherwise would.
- Requires team speed, as well as an athletic QB.
- Limits the ability to manage the clock, an issue for a team with the lead trying to run the clock down.
- Can restrict the running game of the offense.

☐ *Pistol.* Arguably sometimes misunderstood, the pistol is essentially a formation, rather than an offense. An offensive system that is executed from this formation is a hybrid of the traditional shotgun and single back offenses. In the pistol, the quarterback is positioned closer to the LOS (4 yards versus the 7 yards that is typical in the shotgun). The running back sets up directly behind the QB, which gives the offense a variety of run and option plays that may not be available in the shotgun.

Advantages:

- Puts the QB in a better position to initiate the play.
- Allows the QB to be better able to see over the offensive line before the snap.
- Has the ability to freeze defenses with a mix of downhill running plays and passing.
- Forces defenses to play from a balanced set.
- Provides the ability to outnumber defenders at the point of contact.

- Limits the ability of the defense to get a pre-snap read.
- Can flip play sides without moving personnel.

Disadvantages:

- As a rule, requires a "duel-threat" QB.
- Doesn't offer all of the passing advantages when lined up in the shotgun or the running advantages when lined up under center.
- Generally requires an exceptionally athletic and agile offensive line.

☐ *Power.* This offensive system is typically utilized by teams that have a grind-it-out mentality. Featuring a relatively large, physical, and less mobile offensive line, the offense tends to liberally employ drive, base, double, wedge, lead, and isolation-type blocks.

Advantages:

- Can use the formation to shift and gain a numbers advantage no matter what the defensive alignment may be.
- Can see where the weakest areas of the defense may be.
- Can adapt the system to fit the team—its attitude and level of physicality.

Disadvantages:

- Requires a physical offensive line.
- Has relatively limited potential for an effective passing game.
- Offers little-to-no deception, preferring a physical style of offense.

☐ *RPOs.* The RPO (run-pass-option) is the complementary blending of the best aspects of two distinct offenses—the spread option and the pass-first. An RPO is any play on which the offense is given both a run play and some sort of pass or screen play simultaneously. At that point, the quarterback makes a read and a decision about which play gives the offense its best chance of being successful at that particular moment.

Advantages:

- Offers an effective way for the ball to be passed forward.
- Provides the ability to read for the pass pre-snap.
- Most passes have a minimal chance of being intercepted.
- Spreads the entire field.
- Can be added to any play in the offense.
- Doesn't require running backs in order to be successful.

Disadvantages:

- May overly burden the QB, given the plethora of pre-snap and post-snap decisions.
- Can expose the QB to a greater amount of post-throw hits.
- Can thwart the "pass" part of RPO, given the possibility of a defense, with athletically superior players, deploying man-to-man coverage.
- May need two QBs in order to be successful.

☐ *Run-and-Shoot*. This offensive system emphasizes receiver motion and on-the-fly adjustments by the receivers in response to different defenses. As a rule, the run-and-shoot, which typically employs one running back and four wide receivers, is a flexible offense. The receivers are free to adjust their routes on the fly into the defensive coverage they encounter. In turn, the quarterback also reads and reacts to the defensive coverages.

Advantages:

- Do not have to change the personnel combinations.
- Creates wide open running lanes.
- Can spread out the defense.
- Offers a relatively high potential for scoring.
- Forces the defense to switch to four or five defensive back formations.
- Gives the wide receivers a better opportunity to either run routes to uncovered areas or simply beat their defender in coverage.

Disadvantages:

- Requires quick-thinking and alert players, given the complexity involved in this somewhat improvisational system.
- Does not employ a tight end or a fullback to block.
- Involves a lot of technical and complicated pass block schemes.
- Offers a limited ability to control the clock when the offense is ahead.
- Requires a QB who can read a defense pre-snap, fast receivers who are able to run smart routes, and a quick-footed offensive line that can adjust its pass block schemes.

☐ *Single Wing*. A precursor to the modern spread or shotgun formation, the single wing offense is a versatile system in which four backs are positioned in various locations behind the center. As a rule, it is a direct-snap offense that features an unbalanced line with two tight ends, a wingback on the strongside, and no true quarterback. In reality, a wide variety of different variations of the offense exist.

Advantages:

- Has the fastest off-tackle play in all of football, given that there is no quarterback and no handoff.
- Forces the defense to deal with unfamiliarity; opponents most likely won't see this offense more than 1-2 times a year.
- Offers offensive simplicity.
- Is adaptable to almost any personnel.
- Forces the defense to deal with an enhanced level of deception.
- Enables the offense to get four receivers into the pattern quickly.
- Can confuse the defense by employing a variety of motion and formations.

Disadvantages:

- Is not preferred by athletes who would rather play in a wide-open passing attack.

- Does not allow ample time to perfect the passing game, given the time it takes to work on the intricacies involved in its run-blocking schemes and the ballhandling skills and techniques it requires.
- Will cause defenses to respond with nine-man box alignments, which may be a deterrent to a run-heavy offense.
- To a degree, limits the ability of the offensive play caller to be aware of how the defense may respond to the offense, since the offense will rarely face the exact same defense twice.

☐ *Spread.* This offensive system, in which the quarterback is typically (but not always) aligned in the shotgun formation, uses three, four, and occasionally five, receiver sets to "spread" the defense horizontally. While a wide variety of assorted versions of the spread exist, one factor is constant—multiple receivers on the field. Some spread offenses emphasize the running game more; others focus more on the passing attack. Some employ no-huddle; other huddle before every play. Some prefer to use an empty backfield; others favor utilizing motion.

Advantages:

- Creates one-on-one match-ups with the defense.
- Forces the defense to play sound, assignment-driven football.
- Leads to a situation in which missed tackles or blown assignments can result in big plays.
- Dictates the defense's reaction.

Disadvantages:

- Doesn't include either a fullback or tight end to help with blitz pickups.
- Limits the passing attack on occasion because of the lack of a tight end.
- Is somewhat difficult to hold a lead.

☐ *Up-Tempo.* This approach to offense entails running every play relatively quickly (e.g., the hurry-up offense). Its underlying premise is that defenses will be largely unprepared to deal with and adjust to the pace at which the offense is operating.

Advantages:

- Forces the defense to maintain its personnel grouping.
- Forces the defense to limit its playbook.
- Causes problems with defensive communication.
- It takes play-calling away from defensive coordinators, forcing defenders to communicate and adjust on the fly.
- Enables the offense to control the pace of the game and how it wants to play it.
- If the ball is snapped immediately, allows the offense to assess the defense and make appropriate checks.

Disadvantages:

- Can be difficult to practice conducting at a fast tempo.
- Can require simplification in other aspects of the game.

- Limits the opportunity for the coach to have immediate face-to-face interaction with his athletes who have made a mistake.

☐ *Veer*. This offense is a system that emphasizes the veer option, which is essentially considered a "triple option" philosophy. It involves three players engaging with the defense, with one back taking a dive course, another pursuing a pitch course, and yet another serving as a lead blocker on the perimeter of the offensive formation. In this system, the quarterback reads the defense and then distributes the ball, depending on the reaction of the defense.

Advantages:

- Don't have to block everyone—just read them and react.
- Is extremely difficult to defend when it's run properly.
- Is a good ball-control offense.
- Can help even the playing field for teams that are smaller (in size) or slower.
- Enhances an attitude of being aggressive physical.

Disadvantages:

- Requires a lot of practice.
- Limits the passing game.
- Can be predictable.

☐ *West Coast*. This timing-based offensive system features relatively short, horizontal passing routes in lieu of running plays in order to stretch out defenses. The underlying premise is that such a tactic will result in creating the potential for long runs and passes. Arguably, it is more a philosophy and an approach to the game than an array of plays or formations. The underlying premise of the west coast offense is to utilize passing to set up the run.

Advantages:

- Gets the ball out of the quarterback's hand quicker.
- Features high-percentage plays that get everyone involved.
- Enables the offense to control the ball.
- Minimizes dependence on the offensive line.

Disadvantages:

- Must have a mobile QB who is able to throw the ball accurately.
- Requires sure-handed receivers who are comfortable catching the ball in traffic.
- Can be somewhat difficult to master given its complexity as well as its need for precision.

☐ *Wing-T*. This offensive system features a run-first approach that has numerous plays that employ pulling and trapping. This misdirection offense is distinguished by a wingback who is aligned in the slot just behind the tight end and a split end on the weakside. In addition, the formation puts all three running backs in position for counters, other misdirection plays, and fakes.

Advantages:

- Puts the defense in conflict, given the misdirection it employs.
- Is a good ball-control offense.
- Minimizes the amount of time its defense has to spend on the field.
- Provides its offensive line with better angles for blocking, a feature that enables smaller or less athletic players to be productive.
- Can be difficult for the defense to prepare for since the number of teams that employ it is relatively limited.

Disadvantages:

- Places the offense at a disadvantage if it needs to "catch up."
- Has a general lack of offensive balance, given its focus on running.

☐ *Wishbone*. This offensive formation (also referred to as the "bone") is designed to run a triple option with a lead blocker. The underlying premise of the offense is to eliminate two defenders without blocking them, which frees two offensive linemen to block other defenders, usually inside. In essence, the offense anticipates getting a one-on-none in the running game and a one-on-one in open space in the passing game.

Advantages:

- Can be extremely difficult to defend.
- Dominates the time of possession.
- As a rule, does not require superior skills.

Disadvantages:

- Difficult to find a fullback and tight end with the necessary skillset.
- Is not easily adaptable to other types of offensive systems.
- Is not preferred by players who tend to favor a more wide-open style of play.
- Has an increased risk of turnovers.
- Is not a good offense for overcoming a lead.

☐ *Zone*. This offensive system almost exclusively emphasizes zone blocking schemes. Zone blocking requires relatively heavy technique-laden coaching, as opposed to scheme-based instruction. This type of blocking is employed in a number of offensive systems. In this system, there is no "true" hole for the running back, only a point of contact. The offensive line needs to know the direction in which the play is being run. The running back subsequently decides where along the LOS he wants to make his cut.

Advantages:

- Provides a sound and simplistic way of running the football against any defensive front.
- Gives three basic points of contact on every play and forces the defense to account for all of them because each play starts exactly the same way.
- Emphasizes basic fundamentals and techniques.
- Helps players be more physical and simply react to the defense by eliminating hesitation and the need to overanalyze different situations.
- Allows teams to run to any hole or weakness in the defense.

- Can be run against any front or style of defense.
- Makes offenses difficult to prepare for because they are able to run a minimal number of base plays in conjunction with a wide array of formations, motions, shifts, and trades.
- Minimizes weekly adjustments and allows teams to perform the functions they do well, regardless of the opponent or defense being faced.
- Can be used in all field positions and situations (coming out of the end zone, red zone, short yardage, third and long, etc.).
- Complements the play-action passing game, as well as the naked series and the boot series.
- Allows offenses to dictate the tempo of the game and provides them the chance to defeat a defense with patience and consistency.
- Relies on the success of the entire offensive unit instead of one or two individuals, compelling players to depend on one another.

Disadvantages:

- Requires a relatively skilled offensive line.
- Entails an extensive amount of time and practice to master the essential skills and techniques.
- Provides a limited amount of time to practice and have multiple run scheme alternatives.
- May not have sufficient time to have a balanced attack given the time requirements for the run game.

OFFENSIVE PLAYBOOK

Prior to the start of the season, many youth football coaches develop a playbook for their team—either a collective one for every member of the team and the coaching staff or a separate one for each player and staff member working with one of the team's primary units (offense, defense, special teams). This playbook is designed to serve as a blueprint to help a team understand what will be expected of them during the season.

With regard to putting together an offensive playbook, much of what you decide to include in it will be guided by your offensive philosophy. What kind of team do you want to have? What basic principles underlie your offense? What information do your players need to know?

It is important for you to realize that you shouldn't just draw plays and call it a playbook. You should develop your playbook with your players in mind, including as many details and as much information as appropriate. Among the information you should consider including is the following:

- Your philosophy
- Player expectations
- Numbering systems
- Huddle formation
- Cadence
- Formations
- Basic line splits
- Blocking calls
- Block descriptions
- Plays
- Glossary of terms

Plays

Every coach has a set of plays that he believes give his team its best opportunity for being successful. The following plays are examples of different elements commonly included in a team's offense. It should be noted that the formations shown are essentially irrelevant. In fact, the same play can be run from a variety of formations. As such, you need to focus on the inherent concepts involved in the play rather than the formation itself.

Running plays:

☐ *Basic dive play.* In the dive play, the running back runs to the hole with no lead blocker. Because the line is responsible for the defenders closest to them, relative to this quick-hitting play, it is arguably the easiest play to teach blocking.

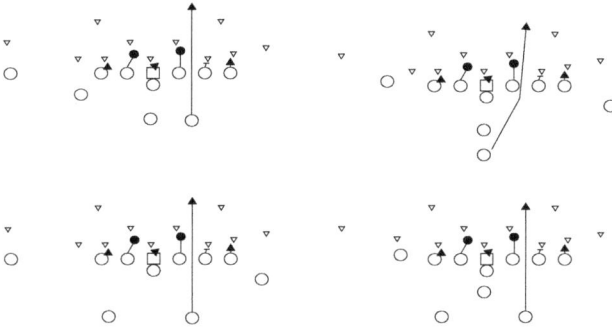

Figure 11-20

☐ *Basic lead play.* In the lead play, the ballcarrier runs to a designated hole, following a running back who serves as a lead blocker. This running back blocks the first player he encounters.

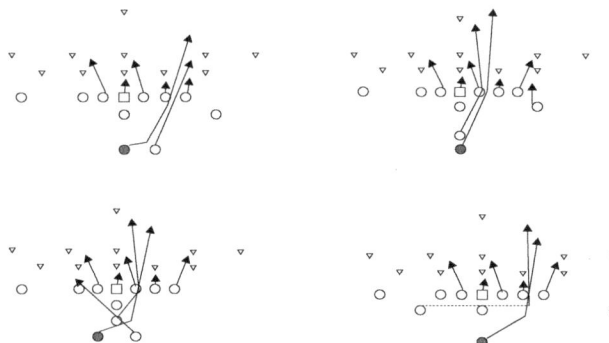

Figure 11-21

☐ *Basic counter play.* In the counter play (shown from an I formation), the backfield starts opposite the direction of the handoff. The ballcarrier takes a jab-step in that direction and then cuts back in the opposite direction and runs through the hole.

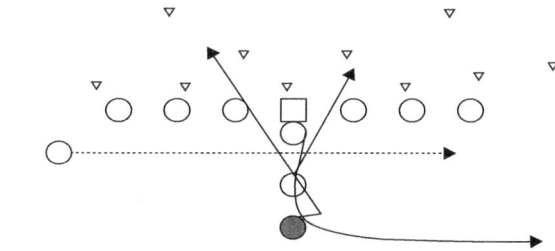

Figure 11-22

☐ *Basic trap play.* The trap play is designed to conflict the defense. It is very similar to the counter play, except that the ballcarrier runs to the designated hole without taking the misdirection jab-step.

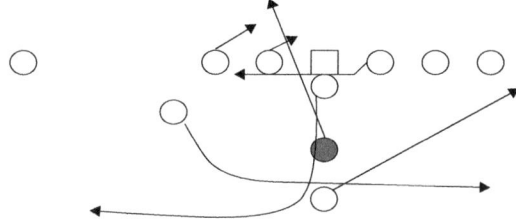

Figure 11-23

☐ *Basic sweep play.* This play (shown from a wishbone formation) involves a power run around the outside with two backs and the outside lead guard blocking.

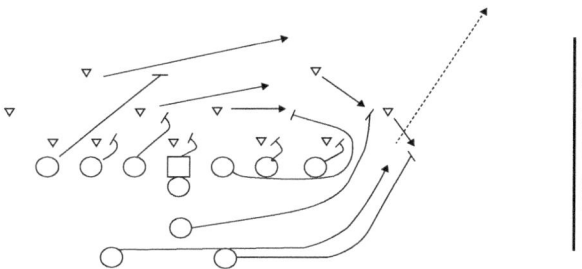

Figure 11-24

☐ *Basic toss play.* In this play, the toss is typically utilized to get to the outside quickly and take advantage of the speed of a particular back. The toss play is more likely to turn the outside corner than a sweep play. The ballcarrier must read the lead block in order to make that decision.

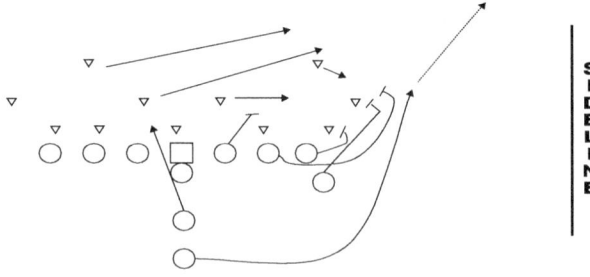

Figure 11-25

☐ *Basic reverse play.* This play is set up by other plays, usually from a running play that has been successful. The underlying concept is to get the defense to flow in one direction while the play goes back in the opposite direction.

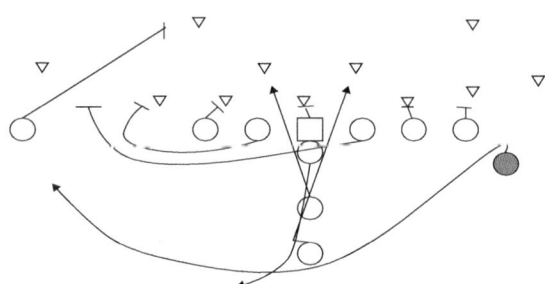

Figure 11-26

☐ *Basic bootleg play.* In this play, the quarterback keeps the ball after a fake to a running back. He then follows the lead block of whatever offensive lineman is leading the play.

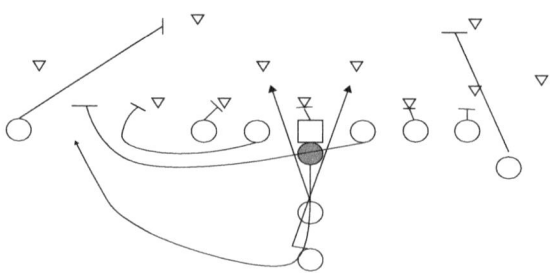

Figure 11-27

Passing plays:

☐ *Basic play-action pass play.* In this play, the pass is derived from the team's running plays. The best play action passes should look like a running play to the defense.

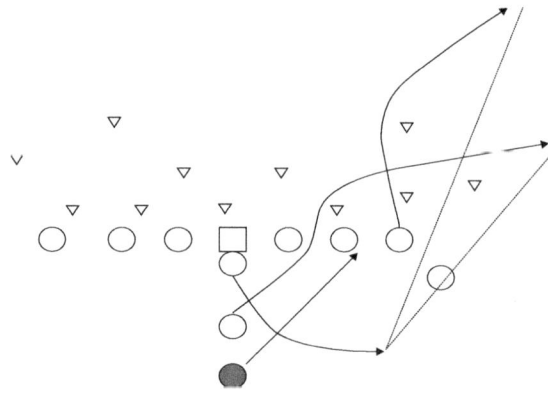

Figure 11-28

☐ *Basic three-step dropback passing play.* A three-step drop is used in the quick passing game. As a rule, this play does not require much of a post-snap read by the quarterback.

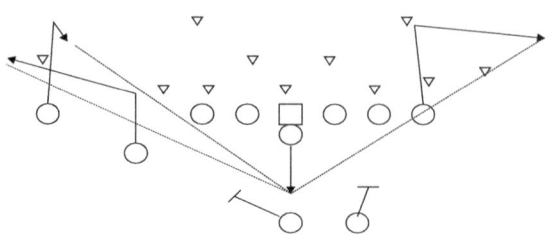

Figure 11-29

- *Basic five-step dropback passing play.* In most offenses, the five-step drop is the most common QB drop and offers more offensive possibilities with regard to the patterns your receivers may run.

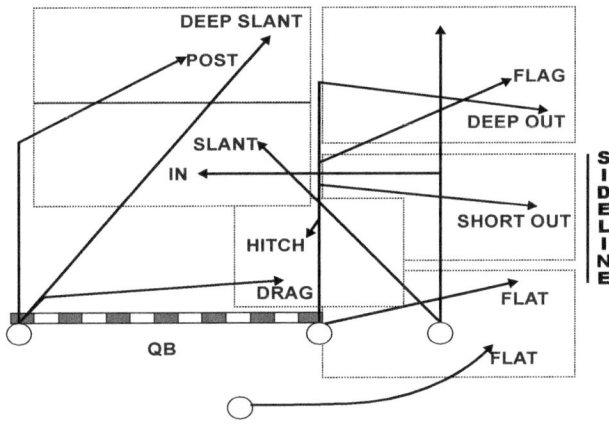

Figure 11-30

- *Basic seven-step dropback passing play.* The seven-step drop is an extension of the five-step drop. These plays, which take longer to develop, are designed to extend the offense vertically.

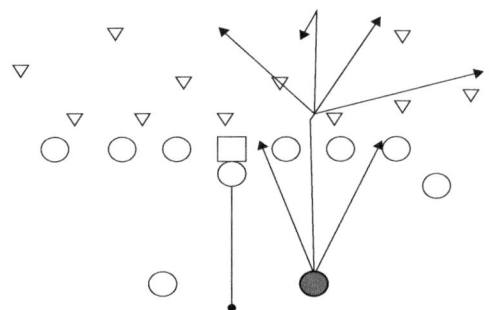

Figure 11-31

Specialty plays:

- *Quarterback sneak play.* This play is used when the offense needs to gain a relatively short amount of yardage (e.g., third and short; on the goal line and short). The key is to block effectively at the point of contact. In this instance, a double-team block is advised.

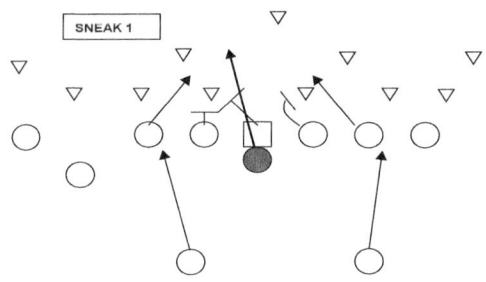

Figure 11-32

- *Screen play.* This play is run from a five-step drop. It requires precise timing and a relatively high level of poise by the QB. The play, which is grounded in deception, is designed to make the defense believe it is a downfield pass.

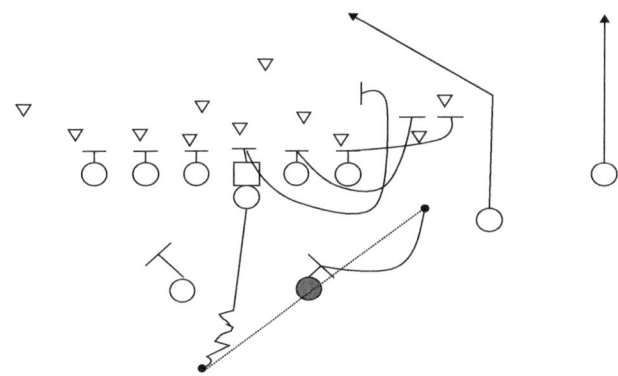

Figure 11-33

CHAPTER 12

HOW TO DEVELOP A DEFENSIVE SYSTEM

Many coaches believe that defense is the cornerstone of winning games. In order for your team's defense to perform well, you need to establish a defensive system that is based on the factors that you believe are necessary for it to be successful.

The connection that links all of those factors together is your defensive philosophy. In other words, what kind of defense do you want your team to have? Do you want an aggressive, physical defense? Or would you prefer that your defense adopt a read-and-react mentality? Your preferences will influence the defensive system you develop.

Whatever way of playing defense you ultimately embrace, it is essential that you put together a plan that fits the skillset of your players. Your efforts to establish a defensive system should be based on what your players can do, as opposed to what you hope they can do or to what you conceive that they should be able to do. Under no circumstances should you try to pigeonhole your players into a role for which they are unsuited.

Similar to your efforts concerning developing an offensive system, your defensive system not only must be simple enough for your staff to teach, it must also be one that gives your team its best opportunity for success. A number of factors should be considered, including the following:

- Does the system take advantage of the individual abilities of defensive players by placing them in situations where they can make a play?
- Does the system minimize a defender's weaknesses and maximize his strengths?
- Does the system keep physical-type defenders close to the core of the formation?
- Is the system able to bring pressure—inside or outside?
- Is the system capable of minimizing the offense's strengths through alignments or favorable match-ups?

- Is the system capable of maximizing the offense's weakness?
- Does the system afford a smooth transition from defense to special teams?

DEFENSIVE BASICS

Your defense will be comprised of three main groups of players—defensive linemen, linebackers, and the secondary (defensive backs). The defensive line is on the line of scrimmage, usually in three- or four-point stances. The line will be backed up by players in two-point stances—linebackers. The secondary will consist of players who align deeper than the linebackers.

The defensive linemen are to defeat the opponent's running game first and rush the quarterback second. On the other hand, in some systems and packages, this premise may not always be true. The defensive linemen may be pass rushers first. Linebackers are equally responsible for the opponent's running and passing game. Deep defenders usually play pass first and run second.

Modern football, sometimes, blurs the distinction between these groups. For example, in an effort to get more speed on the field, coaches are moving defensive backs to linebacker and linebackers to linemen. A linebacker may actually be a defensive back in a nickel or dime package. In turn, a defensive end in a four-down-lineman look may actually be an outside linebacker in a 3-4 scheme.

☐ *Defensive Linemen*

- Spacing. No matter the structure used, a defense has either even or odd spacing. If a defensive player aligns over the center, the defense is odd. A defense is considered even if no defender is on the line of scrimmage over the center.
- Alignments. Defenders can align in one of three places on offensive linemen. Those include head-up, when the defender is directly over the offensive player; shaded, when the defender aligns on the offensive player's inside or outside; and a gap, when the defender aligns in the gap adjacent to the blocker. More often than not, the most commonly used alignment system is one that designates shades. Figure 12-1 depicts even alignments and Figure 12-2 illustrates shaded alignments.

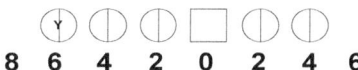

Figure 12-1

Figure 12-2

☐ *Linebackers*

Linebackers either align over offensive blockers, or they stack with a defensive lineman. When linebackers play unprotected over an offensive lineman, they are given a number to distinguish their alignment. For example, if a linebacker aligns over the outside shoulder of the guard, he is said to be in a 30 alignment. A 30 alignment means the linebacker is in a 3 alignments off the ball. A linebacker on the outside shoulder of the offensive tackle would be considered to be in a 50 alignment. A linebacker who lines up behind a defensive lineman is referred to as a stack linebacker. Should he stack with a 3-technique lineman, he is tagged as a 30-stack linebacker. A linebacker aligned behind a 2 technique is a 20-stack linebacker.

The spacing of linebackers is usually reflected by the number of linebackers. Should the defense have an even number of linebackers (two or four), half the linebackers will be on either side of the ball. When the defense has an odd number of linebackers (three or five), one linebacker will usually be directly over the center who, in turn, will be flanked right and left by one or more of the other linebackers. If only one linebacker is used, he will usually be placed over the center.

☐ *Secondary*

Most defensive secondaries will set up in one of the following alignments/shells, from which the defenses can play man, zone, or combination coverages:

- Two-deep box
- Three-deep diamond with either a three-spoke or five-spoke secondary
- Four-deep umbrella
- Four across

Common Defensive Elements

Regardless of what players you have, what defensive system you design, or what scheme you want your team to run as a part of that system, there are certain elements that tend to be common to most defensive systems, including a method for identifying defensive alignment techniques, a procedure for huddling, and a process for communicating.

☐ *Gaps*. It is very important that the players on your defense understand the gap system. Gaps are the designated spaces along the offensive line between the players on the line of scrimmage. Many defensive systems are gap-based systems. These types of defenses assign defenders to gap responsibilities. These responsibilities are called assignments. An offensive blocker has an assignment that gives him a primary blocking responsibility. Defenders should also have assignments that tell them the primary area they are responsible to protect. These areas are called gaps. Figure 12-3 shows where each gap is located. The letters represent the gaps on the offensive line.

- The A gap is the space between the center and the guard.
- The B gap is the space between the guard and the tackle.
- The C gap is the space between the tackle and the tight end or the ghost TE (the space where the TE would normally be, but isn't in the formation the offense is employing).
- The D gap is the entire area outside the tight end or the ghost TE (Figure 12-4).

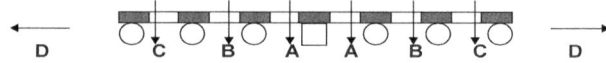

Figure 12-3

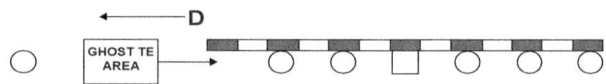

Figure 12-4

☐ *Defensive Alignment Techniques*. A technique can simply be described as the area in which the defender aligns himself prior to the snap of the ball. This system is a universal defensive language. If you are putting together your defense, you must learn and understand this system.

Figure 12-5 demonstrates the head-up techniques. The even numbers represent defensive linemen in head-up alignment with the offensive linemen. For example, if a defender is lined up directly over the guard, he is said to be in a 2 technique; head-up on a tackle is a 4 technique; over the TE is a 6 technique; and over the center is a 0 technique. If there is a linebacker lined up head-up on a guard, he, too, is considered to be lined up in a 2 technique, even if he is lined up three yards off the LOS. Some defensive numbering systems will add a zero to the end of the number for the alignment of a linebacker. For example, the same linebacker previously described would be in a 20 technique.

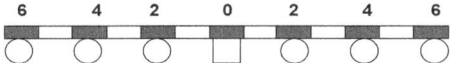

Figure 12-5

For instance, if there is no tight end in an offensive formation and the defender's alignment still calls for a 6 technique, the defender lines up over the ghost TE. In other words, he lines up exactly where he would if the tight end were there. The defender aligned in a 6 technique, as shown in Figure 12-6, is lined up over the ghost TE.

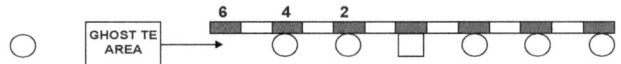

Figure 12-6

The numbers and letters in Figure 12-7 describe an inside shade technique by the defensive linemen. As such, they are lined up on the inside shoulder of the offensive linemen. For example, a man lined up on the inside shoulder of the guard is in a 2i technique; the inside shoulder of the tackle is a 4i technique; and the inside shoulder of the TE is considered a 7 technique.

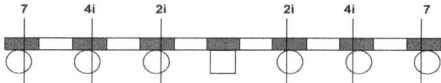

Figure 12-7

The numbers in Figure 12-8 represent an outside shade technique by the defensive linemen. In other words, they are lined up on the outside shoulder of the offensive linemen. No matter which side of the center they are lined up on, it is considered a 1 technique. If they are lined up on the outside shoulder of the guard, they are in a 3 technique; the outside shoulder of the tackle is a 5 technique; the outside shoulder of the TE is a 9 technique.

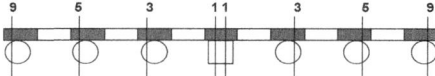

Figure 12-8

There are several possible alignment techniques for the defense. Each has its own set of rules, keys, and responsibilities:

0 Technique:

0 Alignment

- A player who is in a 0 technique is aligned head-up on the center (Figure 12-9).
- This would be used in an odd defense.

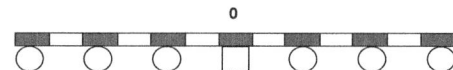

Figure 12-9

0 Assignment

- This technique is widely used in 5-0 defenses. The responsibility of this player can vary. In some base 50 defenses, this player would have two gap responsibilities. The two gaps would both be A gaps.
- The key is the center's head; the defender shouldn't allow it to cross his body. Whichever side his head goes to will likely be the playside.
- Other base 50 defenses will require this player to have strongside A gap responsibilities. In this situation, the player doesn't know which gap he is responsible for until the offense is set up and a strongside is determined.

1 Technique:

1 Alignment

- A player lined up in a 1 technique is lined up in a shade of the center (Figure 12-10).
- An odd number technique represents an outside shade; both sides of the center could be considered outside.
- The facemask of the defender is aligned with the center of the outside shoulder of the center.

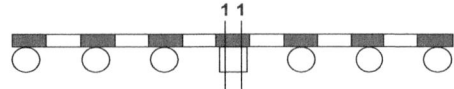

Figure 12-10

1 Assignment

- The base responsibility for a defender in a 1 technique is the A gap to the shade side of the center.
- It is imperative that he never allows the center's head to cross his body.
- If the center blocks down on him, he should work to get himself to the other side of the center's body.
- The guard to the shade side will be the other key. If he tries to block down, the player should work to his outside. This will likely be the playside.
- The defender should not allow himself to be double-teamed. If possible, he would work to the outside of the guard in this situation and try to break the double-team.
- If the guard pulls, the defender should read and react quickly in that direction. He will likely lead him to the play.
- On passes, he must stay in his rush lane. The rush lane is a direct line between the defender and the QB.

2i Technique:

2i Alignment

- A player lined up in a 2i technique is lined up in an inside shade of the guard (Figure 12-11).
- The facemask of the defender is aligned with the center of the inside shoulder of the guard.
- This type of alignment is commonly found in even defenses.

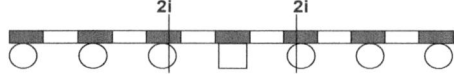

Figure 12-11

2i Assignment

- The base responsibility for a defender in the 2i technique is the A gap.
- It is imperative that he never allows the guard to cross his body.
- If the guard blocks down on him, he should work to get himself to the other side of the guard.
- The center will be the other key. If he tries to block down, the defender should work to his outside. This will likely be the playside.
- The defender should not allow himself to be double-teamed. If possible, he would work to the outside in this situation to try to break the double-team.
- If the guard pulls, he should read and react quickly in that direction. He should work his way down the line of scrimmage, mirroring the guard until he reads the play. This will likely lead him to the play.
- On passes, he must stay in the rush lane. The rush lane is a direct line between the defender and the QB.
- If the guard releases beyond the defender for a linebacker, he should watch for a trap block coming from the opposite side.

2 Technique:

2 Alignment

- A player lined up in a 2 technique is lined up head-up on the guard (Figure 12-12).
- This type of alignment is commonly found in even defenses.

Figure 12-12

2 Assignment

- The base responsibility for this player can vary greatly. The base assignment is either the A or B gap. This will be determined by the base scheme of your defense.
- The 40 defense is an even defense that will vary the assignment according to the defensive call. The linebacker will always be responsible for the gap opposite the defensive lineman's responsibility.
- He should try to not allow the guard to cross his body.
- The center and the tackle will be the other keys. If they try to block down, the defender should work to their outside, which will likely be the playside.
- The defender should not allow himself to be double-teamed. If possible, he would work to the outside in this situation and break the double-team.
- If the guard pulls, he should read and react quickly in that direction, working his way down the line of scrimmage, mirroring him until he reads the play. He will likely lead him to the play.
- On passes, he must stay in the rush lane. The rush lane is a direct line between the defender and the QB.
- If the guard releases beyond the defender for a linebacker, he should watch for a trap block coming from the opposite side.

3 Technique:

3 Alignment

- A player lined up in a 3 technique is lined up in an outside shade of the guard (Figure 12-13).
- The facemask of the defender is aligned with the center of the outside shoulder of the guard.

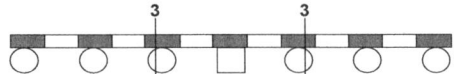

Figure 12-13

3 Assignment

- The base responsibility for a defender in a 3 technique is the B gap.
- He should try to not allow the guard to cross his body.
- If the guard tries to reach block him, he should work to get himself to the outside.
- The tackle will be the other key. If he tries to block down, the defender should work to his outside. This will likely be the playside.
- The defender should not allow himself to be double-teamed. If possible, he would work to the outside in this situation and break the double-team.
- If the guard pulls, he should read and react quickly in that direction, working his way down the line of scrimmage, mirroring him until he reads the play. He will likely lead him to the play.
- On passes, he must stay in the rush lane. The rush lane is a direct line between the defender and the QB.
- If the guard releases beyond the defender for a linebacker, he should watch for a trap block coming from the opposite side.

4i Technique:

4i Alignment

- A player lined up in a 4i technique is lined up in an inside shade of the tackle (Figure 12-14).
- The facemask of the defender is aligned with the center of the inside shoulder of the tackle.

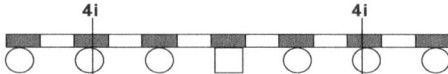

Figure 12-14

4i Assignment

- The base responsibility for a defender in a 4i technique is the B gap.
- He should try to not allow the guard to cross his body.
- If the tackle blocks down on him, he should work to get himself to the other side of the tackle.
- The guard will be the other key. If he tries to block down, the defender should work to his opposite side. This will likely be the playside.
- The defender should not allow himself to be double-teamed. If possible, he would work to the outside in this situation and break the double-team.
- If the guard or tackle pulls, he should read and react quickly in that direction, working his way down the line of scrimmage, mirroring him until he reads the play. He will likely lead him to the play.
- On passes, he must stay in the rush lane. The rush lane is a direct line between the defender and the QB. He should never spin to his inside, unless he is blocked beyond the passer.

- If the guard releases beyond the defender for a linebacker, he should watch for a trap block coming from the opposite side.

4 Technique:

4 Alignment

- A player lined up in a 4 technique is lined up head-up on the tackle (Figure 12-15).
- This technique is commonly used in both 50 and 60 defenses.

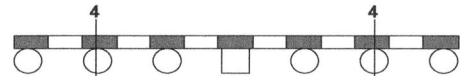

Figure 12-15

4 Assignment

- The base responsibility for this player can vary greatly. The base assignment is either the A or B gap. This will be determined by the base scheme of your defense.
- This player will have C gap responsibility in many 50 base defenses. This defense may vary the responsibility, depending on alignment and assignment of the linebackers.
- It is imperative that he never allows the tackle to cross his body.
- The guard and the tight end will be the other keys. If they try to block down, he should work to their outside. This will likely be the playside.
- He should not allow himself to be double-teamed. If possible, he would work to the outside in this situation and break the double-team.
- If the guard or tackle pulls, he should read and react quickly in that direction, working his way down the line of scrimmage, mirroring him until he reads the play. He will likely lead him to the play.
- On passes, he must stay in the rush lane. The rush lane is a direct line between the defender and the QB.
- If the guard releases beyond the defender for a linebacker, he should watch for a trap block coming from the opposite side.

5 Technique:

5 Alignment

- A player lined up in a 5 technique is lined up in an outside shade of the tackle (Figure 12-16).
- The facemask of the defender is aligned with the center of the outside shoulder of the tackle.

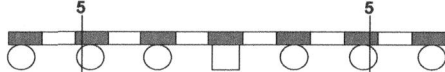

Figure 12-16

5 Assignment

- The base responsibility for a defender in a 5 technique is the C gap.
- It is imperative that he never allows the tackle to cross his body.
- If the tackle tries to reach block him, he should work to get himself to the outside.
- The tight end will be the other key. If he tries to block down, the defender should work to his outside. This will likely be the playside.
- He should not allow himself to be double-teamed. If possible, he would work to the outside in this situation and break the double-team.

- On passes, he must stay in the rush lane. The rush lane is a direct line between the defender and the QB.
- If the tackle releases beyond the defender for a linebacker, he should watch for a trap block coming from the opposite side.

6 Technique:

6 Alignment

- A player lined up in a 6 technique is lined up head-up on the tight end or ghost tight end area. Some defensive schemes may call for him to slide into a 5 technique if there is no tight end (Figure 12-17).
- This technique is commonly used in even defenses.

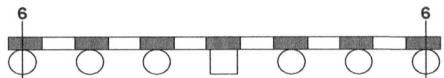

Figure 12-17

6 Assignment

- The base responsibility for this player can vary greatly. The base assignment is either the C or D gap. This role will be determined by the base scheme of your defense.
- It is imperative that he never allows the tight end to cross his body.
- He should never allow the tight end to release from the LOS cleanly. He should jam him at the line and mirror his initial movements.

7 Technique:

7 Alignment

- A player lined up in a 7 technique is lined up in an inside shade of the tight end or ghost tight end (Figure 12-18). Some defensive schemes may call for him to slide into a 5 technique, if there is no tight end.
- The facemask of the defender is aligned with the center of the inside shoulder of the tight end or ghost area.
- He should align on the tight end up to a three-yard split from the tackle. If he is any further, it should be considered a ghost situation.

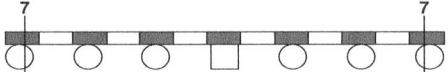

Figure 12-18

7 Assignment

- The base responsibility for a defender in a 7 technique is the C gap.
- If the tight end blocks down on him, he should work to get himself to the other side of the tight end.
- The tackle will be the other key. If he tries to block out, the defender should work to his opposite side. This will likely be the playside.
- He should not allow himself to be double-teamed. If possible, he would work to the outside in this situation and break the double-team.
- On passes, he must stay in the rush lane. The rush lane is a direct line between the defender and the QB. He should never spin to his inside, unless he is blocked beyond the passer.

- If the tight end releases beyond the defender for a backer, he should watch for a trap block coming from the opposite side. This may also indicate a play-action passing situation.
- If the tight end blocks down the line, he should jam down on his outside shoulder and work down with him. He should look for a kick out block from a running back or pulling lineman. If he encounters this situation, he should drive the kick blocker back into the ballcarrier who is likely following him.
- He should align on the tight end up to a three-yard split from the tackle. If he is any further, it should be considered a ghost situation.

9 Technique:

9 Alignment

- A player lined up in a 9 technique is lined up in an outside shade of the tight end. This player will likely be in a two-point stance.
- The facemask of the defender will be aligned with the outside shoulder of the tight end.
- If there is no tight end, but there is a slot back in his area, he should align himself with the slot back as he would have the tight end.

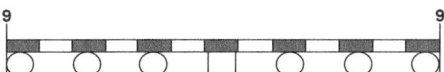

Figure 12-19

9 Assignment

- The base responsibility for a defender in a 9 technique is the D gap. This means he has outside containment responsibilities. On outside running plays, he is responsible to either turn the play inside or string it out-of-bounds.
- It is imperative that he never allows the tight end to cross his body. If the tackle tries to reach block him, he should work to get himself to the outside.
- The near back will be the other key. If he releases toward the outside of the tight end, he should release the tight end and work to the outside shoulder of the back.
- If the tight end blocks down the line, he should jam down on his outside shoulder and work down with him. He should look for a kick-out block from a running back or pulling lineman. If he encounters this situation, he should drive the kick blocker back into the ballcarrier who is likely following him.
- On passes, he must stay in his rush lane. The rush lane is a direct line between this player and the QB. He should never allow himself to get deeper than the ball.

☐ *Huddling*

Some defenses huddle before the ball is snapped to get the defensive play call; others don't. Teams that huddle typically have their linemen and linebackers involved, since the defensive backs often have further to go to get back into position. DBs often base their coverage on the look the offense is presenting. As a rule, the defensive playcall is given in the defensive huddle by a designated player (typically the middle linebacker), who gets the signal from the sideline. How a defense lines up to huddle (e.g., stack, circle, etc.) may vary from team to team.

If the defense does not utilize a huddle, the entire defense looks to the sideline and gets the defensive call from a designated source (it could be either a coach or another player). Among the information transmitted in a defensive call are blitz schemes and coverage calls.

☐ *Defensive Communication*

One of the keys to effective defensive play is verbal communication between defenders during the game. From alerting teammates to what the offense is doing (e.g., "pass, pass, pass;" or "run, run, run"), to what situation may be imminent (e.g., "look out for a reverse;" "look out for #32;" etc.), to offering words of encouragement (e.g., "way to go;" "great effort;" etc.), the importance of on-the-field communication between the various members of the defense cannot be overemphasized. Not only does it help keep the defenders alert and focused, it can also help foster a uniting atmosphere.

PLANNING FOR SUCCESS

Defensive success on the gridiron does not occur by accident. It requires systematic planning. One of the most important factors is determining what you want your defense to embody. What attributes will characterize it? What traits will your defensive players possess?

You also need to ascertain what style of defense you want to employ—aggressive, reading, or a combination of both. In addition, you need to determine, within the three basic styles of defense, which theory is most suitable for your team. Finally, you need to decide what defensive scheme best fits the skillset of your players and coaches, as well as your defensive philosophy.

Another consideration when deciding on the defensive system that best accommodates your team is how will the proposed defense affect other aspects of your team. For example, if you believe that your team may surrender a lot of points, you may need to implement a ball-control offense to keep your defense off the field. On the other hand, if you have a strong defense, your offense may be able to take more shots down the field.

Desirable Defensive Attributes

There are nearly as many ways of thinking about how to play sound defense as there are coaches with opinions on the subject. On the other hand, most (if not all) defensive players and teams that perform well share certain characteristics, including the following:

☐ Common attributes of effective defensive players:

- Love to play football.
- Are intelligent.
- Always do their best.
- Are competitive.
- Are disciplined.
- Are dependable.
- Play with confidence and have fun.
- Learn from their mistakes.
- Are coachable.

☐ Common attributes of effective defensive teams:

- Love to play the sport and have fun doing it.
- Always do their best.
- Play aggressively.
- Master the fundamentals.
- Have a sense of unity and teamwork.
- Tend to win first down (allow three yards or less).
- Are successful on third down (get off the field).

- Win the field position game (play on the opponent's side of the field).
- Limit yards after contact (on both running and passing plays).
- Win the turnover ratio (fumble recovery; interceptions).
- Score on defense.

Styles of Defense

Regardless of the defensive teams and formations used, defenses typically employ one of three approaches to defend on a particular play:

- Read and react—players diagnose the play and then react.
- Be aggressive and read—players pursue, while diagnosing the play.
- Combination—some players read and react, while others pursue while reading the play.

☐ *Read and React*

Defenses in the read-and-react style usually play horizontally along the line of scrimmage. Upfield charges, which press the line of scrimmage, are limited in favor of looking for certain keys or reads before players act. Defenders only react when they process the offense's intentions. The defense has a "bend-but-don't-break" philosophy, which involves giving up bits of ground slowly. This type of defense seeks to play field position and make the offenses go the long way while counting on the offense to eventually make a mistake. Defenses try to match up with offensive personnel packages as well as offensive formations. Defenses seek to cheat their alignment to play off offensive tendencies. Defenses may have to substitute a heavy lineman or a defensive back package to offset offensive intentions. Simply stated, read-and-react defenses tend to allow offenses to dictate the situation.

☐ *Be Aggressive and Read*

An aggressive style of play results in the defense dictating to the offense. Be-aggressive-and-read defenses want to turn the tables on the offense and force them to react to the defense. Aggressive defensive play results in defenders pressing the line of scrimmage to force the issue. Defenses attack points on the field, personnel, or formations in an attempt to disrupt the flow of the play, and, as a result, create big plays for the defense (i.e., fumbles, interceptions, sacks, minus yardage plays, etc). A drawback to the use of this aggressive mindset is that defenses leave themselves open to giving up big plays to the offense because of the need to use man coverage in many pressure schemes. Many teams are finding that to offset this liability, they can zone blitz. Some 3-4 teams, for example, are very adept at applying pressure, while backing it up with zone.

☐ *Combination*

Effective defenses have the capability to combine aggressive and read/react techniques within individual defensive calls. Within a particular defensive call, some defenders may be reading and reacting, while others run an aggressive maneuver. Even though basically three styles of defense exist, not many teams subscribe to a particular style 100 percent of the time. Teams that primarily use the read-and-react approach attempt to buy time until the offense makes a mistake (i.e., turnover, penalty, or missed assignment). Because physically overmatched teams can't use this philosophy, they may have to turn to an aggressive and pressing style of play, which could conceivably give them a chance to be successful. Even then, stunting should be used judiciously to avoid giving up chunk plays. As a rule, effective defenses use all three styles or philosophies: read and react, be aggressive and read, and combination.

Theories of Defensive Execution

Six different theories exist concerning how the defense seeks to shut down the offense. Each theory has advantages and disadvantages.

☐ *Base*

In a base look, defensive linemen are not slanting, linebackers are not stunting, and the secondary plays pass first with force rules well-defined.

Advantages:

- Simple
- Defensive mistakes held to a minimum.
- Fosters excellent team pursuit.

Disadvantages:

- Defense can be overmatched personnel-wise.
- Offensive blocking assignments will be well-defined.
- The offense dictates to the defense.

☐ *Stunting*

Stunting involves linemen moving from one position to another on the snap with linebackers and/or defensive backs crossing the line of scrimmage on the snap.

Advantages:

- Covers up mismatches.
- Element of surprise; defenders show up in unexpected areas.
- Confuses pass- and run-blocking schemes.
- Creates minus-yardage plays—tackles for loss/sacks.
- Free rushers at the quarterback
- Turnovers—fumbles and interceptions
- Defense dictates to the offense.

Disadvantages:

- Defenders can stunt themselves out of a play.
- Can result in lost gap integrity on missed assignments.
- Pursuit can suffer.
- Offense has the potential for a big play.

☐ *Angling*

Angling or slanting occurs when defensive linemen move from one position or alignment to another alignment on the snap. Defenders will either key the lineman they are slanting to and will feel the offensive lineman they originally aligned on, or they will charge into the assigned gap. Once the slant is executed, the defender will diagnose ball direction and get in a good pursuit angle.

Advantages:

- Element of surprise
- Confuses pass and run blocking schemes.
- What the offense sees pre-snap is not what they will get post-snap.
- Suits the skillset of smaller, more agile players.

Disadvantages:

- Pass rush can suffer with defenders working parallel instead of vertical.
- May slant away from the play.
- Effective zone blocking can pick up the slant.

☐ *Pre-Snap Movement*

Defenses present one look to the offense and then shift into another configuration just prior to the snap. This pre-snap movement can be done a number of ways. One way is the "move to," which begins on command. For example, on the "move" command, the defense can move as one from a 4-3 shell to a Bears (or 46) look. This is called a "move-to" defense. The same objective can be realized with a stem concept, where defenders move on their own from the 4-3 look to the 46 defense. With this look, players move individually, so a steady stream of players move in and out (or up and back); it isn't synchronized like the move-to call. Another simple pre-snap movement that could cause offensive problems is a simple individual move undertaken by only one or two defenders. This "prowl," which a player can be coached to do on his own, could necessitate an at-the-line-of-scrimmage blocking adjustment. For example, a defensive tackle in a 4-3 defense, moving from a 3 technique to a 4i technique alignment, presents the offense with a completely different defense.

Advantages:

- Surprise tactic.
- May force the offense to alter its cadence.
- Forces the offense to go on quick counts, which may eliminate checkoffs.
- May force the offense to run a lot of check-with-me calls, which could result in missed assignments.
- Confuses pass- and run-blocking schemes.

Disadvantages:

- The defense may be caught moving on a quick count.
- A defensive misalignment may result in an unmanned gap.
- Approach makes it harder for defenders to read pre-snap cues, such as offensive line stances.

☐ *Base-Stunt Combination*

A defense that combines base and stunt techniques on a particular play reaps the advantages and disadvantages of both styles.

☐ *Angling-Stunt Combination*

This theory has linemen slanting, while a linebacker or linebackers run a stunt either with or opposite the line charge. This premise has all the inherent advantages and disadvantages of both angling and stunting strategies.

Defensive Schemes

Similar to offensive formations, a number of combinations of formations can be employed to set up a defense. In each set-up, the defensive players have relatively specific alignments and assignments. The popularity of each of these set-ups, referred to as defensive schemes, tends to vary from team to team. As a coach, the basic key is to adopt a scheme that is compatible with the skillset of your players, your philosophy concerning how you want your team to play defense, and the defensive approach you believe gives your team the best chance for success. Each scheme has its strengths and vulnerabilities.

☐ 3-4-4

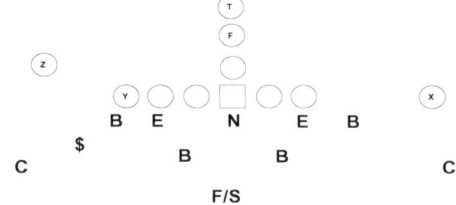

Figure 12-20

Strengths:

- Defense can be bend-but-don't-break, or an aggressive-upfield defense. This mix in philosophy can change from play to play.
- Defenders can be schemed using a two-gap technique or can be placed on the edge of offensive players and defend one gap.
- Defense is flexible enough to adjust to pro-type offenses with their attendant motions, multiple formations, and balanced run/pass game.
- Since most teams use the popular 4-3 defense, the 3-4 defense is hard to prepare for. Its unfamiliarity is an asset.
- The defense mentally stretches offenses with various alignments and different combinations of pass rushers.
- Defenses put more speed on the field with added linebackers.
- Eight men in two-point stances enhances the coverage package.
- Easy to incorporate nickel, dime, and quarter packages.

- Easy to get an eighth man in the box.
- Defense covers a center who is used to playing against an even front.
- A linebacker placed over the tight end can impede his release.

Weaknesses:

- Wide line splits can cause problems and isolate the nose tackle.
- Ends are in position to be double-teamed.
- Ends aligned primarily over the tackles can be outsized.
- An extra tight end adds an eighth gap to a seven-man front.
- Two bubbles exist over the guard areas.
- If the defense flip-flops with a strongside and weakside, problems can occur if the offense trades the tight end. The weak or quick side then has to play the strongside of the offense, and the strongside of the defense must play to the quick side of the offense. Mismatches may occur.

☐ 3-3-5

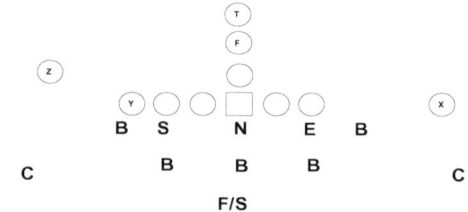

Figure 12-21

This defensive concept can either be a 3-3-5 with three linemen, three linebackers, and five defensive backs, or a 3-5-3 configuration with three linemen, five linebackers, and three defensive backs. The decision concerning which alignment to utilize depends upon your competition and roster.

Strengths:

- This scheme has many of the same benefits found in a 3-4 defense. As a matter of fact, the 3-4 and 3-3 can be interchangeable.
- Speed is placed on the field, with three linemen and eight defenders in a two-point stance.
- The defense can be designed as a two-gap scheme or one-gap defense.
- The base front is an eight-man look.
- A 3-on-2 ratio is employed off tackle.
- The tight end can be covered to impede his pass release.
- This defense allows a multitude of rushers in different combinations.
- It includes the availability of line slants with possible linebacker blitzes.
- Uniqueness of the defense makes it unfamiliar to offenses.

Weaknesses:

- Many of the deficiencies found in the 3-4 are also found in the 3-3.
- Offenses will pass against 3-5 (five linebackers).
- Offenses will run against 3-3 (five defensive backs).
- Effective zone-blocking teams can pick up line slants.
- Nose can be isolated with aggressive line splits.
- Tight end trades are effective versus flip-flopping personnel.

☐ *46 Bears Defense*

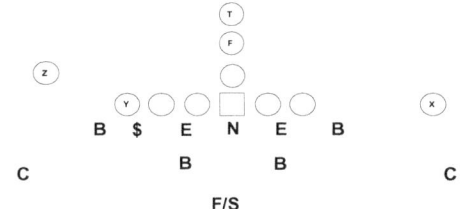

Figure 12-22

This defensive scheme was popularized by the Chicago Bears teams of the 1980s.

Strengths:

- Offers a great change-up or change-of-pace to an even-front defense.
- Adaptable to any defensive system, 5-2, 3-4, 3-3, 4-3, 6-1, and split-4 systems are all receptive to the Bears' look.
- Limits an offense's game plan so that offensive coordinators can't use all of their playbook.
- Forces major adjustments in run/pass-blocking schemes.
- Can be used versus a wide variety of offensive philosophies (power I, wing-T, run-and-shoot, pro I, etc).
- Can be used in any field zone.
- Is applicable for any down-and-distance situation.
- Can result in a five-man overload or a balanced 4-4 ratio, given the placement of the nose.
- With eight potential rushers within five yards of the ball, presents an eight-man look.
- Applies pressure without stunting.
- Pressures quarterbacks by alignment.
- Has a wide and varied stunt package.

- Offers a wide and varied coverage package.
- Enables second-level defenders free to run to the ball because it is difficult for blockers to get to the second level.
- Is a great way to get pressure on first and second down without stunting.
- Outnumbers the offense from tackle to tackle.
- Can be beneficial for teams that may not have exceptional team speed.
- Speeds up fast players.
- Includes two outside-edge rushers.
- Has a three-on-three match-up in the middle.
- Precludes the offense from double-teaming the best pass rusher.
- Funnels all runs to the middle of the defense.

Weaknesses:

- Effective dive-option games can exploit this scheme.
- Off-tackle power plays with angle blocks can hurt.
- Must be able to cover the tight end with a linebacker unless the defense subs a nickelback.
- The defense is predictable coverage-wise, if it predominantly uses man-free coverage.

 4-3-4

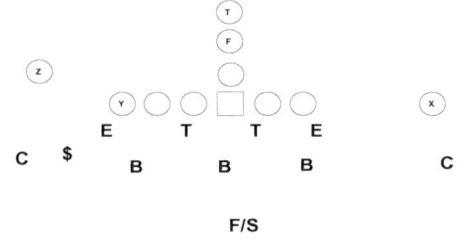

Figure 12-23

The 4-3 may be the most popular defensive scheme on every competitive level of football.

Strengths:

- Allows a wide and varied assortment of coverage packages. Man, zone, and combination coverages are used.
- A flexible and effective stunt package is available.
- A small and quick team can be effective with an aggressive mindset since this defense allows more speed on the field.
- Nine men in the box is possible.
- In many instances, defensive tackles will be larger than offensive guards.
- The offense's biggest players, the tackles, must be able to operate in space.
- The offensive tackles must be able to block quick and agile ends in space.
- If the strong defensive end is placed on the tight end, he can harass the tight end's pass release.
- Since no defender is in the C gap, the tight end and tackle cannot double-team.
- Defenders, who are usually aligned on the edge of blockers, are assigned one gap, which allows smaller, quicker defenders to be successful.

Weaknesses:

- Offenses will trap and draw if the defense is pressing the line of scrimmage with a vertical mindset.
- The addition of a second tight end adds an eighth gap to be defended by seven defenders.

- Three bubbles exist. Two bubbles are in the off-tackle areas with the third over the center.
- Wide line splits between the guards widens the defensive tackles.
- If the defense is built on speed, offenses with a power running game can be successful.
- Because of its popularity, offenses have seen it before (usually several times a year).

☐ *4-2-5 Nickel or Dime Defense*

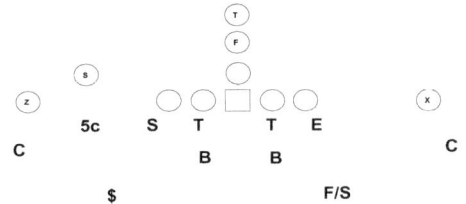

Figure 12-24

Some teams employ the 4-2 as their base, while others use it in long-yardage situations.

Strengths:

- Can employ six or seven defensive backs.
- Field speed is enhanced with all of these defensive backs on the team.
- Defenses can use outside linebackers at the end position.
- Inside linebackers can be utilized at the tackle positions.

Weaknesses:

- Not as effective against the run, given the number of defensive backs on the field.
- Only six defenders are in the box.

☐ *Nickel or Dime 3-3 Defense*

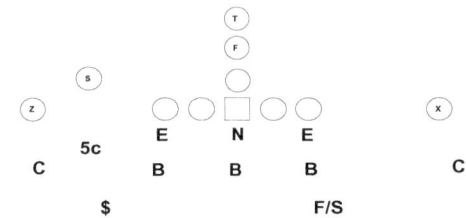

Figure 12-25

A number of teams use the 3-3 scheme as their nickel package (Figure 12-25). This odd look is a more effective change-up than the even spacing of the 4-2 package. Many of the same advantages and weaknesses are inherent in the 3-3 package as in the 4-2 look.

☐ *Wide-Tackle 6 Defense*

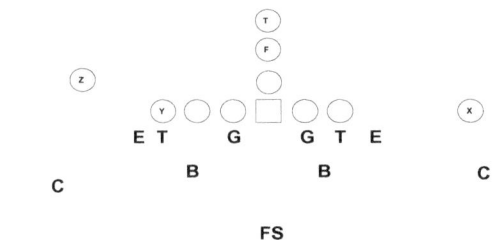

Figure 12-26

Strengths:

- Base is an eight-man front.
- Guards can shade the offensive guard inside, outside, or head up.
- Tackles can shade the offensive end inside, outside, or head up.
- Ends are in great position to contain wide runs or sprint passes.

- Ends are in great position to play bootlegs, counters, and reverses.
- Defense is flexible enough to adjust to offensive sets.
- A multitude of stunts are available.
- Defense can easily shift to a 7-1 look, with a linebacker on the LOS over center.
- Tackle can hold up the tight end's release.
- Defense is very strong in the C gap with a 3-1 ratio.
- Position of the tackle eliminates the double-team in the off-tackle area.

Weaknesses:

- Engage with the defensive guards by running outside if the guards align in A gap.
- Engage with the defensive guards by running inside if the guards align in B gap.
- Engage with the defensive tackles by running outside if they align inside the blocker.
- Engage with the defensive tackles by running inside if they align outside the blocker.
- Offensive-guard splits can weaken the middle.
- Offense has a 3-2 ratio in the middle.
- Quick hitters, sneaks, and wedges are effective in A gaps.
- Short trap game is effective, especially with good line splits.
- Tackles should have the speed and agility to contain the quarterback.
- If the end is a true end, he may have to play in space.
- Inside-outside fold blocks are effective.

☐ *Split-6 Defense*

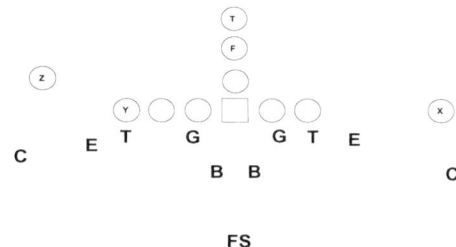

Figure 12-27

In many respects, this defensive scheme is similar to the wide-tackle-6 package.

Strengths:

- Inside linebackers are protected.
- 4-3 ratio favors the defense in the middle.
- Offers a very effective stunt game.
- It is easy to get a wide-tackle-6 look by reducing the guards and widening the linebackers.
- Provides good contain versus wide runs or sprint passes.
- An eight man front.

Weaknesses:

- Can be successful in the middle area with the addition of an extra blocker (isolation).
- Sneak and wedge plays are effective, especially on short-yardage and goal-line plays.
- Inside-outside fold blocks are effective.
- If the defensive guards are outside, can run inside.
- If the defensive guards are inside, can run outside.
- Guards can be double-teamed.

- Tackles may have to contain on level-three passes.
- Flat areas are weak.

☐ *Stack 4-4 Defense*

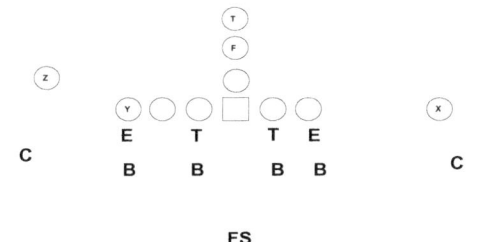

Figure 12-28

The stack 4-4 can be used as a change up from the split-6 and wide-tackle-6 packages. A 4-3 defense can easily present a stack 4, with an eight-men-in-the-box look, by sliding the linebackers to the tight end and inserting the free safety as a linebacker to the weakside, or shading the linebackers weak and walking down the strong safety to linebacker depth.

Strengths:

- Eight-man front.
- Hard to block stacked linebackers.
- Easy to get into a wide-tackle-6, split-6, or gap-8 configuration.
- Each gap is threatened.
- Line slants are good, especially from head-up alignments.
- Good package for smaller, quicker players.
- Linebacker positions can be interchangeable with other linebackers or defensive backs inserted.
- Forces offense to block area instead of man to man.
- Difficult to prepare for.

Weaknesses:

- Flat areas are weak.
- Must play a lot of man coverage unless defensive coordinators dilute the core of the defense.
- Effective zone blocking can nullify parts of the stunt package.

☐ *Gap-8 Defense*

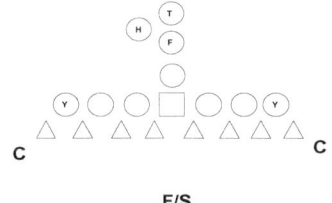

Figure 12-29

A gap-8 look is effective in short-yardage or goal-line situations.

Strengths:

- Each gap is filled.
- Penetration is a high priority.
- Forces minimum offensive-line splits.

Weaknesses:

- Plays that break the line of scrimmage are usually successful.
- Pursuit is poor.
- With all-out penetration, trap plays are effective. Quick-hitting traps with the center turning back are highly effective, especially with no middle linebacker.
- Is susceptible to a down block and kick-out in C gap.

PUTTING IT ALL TOGETHER

In many instances, football is a fairly straightforward game. For example, the underlying premise of the game is clear-cut—the winner of a game is the team that outscores its opponent. If a team can't score, it can't win ... hence, the importance coaches place on defense.

The fundamental role of the defense is to stop the offense from scoring and to do what it can to regain possession of the ball. Regardless of whether the defense is facing a "running" team or a "passing" team, it addresses this responsibility in three specific ways—intercepting passes, recovering fumbled balls, or causing three-and-outs.

Defending the Run

Arguably, the long-held football expression, "some teams can beat you through the air, but every team can beat you on the ground," has merit. Accordingly, regardless of the focal mindset of the offense (running, passing, or multiplicity), the first consideration of the defense should be to stop the run, which will make the offense one-dimensional. It should be noted that even passing teams feel the need to be able to run the ball, to some extent, in order to be successful.

Truth be known, there is no one-size-fits-all approach to successfully defending the run. There are, however, a variety of factors and elements that should be considered that can be helpful in that regard, including the following:

- Determine the type of run game your opponent employs (e.g., option, power, wing-T, pro-style, etc.).
- Scheme to take away what the offense likes to do by formation, down-and-distance, field zone, etc.
- Undertake the basic adjustments that have the best chance of stopping the offense's best 3-4 run plays.
- Strategize to win the numbers game in the box to take on the run.
- Be aware that a team's pass coverage can have an impact on its ability to defend the run. For example, if its corners match up well with the offensive wideouts and can cover them with little or no help, its safeties can be committed to the run and be inserted into the box.
- Attack the offense by varying the shades of the defensive linemen or making adjustments in the alignments of the linebacker.
- Design a defensive game plan that addresses run force. Tie in the run force with the pass coverage. Analyze the offense's perimeter run game, including the basic blocking schemes it utilizes (e.g., stalk, crack, run-off, crossing, etc.). Have three elements of pursuit in place to meet the outside run in its formative stage:
  - Primary force—make the tackle force the cutback, or drive the ball deep.
  - Cutback—fit between the primary force and the first inside-pursuit defender.
  - Secondary support—responsible for a run-pass; never crosses the LOS or comes up on a run until the ball crosses the LOS or until he replaces a defender who is being cracked.
- Consider your most aggressive and strongest players for the front seven of the defense.

Defending the Pass

Successful pass defense is the epitome of "team concept." Effective pass defense requires contributions from all parts of the defense. While each part is independent, collectively, they collaborate to get the job done.

The defensive line rushes the quarterback and applies pressure. The linebackers and secondary cover. Concurrently, each group feeds off the other. For the coverage unit to be successful, the defensive line must exert pressure on the quarterback and not allow him to hold the ball and wait for one or more of his receivers to come open. Conversely, the coverage defenders can cause the QB to hold the ball longer with good coverage, which enhances the likelihood of the pass rushers being able to get to him. In other words, the more effective the rush, the better the coverage. In turn, the more effective the coverage, the better the rush.

☐ *Pass Rush Objectives*

One of the major responsibilities for defensive linemen is to rush the passer. As in any endeavor, attitude is vital. The coach must define success. If players think the only definition of pass rush success is a sack, a lot of players are going to be disappointed. Players should understand that success can mean many things. A list of possible successful objectives for pass rushers includes the following:

- Squeeze the quarterback's area. The ends attack his upfield shoulder. The tackles attack the near number. The goal is to force the QB closer to another rusher.
- Don't allow the quarterback to go to the second receiver.
- Force him out of the launch point. However, contain an athletic quarterback.
- Force the quarterback to throw on the run.
- Make the quarterback aware of pressure.
- Inside rushers push the pocket to reduce the quarterback's ability to step up. Outside rushers force the quarterback to step up.
- Sack the quarterback.
- The ultimate contribution is the trifecta. Get to the quarterback, force a fumble, then scoop and score.

Even if a pass rusher cannot reach the quarterback, he can still be beneficial to an effective pass rush. A rusher simply getting his hands up is a benefit to the rush. The objectives when getting the hands up include:

- Divert the quarterback's attention.
- Bat the ball down.
- Tip the ball for an interception.
- Force a bad throw.
- Force the quarterback to tuck the ball and run.
- Force the elevation of the pass.
- Make the quarterback move his feet, which throws off his timing.
- Throw off the receiver's timing.
- Obstruct the quarterback's vision.

Even if the pass is delivered, there can still be positive results for the defense, if defensive linemen disengage and aggressively pursue the play. The possible objectives when covering after the ball is thrown include:

- Knock the ball loose from the receiver.
- Gang tackle.
- Get in position to block for an interception.

☐ *Pass Rush Tips*

Anticipation in the pass rush is vital. Players should know the down-and-distance situation and the game plan. Field position and down-and-distance are tipoffs. Immediate pass recognition predicated on offensive movement comes from preparation in practice. What moves first? In some cases, a quarterback's body part may move just prior to the snap. For example, the quarterback may move his foot just before the snap. Some quarterbacks will open their hands just before the center-quarterback exchange. Players should also watch for the blocker's head to pop up (high helmet).

Quickness and decisiveness of the initial move are important to the pass rush. Coordination of the rusher's hands, feet, and head movements make all the difference. Rushers should keep momentum going toward the passer. A one-move, one-counter mindset is key, since seldom is there time for multiple moves. The clock is ticking. Rushers should be quick and decisive on their initial move.

Effective rushers get their hands inside the blocker, while keeping their shoulders forward of the feet to prevent the blocker from getting under the rusher's pad level. An effective rusher never shows his numbers and should not give up his chest to the blocker.

Linemen should keep their eyes on the quarterback, while head, hands, and feet get them there. A competent rusher runs through the quarterback and tackles him high. Cage players make the quarterback step up by staying on the quarterback's upfield shoulder. The tackles attack the near number.

If the rusher hasn't reached the quarterback, he should get his hands up, as the quarterback starts to throw. He should stay out of the blocker's middle by working half-man on the blocker and applying pressure to the blocker's outside shoulder, while staying in the assigned rush lane. Working down the middle of the protector turns into a strength tactic, which takes time. The clock is running, and a rusher has no time to wrestle with the blocker.

Pass rushers must understand that the right arm works with the right leg and the left arm works with the left leg. They must close the critical area with speed and quickness, allowing no separation between rusher and blocker by making pass rush moves at an arm's distance.

The offensive man's only ally is distance. The pass rusher must run in straight lines, keeping his feet, weight, and upper body going forward (i.e., advance—don't dance). Rushers should try to make offensive linemen move their feet. Once a lineman makes a stand, however, he should use his leverage to defensive advantage (i.e., if the blocker pushes, the defender pulls; or if the blocker pulls, the defender turns him). Sound pass rushers take advantage of offensive pass sets. Among the effective ways to attack various pass block techniques are the following:

- *Soft deep set:* The defender should use an early power rush.
- *Hard set (blocker pops up):* The defender should make the blocker move his feet. Speed moves or a run-around are good. Also, the blocker is open to a push-pull move.
- *Head or shoulders are down:* The defender should use a quick swim.
- *Leaps forward:* The defender should use a quick swim or run-around.

- *Deep setter:* The rusher should use a power move. Also, the blocker can be beaten inside using a spin, hump, or foot fake.
- *Chaser:* The defender should run around the blocker.
- *Rider:* The defender should get low and speed rush. However, he shouldn't allow himself to be ridden past the quarterback.
- *Sets and cuts:* This technique is employed by shorter offensive players or on three-step passes. Effective use of hands by the rusher is vital. The defender should use a limp-leg technique, and get the hands up. The ball is coming out quick on the three-step drop.

As a general rule, rushers should use finesse moves on power blockers, and utilize power moves on finesse blockers.

☐ *Pass Blocker's Pressure Point*

Rushers should see the pressure point of the blocker, which is the inside or outside shoulder of the blocker, depending upon which lane the defender is pursuing. Tips on engaging the blocker's pressure point include the following:

- The rusher should keep his hands inside the blocker's hands.
- The rusher should never stop his feet. He should always work north and south. He should never chop his feet or bring them back to parallel.
- The rusher should stay tight to the blocker (half-man). Once the rusher disengages from the blocker, he should accelerate to the quarterback.
- If the blocker sets short and soft, the rusher should use a power rush.
- The rusher should feel the pressure point of the blocker. If he leans, the rusher should pull. If he squats, the defender should push.
- Versus a hold, the rusher should grab his wrist and lift and follow with a rip move.
- When being driven past the quarterback by the blocker, the rusher can use a power rush by pointing his toes toward the quarterback and bull-rushing. Counter pass rush moves are automatic at the quarterback level. The worst place to be is behind the quarterback.

☐ *Speed Rush Tips*

Speed rushers should have a big first step with a four-yard spot behind the blocker as the target spot. The rusher will decide at that point which move to use. This is the critical area. If the rusher gets to the target spot and he is deeper than the blocker, he should continue on with a speed move. To do this, the rusher should simply take his inside hand and press the blocker's hand down and turn the corner. The goal of a speed rush is to turn the shoulders of the blocker, which weakens his ability to stay strong. Rushers should plant the "seed of speed." When the blocker becomes concerned about a speed rush, he is open to other pass rush moves.

Rushers can use speed, alignment, and technique to turn the shoulders of the blocker. If the rusher can get hip-to-hip with the blocker, he has a decided advantage. Anytime the hips are even and the rusher is facing the quarterback, the blocker should not be able to prevent the rusher from bursting to the quarterback without an obvious holding infraction. The previous information on pass play is generic in nature. These principles and concepts are applicable to any defensive system.

☐ *Pass Rush Concepts*

For every defensive call, there will be well-defined cage responsibilities. Cage players must reach the quarterback and squeeze the pocket, making a quarterback step up. Cage defenders must be very careful when using an underneath path on a blocker on a pass rush move (a spin move, for example). The defense must have solid cage with pressure calls, since most quarterbacks try to escape outside. The quarterback cannot be allowed to escape; cage players must make him stay in the pocket.

Most defensive systems specify inside pressure lanes on both sides of the ball. These lanes will be filled according to the defense, stunt, or pressure called. All pass rushers should understand the concept of balance and containment. Defenders cannot be freelancers. Everyone should know their responsibility.

☐ *Types of Coverages*

One of the most important decisions you can make when putting your defense together is what type of pass coverages to use. Most coverages can be categorized into one of four basic types—zone, man-to-man, combination, and blitz. Each type has its pros and cons. While most defenses employ components of each type, at one time or another during the course of the game, teams are usually more proficient in one coverage than in the others. The two main types of pass coverages, zone and man-to-man, have their own advantages andDisadvantages:

Advantages of Zone Coverages:

- Defends the field.
- Makes the ball the issue.
- Offers better run support.
- Allows defenders to better see the ball and break when the ball is thrown.
- May give up completions but shouldn't allow deep completions. Hard to blow the top off the coverage.
- Makes the offense go the long field.
- Results in more interceptions than man coverage because all defenders see and rally to the ball.
- Gang tackling is better in zone than man.
- Less talented players can be used.
- Handles crossing routes, picks, and rub-offs better than man coverage.

Disadvantages of Zone Coverages:

- Defenses must get pressure with a base rush.
- Quarterback has time to throw. He can get in a rhythm.
- Allows a high completion rate.
- Pass-protection schemes allow help to be given to offensive linemen.
- Zones can be flooded.

Advantages of Man Coverages:

- The ball is the issue.
- Completion rate is lower.
- Defense can use numbers to attack protection schemes.
- Various games and stunts are available.
- Added number of rushers pressure the quarterback. The result is hurried passes and sacks.

- Quarterback may have to hold the ball longer, waiting for a receiver to break free.
- With tighter coverage, the quarterback must be more accurate.
- Man coverage is better in short and medium down-and-distance situations.
- A linebacker can insert or drop to find work, if his assigned man blocks.
- Insertion of a linebacker when his man blocks can disrupt screens.

Disadvantages of Man Coverages:

- Requires more athletic players.
- Completions usually mean long gains.
- Interceptions are less likely because more defenders will have their back to the ball.
- Defenders can be isolated. Mismatches can occur.
- A scrambling quarterback is a problem to underneath defenders as they usually have their backs to the ball.
- Coverage busts are more costly than zone. There may be no help in man coverage.
- Offenses can use play-action to present a conflict between run/pass responsibilities.
- Mismatches are possible, especially with formational changes or motion.
- The defense must get to the quarterback with pressure or defenders will be left high and dry.
- The strong safety may give away the coverage by his alignment on the tight end.
- Underthrown deep route is harder to play in man.

☐ *Base Coverage Packages*

Certain basic coverage packages are commonly part of the defensive system in most defenses. These packages, which are shown from only one defensive formation in the following diagrams, feature coverages that can be adapted to most defensive alignments. Among the more popular of these coverage packages are cover 2, cover 3, cover 4, and cover 1.

Cover 2

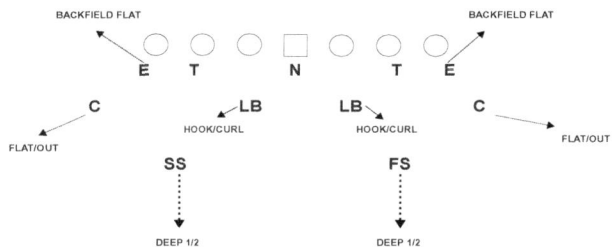

Figure 12-30

The cover 2 is a two-deep zone defense. This simply means that there are two defenders responsible for the deepest zone. They each are responsible for half of the field in that zone.

- This alignment has two safeties, who are responsible for the deep zone.
- The linebackers are responsible for the middle intermediate and short zones.
- The cornerbacks are responsible for the outside intermediate zone.
- The defensive ends will pick up the flat in the backfield.

Cover 3

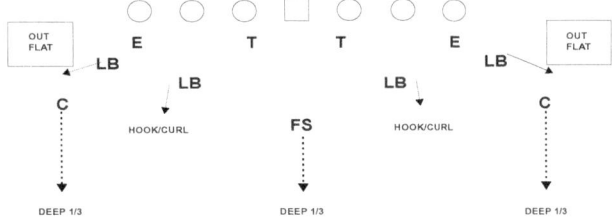

Figure 12-31

The cover 3 is a three-deep zone defense. This simply means that there are three defenders responsible for the deepest zone. They each are responsible for one-third of the field in that zone.

- This alignment entails one safety and two cornerbacks who are responsible for the deep zone.
- The linebackers are responsible for the middle, intermediate, and short zones.
- The outside linebackers are responsible for the out and flat zones.

Cover 4

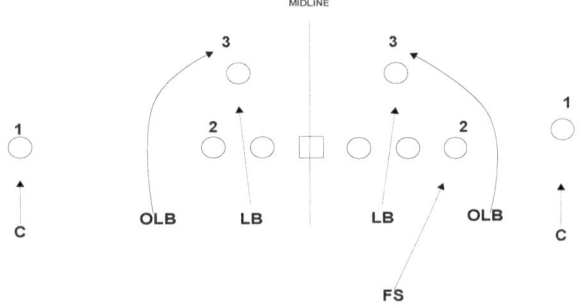

Figure 12-32

A cover 4 defense, also referred to as quarters coverage, is a four-deep, three-under zone defense. It utilizes man-to-man principles, while creating opportunities for both safeties (the free safety and the strong safety) to double (i.e., bracket) the two best wide receivers of the offense.

- This alignment employs a standard four-deep look (two cornerbacks and two safeties).
- The corners are positioned 7-8 yards from the LOS, while the safeties are aligned at 10-12 yards off the ball.
- This alignment also has two underneath flat defenders and a linebacker playing the "middle-hook area" to wall off any inside-breaking receiver.

Cover 1

A cover 1 defense, also called man defense, entails having every potential receiver covered by a defender, using a man-to-man technique. In this situation, all defensive linemen have a pass-rush mentality. The linebackers and the defensive backs are responsible for coverage. There will always be one or two cover defenders (linebackers or defensive backs) who may not have a cover responsibility. In these instances, they will either rush the passer, cover a hot zone, or double-cover a receiver.

To determine which receiver the defender will cover, they must communicate. The best way to do this is to label every potential receiver. A very common way to do this would be to number the eligible receivers as shown in Figure 12-33. First, the offense is split in half, using the midline as the dividing point. Then, every eligible receiver is numbered, starting from each sideline and ending at the midline.

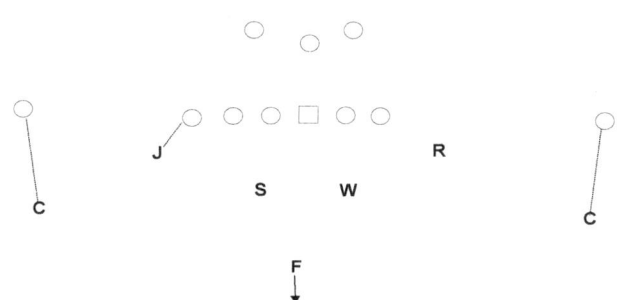

Figure 12-33

Most defenders will know which receiver they are responsible for when their coverage package is called in the huddle. If there is any confusion, they can communicate with each other by pointing and by calling out a receiver's number.

☐ *Designing a System to Defend the Pass*

Before a scheme and system to defeat the opponent's passing game is developed, the coach should first understand how the offensive signal caller studies the defense. To stop the opponent's passing game, the coach should understand what the offense is looking for and how it will address his team. A typical offensive breakdown of the defense would include the following information:

- Basic defensive philosophy.
- Coverages by down-and-distance.
- Coverages by field zone.
- Coverages by offensive formation.
- Personnel pass/drop ratios.
- Blitz coverages.
- Defensive adjustments to motion. How does motion affect factors such as force, coverages, blitzes, and so forth?
- How do the wideouts match up with the corners?
- Where is a height or speed mismatch likely?
- Who is the best and worst cover man? The offense will seek profitable match-ups.
- How effective is the underneath coverage?
- How do running backs match up with linebackers?
- Short-yardage coverages.
- Two-minute coverages.
- Substitution packages.
- Five- and ten-cent coverages.
- Prevent defense.

- However you decide your team should defend the pass, your plan should: Fit into the basic scheme.
- Fit the personnel.
- Be teachable.
- Be adjustable to all formations and motions.
- Have sound run support. All the elements should be in place (i.e., primary force, cutback, and secondary support).
- Avoid easy pre-snap reads by the quarterback.
- Be able to take away an offense's best receiver, which can be done through personnel match-ups, double coverage, rolls, or help schemes.
- Pressure and disrupt when desired.

CHAPTER 13

HOW TO DEVELOP A SPECIAL TEAMS UNIT

One of the most accepted axioms in football is that "football is a game of inches," which underscores the importance of field position. The further your opponent has to travel to score, the greater the chance your defense has in stopping them.

Successful teams usually win the battle of field position. The biggest change of field tends to occur on a special teams play. Large chunks of field position are often gained or lost on a special teams play. Coaches who do not believe that special teams play is as important as offense or defense provide opponents with a competitive edge.

The potential significance—and fun—of special teams play, goes well beyond field position. Aggressive special teams play not only can help set the tempo (pace) of the game, it can change the momentum of the game, if and when a "big play" occurs. Sound special teams play also can help instill confidence and mental discipline in your players.

It is also important to be aware of the fact that a special teams down is not like a down on offense or defense. A bad play on special teams can lead to disaster. More often than not, such a situation involves a one-and-done scenario. In contrast, the impact of a bad play on offense (e.g., being tackled behind the line of scrimmage) or defense (e.g., being fooled on a trick play) may be temporary, lasting only as long as the next down.

Successful special teams play is no different than either offense or defense. It requires planning and action. Both aspects start at the top—with you, the head coach. You have to realize how critical special teams play is to the overall success of your *team*. You have to be committed to prepare your special teams to be effective, including devoting sufficient practice time to this phase of the game.

SPECIAL TEAMS UNITS

As with any other phase of a football game, give adequate time and energy to special teams. Such an investment will pay off. On the other hand, less than an appropriate level of commitment on your part will shrink your chance for success.

The organization and execution of your special teams units should not be an afterthought. After all, 20 to 30 percent of all plays in a game involve the kicking game. Statistics indicate that approximately 30 percent of all points in a game come from special teams. Your special teams units will often play a significant role in your team's success.

As with any other phase of a football game, you must be able to teach the players on your special teams units how to undertake their responsibilities in the right way, each and every time. Among the assorted skills and movements you must address are the following:

- Catch a kickoff
- Cover the kickoff
- Return the kickoff
- Punt
- Snap for a punt
- Catch a punt
- Cover a punt
- Block for a punt
- Block a punt
- Kick an extra point
- Snap for an extra point
- Hold for an extra point
- Block for an extra point
- Block an extra point
- Kick a field goal
- Snap for a field goal
- Hold for a field goal
- Block for a field goal
- Cover a field goal attempt
- Block a field goal

In general, a team will have up to 10 special teams units, six core and four supplemental. Depending on the circumstances and your philosophy, the supplemental units are optional.

Core

- Kickoff cover team
- Kickoff return team
- Punt team
- Punt return team
- Field goal and extra point team
- Field goal and extra point block team

Supplemental

- Onside kickoff team
- Hands team
- Punt-fake team
- Field goal/PAT-fake team

Kickoff Cover Team

- *Objectives.* To give the defense good field position by keeping the receiving team as close to its own goal line as possible; to create turnovers.
- *Specialist.* A kicker who kicks the ball to the goal line with good hang time to delay the return and allow the coverage to get down the field. He must also keep the kick inbounds.
- *Team.* Fast and sure tacklers who stay evenly spaced.

The primary goal for the kickoff cover unit is to stop the return as deep as possible. To achieve this objective, the ball must be kicked deep, and the coverage players must sprint from the start of the ball being kicked, be aggressive, and be fundamentally sound tacklers.

☐ *Coverage Guidelines:*

- It is imperative that everyone stays onside. Everyone must stay behind the kicker. The kickoff team should reach the line as a unit at full speed.
- The unit's goal is to be aggressive, tackle well, and either cause a turnover or make the tackle as close as possible to where the ball is caught.
- The coverage must be an all-out sprint from the start.
- At the "contact point," the ball must be leveraged from the outside-in. Everyone should squeeze down the running lane as fast as possible, but under enough control to make the tackle.
- It is important that every member of the kickoff team stays in his coverage lane only as long as it takes to read the return. When an opponent seeks to block early, they avoid him by releasing past his backside hip and then quickly get back into their lanes. Each member of the kickoff unit should use his hands and push off blockers who cross his path. If the ballcarrier is within 10 yards, everyone must stay in their lane and move the blocker down the middle, using their hands to control him. Everyone must shed the blocker quickly and either slide laterally to make the tackle or run him into the returner if he is in a backpedal.
- The contain men must stay outside the other 21 players on the field. They should keep the other 21 players on their inside shoulder and in front of them. If the ball comes toward them, they should turn it back inside. If the ball goes away from them, they should check for a reverse and then pursue.
- Safeties must stay behind the other 20 players. They should keep the ball in front of them and between them and the other safety, or between them and the sideline if the return is to the sideline.
- Everyone must have the presence to feel where the ball is being returned. The "return indicator" may help. This can provide everyone with a jump on adjusting their coverage lanes. Members of this unit must avoid the blockers and find the return lane.
- If someone gets blocked, he cannot stay blocked. The kickoff-cover unit cannot trade one-for-one. Each player should engage two opponents.
- Players on this unit must never follow a teammate downfield. If a member of the kickoff cover unit comes off a release and sees a teammate crossing in front of him, he should work to the open lane.
- The first man to the ball should try to make a controlled tackle on the ballcarrier, attempting to: first, make the tackle; second, cause a fumble; and third, slow him by forcing him to change his course. This technique will give his teammates time to get there and make the tackle. The ball should be covered. Turnovers should be created.
- They must tackle with balance and control. Gang tackling is a mark of effective kickoff coverage.
- The reason a player is on the kickoff team is that he is one of the fastest and fundamentally sound tacklers on the *team*.
- They should hustle and pursue with enthusiasm.
- This unit must get past the front-five blockers.

Kickoff Return Team

> - *Objective.* To return every kickoff to at least their own 30-yard line.
> - *Return specialist.* Returners with speed, the ability to catch every kicked ball, and the desire to make a big play.
> - *Team.* Open-field blockers who will block on the run. This group includes players who make good decisions on squib and bloop kicks.

The primary goal for the kickoff return unit is to gain possession of the ball in good position when the play is over. Each player has a job to do and has to do it penalty-free.

☐ *Return Guidelines (All Players)*

- The kickoff return team fields all kicks, remembering that it is a free ball after it travels 10 yards. The returner must down or return the ball unless he is sure it is going out of bounds.
- Members of the kickoff return team need to see the ball kicked. They need to know the direction of the kick to set their blocks properly. They must also react to surprise onside kicks, squibs, and bloops.
- They must block in front and above the waist. Clipping or an illegal block in the back or below the waist puts players at risk of injury. A player must hold off if he cannot block an opponent legally.
- After making an initial block, they try to block a second player as close to the ballcarrier as possible, but never behind the ballcarrier.
- The front five blockers must have the desire to spring their kick returner for a long run.
- The front-five blockers must be able to "contact-fit" and stay with their blocks.
- The members of the kickoff return unit may fair catch a kickoff that is a bloop or pooch kick.
- Members of this unit should always anticipate an onside kick, especially if the other team is kicking off from midfield following a penalty on the return *team.*

☐ *Position Guidelines for the Front Five (Center, Guards, and Tackles)*

- Never line up directly in front of the ball. Always offset to avoid a hard kick directly at them
- Always expect either a hard kick at them or an onside kick. Fall on the onside kick. Let the hard kick go by them.
- Know their blocking assignment. Make the correct count, usually 1 through 10, from right to left. Communicate with their teammates.
- Align behind the front restraining line until the ball is kicked.
- After they see the ball kicked deep, turn and sprint back to their blocking point. Find their assigned player. It is important that they see the direction and distance of the kick.
- Make their blocks at least 5 to 10 yards in front of the second-level blockers.
- Listen and look for calls requiring them to adjust their blocking angle.
- The center is responsible for noticing directional kicks by the laces on the ball, and/or the position of the kicker.
- When the center yells "squib" or "bloop," the front five should short set (i.e., drop only 10 yards before turning to block).

☐ *Position Guidelines for Second-Level Blockers*

- Always be alert for line-drive kicks, bloop kicks, squib kicks, and onside kicks.
- Have a designated blocker to make the calls (squib, short, etc.).
- Be good blockers, runners, and ball handlers.
- Listen for calls to adjust their blocking responsibility.
- See where the ball is kicked (during flight) and get into position to block.
- Never back up to catch a kick; they should only catch balls kicked in front of them when the returner doesn't call for it.

☐ *Position Guidelines for the Returners*

Most teams employ two return men, who typically position themselves side by side.

- Practice sound fundamentals when handling the ball. Look the ball into the hands. Tuck it away tight (four points of pressure). Get in the habit of keeping a tight grip on the nose of the ball with the fingers and hands. Put pressure on the rear of the ball with the elbow and arm. Learn to run with the ball in a secure position. Let the ball swing back and forth in a natural rhythm and keep the ball in close to the body with pressure tightly applied front and rear. When trapped, bring the ball in close and protect it with both hands. Focusing on these fundamentals in practice will help them to become second nature.
- Handle all kickoffs (unless they're "short" kicks). Any muffed kickoff into the end zone needs to be covered and downed. If the opponent recovers the ball in the end zone, it is a touchdown.
- If bringing a ball out of the end zone, continue to return it upfield. Going back into the end zone will give the opponent a safety (whether the ballcarrier downs the ball or is tackled).
- A cool head is required in the job. Always be thinking.
- A bouncing kickoff that ricochets off a returner or one of his teammates into the end zone can be downed there for a touchback.
- Watch the kicker's angle to anticipate a corner kick. Also, notice where the laces of the ball are pointing. Be thinking about what to do if the kickoff goes into a corner of the field. The center will help by raising his hand to the side of the kick.
- Catching a kick going forward is one basic fundamental of achieving good returns. Because the kicking team knows this fundamental, as well, they frequently try to prevent it from happening by kicking the ball to the corner. If they can get the returner to field the ball going sideways or backward, his momentum will be effectively slowed.
- Another tactic to neutralize a good kick returner is to squib kick. A returner should field these types of balls as quickly as possible and get as many yards as possible.
- A kick that goes into the end zone requires good judgment regarding whether the returner should run it out. Players should talk to each other. The height of the kick should also help the returner make the appropriate decision. The yard line the ball has been kicked from is another consideration.
- Know the kicker (e.g., where he puts the ball, average distance, height, and hang time).

- Be conscious of the wind. Is the ball being kicked with or against it? How strong is the wind?
- Talk to each other to be sure who is catching the ball. The "right returner," for example, should give a loud and clear "you … you … you" or "me … me … me" call. He should pound his chest with his right hand on "me … me," and point with his left hand on "you … you."
- Know the coverage—how the kickoff team comes down the field and any habits they may have.
- Play smart.
- Have fun.
- Give a best effort.
- Finish the play.

Punt Team

> - *Objectives.* To gain good field position; to allow fewer than three yards per return; to force a fair catch; to cause a fumble and recover it; to down the ball as close to the opponent's goal line as possible.
> - *Specialists.* A punter who gets good height and distance and also consistently places the ball on or inside the 10-yard line; a center who makes an accurate snap every time.
> - *Team.* Speed is necessary to get to the ballcarrier. Block first, maintain spacing, and never follow the same colored jersey. Break down and then gang tackle—block—release—cover—tackle.

Nowhere in football is field position gained or lost as rapidly as it is in the punting game. Some coaches believe the punt is the most important play in football. The punt team has three primary responsibilities: protect the punter, punt the ball, and cover the punt.

☐ *Factors That Help Minimize Net Yardage on Punts:*

- Good snap
- Firm protection
- High-hanging punt
- Aggressive coverage
- Sound tackling

☐ *Pre-Snap Guidelines:*

- Be ready on the sideline on third down.
- Huddle on the sideline for any special instructions.
- Hustle onto the field and get lined up quickly.
- Take the proper split and stance, and listen to the calls.
- See the ball with peripheral vision and move on the snap.
- Communicate clearly, when necessary.

☐ *Personal Protector Guidelines:*

- The designated personal protector should look to make sure that his teammates are on the field in proper position. He then makes a "ready" call to alert the team to listen to his calls.
- Initially, the personal protector should make a front call, and then a protection call.
- After the protection call, the punt team should communicate with each other, if necessary.

- Next, the personal protector should recheck the front before saying "set." No movement can occur after the set call. The snapper should pause after set, and then snap the ball.

☐ *Ideal Times for the Basic Elements of the Punt:*

- Center snap—The center should try to get the ball to the punter in under one second.
- Punter's "in-hand time"—The punter must be able to get the ball off in less than 1.5 seconds on a two-step approach.
- Hang time (the time the ball is in the air)—The punter should strive to keep the ball in the air for four seconds to allow the coverage the opportunity to either keep the return to a minimum of force a fair catch.

Punt Return/Block Team

Return Unit

> - *Objectives.* To return each punt a minimum of 10 yards; to always give the offense good field position; to handle each punt properly; to limit the punt team to 33 net yards or less per punt.
> - *Return specialist.* Punt returners who have sure hands and are able to use their blockers. They must catch the ball (i.e., seldom let the ball hit the ground).
> - *Team.* Fast, open-field blockers who use good judgment to avoid blocking illegally. Must stay onside and avoid roughing the kicker.

The punt return unit involves a collective effort to return a punt as far as possible. Based on the coverage employed by the punt team, the type of punter, and the punt protection, a variety of types of returns can be used. Other variables, such as field position, game situation, and the weather, can also be a consideration of return type.

☐ *Return Guidelines*

- Stay onside (see the ball snapped).
- Stay off the punter (unless the kick is blocked).
- Block above the waist and in front on returns.
- Pressure the punter and attempt to break his rhythm.
- Do not let the ball hit the ground (i.e., the return man should try to catch all punts).
- Make the proper "fair catch" signal.
- Know the return call.
- Have a predesignated signal, a short keyword, to alert teammates that the ball is hitting the ground. Players must locate the ball and get away from it. The returner also should use a visual "wipe-away" hand signal.

Block Unit

> - *Objectives*. "Block, scoop, and score." Try to advance a blocked punt that hasn't crossed the line of scrimmage.
> - *Block specialists*. Reliable punt rushers who are quick and aggressive and who want to block kicks. They should aim for the "block point" and put their "eyes and hands" on the ball.
> - *Team objective*. To achieve an all-out effort by blockers who are intent on blocking the punt.

This unit engages in an attempt to either block the kick or, at the least, force a bad kick. A variety of types of rushing techniques can be utilized. As a rule, a block attempt is based on such variables as timing, the protection, the time left on the scoreboard, field position, and the score in the game.

☐ *Block Guidelines*

- Start in a sprinter's stance, with the feet staggered and most of his weight on the down hand.
- Crowd the ball as much as possible.
- See the ball to facilitate a great takeoff.
- Be ready as soon as the center possesses the ball.
- Take advantage of any mannerisms or tells of the center.
- On the takeoff, stay low and make himself small by turning his shoulders perpendicular to the line of scrimmage.
- Maintain rush lane integrity.
- If taken on by a blocker head-up, work to his assigned gap.
- If blocked from the side, dip the nearest shoulder, rip through, and redirect toward his assignment.
- At the launch point, extend his arms and surge, as opposed to jumping or leaving his feet.
- Keep his layout flat and parallel to the ground.
- At the contact point, keep his eyes open and his hands together, with thumbs touching.
- Look through the V formed by the hands, with his eyes on the ball.

Field Goal and Extra Point Team

> - *Objective*. To score (three points for a FG and one for a PAT).
> - *Specialists*. Three-man partnership:
>   ▸ A kicker who gets quick height (to avoid the block) and has consistent accuracy
>   ▸ A holder with sure hands and the ability to quickly and accurately place the ball
>   ▸ A center with snapping accuracy.
> - *Team*. No penetration! Take the proper stance and steps; see the ball snapped.

☐ *Position Guidelines:*

- Center (after the "set" command):
  ▸ Snap the ball any time he is ready.
  ▸ Make the snap sharp and accurate.

- Help ensure that smooth rhythm exists with the snap, hold, and kick.
- Use head movements to prevent the rushers from getting a jump on the snap.
- After the snap, set and rise up under control.
- Do not fire out or get pulled, which would create a rush lane.

- Guards and tackles:
  - Set low and rise high and tight to the inside-block area.
  - Initially, take a quick set step with their inside foot, sharply planting it just inside and behind the heel of the outside foot of the player inside of them.
  - Keep the outside foot planted and stationary, with their hips and shoulders square to the line of scrimmage.
  - Keep their hands high to block, as in pass protection.
  - Remember that they are responsible for the inside gap first.

- Ends and wingbacks:
  - Remember that they are responsible for the inside gap first, and then the outside gap.
  - Take their first step to the inside to secure that gap.
  - Strike the inside rusher with their inside hand as they step inside and drop their outside foot back at a 45-degree angle; strike the outside rusher with their outside hand.
  - The wingbacks should always peel back and spy for a blocked kick. If a kick is blocked, they should either recover it or make the tackle.

- Holder:
  - Ensure that the 11 men of the kicking unit are on the field.
  - Help ensure that smooth rhythm exists with the snap, hold, and kick.
  - Place his down-hand on the spot on which he'll set the football.
  - Check to see that his teammates and the kicker are ready.
  - Be ready to yell a predesignated signal if an error happens.

- Kicker
  - Pick his spot for lining up directly behind the ball.
  - Offset his position if the ball is on the hash.
  - Begin his approach when the ball is snapped.
  - Be ready to yell a predesignated signal if an error happens.

Field Goal and Extra Point Block Team

- *Objectives*. "Block, scoop, and score." Block the field goal, giving the field goal block team a touchdown or good field position; always try to advance a blocked kick that hasn't crossed the line of scrimmage. Yell out a predesignated signal when a partially blocked kick crosses the line of scrimmage.
- *Block specialists*. Blockers, jumpers, and swimmers that pressure inside and outside. Inside blockers—"penetrate and elevate."
- *Team*. Take care of assignments to defend against the fake while attempting the block.

The field goal and extra point block unit needs to be fundamentally sound with their alignment and responsibilities; be able to perform when the pressure is on; be alert and aggressive to stop all fakes; and know all of the rules pertaining to blocks, kicks, etc.

☐ *Block Guidelines (Everyone):*

- Be ready. Always be alert for a fake. Call it out!
- Know their alignment and assignment responsibilities.
- Go all-out. They never know when one or three points will make the difference in the game.
- Know their "pass" responsibilities.
- Know who has "contain run" responsibilities.
- Stay onside and get off on the snap. (See the ball in their stance.)
- Treat a blocked kick the same as a blocked punt. Know the rules. If a blocked kick goes beyond the line of scrimmage, get away from it.
- Block the ball with their hands. Timing is important.
- Pick up and run with blocked balls that haven't crossed the line of scrimmage (i.e., "scoop and score").
- Tackle the opponent if they should pick up a blocked kick. *Note:* A blocked kick that is behind the line of scrimmage can be advanced by either *team.*

☐ *Block Guidelines (Outside Rushers):*

- Align as close to the line of scrimmage as possible. Use a sprinter's stance.
- Get off on the snap. Watch the snapper for tells (e.g., moves his fingers, tightens his grip on the ball, bounces his backside or knees, has a rhythm after the "set" call).
- Run as close to the wing as possible. Keep their shoulder level low. After their second outside step, drive flat for the ball. Accelerate hard to the block point, and keep their eyes on the ball.
- On the fourth or fifth step (depending on their stance), lay out flat across the path of the ball, turning their body in slightly.
- Block the ball four to five feet from the ground with both hands. The block point is three yards in front of the spot.

Onside Kickoff Team

- *Objectives.* To recover a deliberately short kick and give the offense an enhanced opportunity to score.
- *Specialist.* A kicker to kick the ball a legal minimum of 10 yards.
- *Team.* Swarm to the ball and recover it.

Various situations exist when an onside kick should be considered. Some coaches employ an onside kick as a surprise move. Some coaches use a surprise onside kick to establish or change momentum. Some teams utilize an onside kick when they are trailing on the scoreboard to get the ball back quickly.

☐ *Onside Kick Guidelines:*

- The ball must go 10 yards or be touched by the receiving team in order for it to be recovered by the kicking *team.*

- Do not be offside.
- Know the call and direction of the kick.
- Know who has safety responsibility.
- Each player should know his role. Members will be divided into blockers and recoverers. Blockers attempt to recover only if the ball is kicked to their assigned man.
- Do not try to pick up the ball. The kicking team may not advance the ball. Possession is all-important.

Hands Team

> - *Objectives.* To recover the ball and protect the player who recovered it.
> - *Specialists.* Quick, aggressive players with good hands and decision-making skills.
> - *Team.* Field the ball; block to protect the recovery players; two returners to handle kicks that travel past the front line.

The hands unit is utilized by the kickoff return team when they expect to receive an onside kick. Most of the players on this unit are skilled at catching the ball, e.g., receivers, tight ends, running backs, and defensive backs. As a rule, the hands team is deployed as a mirror to the kickoff team directly in front of them.

☐ *Hands Team Guidelines:*

- Know the rules concerning onside kicks.
- Be aware that the kicked ball must either travel at least 10 yards or be touched initially by a member of the hands unit for it to be legally recovered by the kicking *team*.
- Line up as close as possible to the neutral zone so that once the ball crosses the zone line they can try to recover it.
- Always offset to avoid a hard kick directly at them. Let a hard kick go by them to the next level of returners.
- If possible, fall on an onside kick, wrap up the ball, and recover it.
- Be aware that an onside kick can be fair caught.

Punt-Fake Team

> - *Objective.* To get the first down or score a touchdown.
> - *Specialist.* A personal protector who uses good timing and judgment concerning when to use an automatic run or pass. The most important factor is to get the first down.
> - *Team.* Be alert to when and why a fake is called. Be alert to check to a punt.

On rare occasions, the punt team will fake a punt and run or pass the ball instead. Fake punts, which are undertaken as a surprise move, can be a momentum-changer when successful.

☐ *Fake Punt Guidelines*

- Adhere to all rules concerning the punt game, particularly those involving blocking on a fake punt.
- Avoid mannerisms or tells that may tip off the return team that a fake punt may be coming.

- As with any offensive or defensive play, know their assignments and handle them to the best of their ability.
- Take advantage of an opponent's tendencies/weaknesses.

Field Goal/PAT-Fake Team

- *Objective.* To get the first down or score a touchdown on a field goal; to score two points on a PAT.
- *Specialist.* A holder with running and passing ability.
- *Team.* Carry out responsibilities. No tip-offs.

Depending upon the circumstances, a team may use a fake play on a field goal or PAT attempt. This trick play can involve either a running, option, or passing play from a kick formation.

☐ *Fake Field Goal/PAT Guidelines:*

- Adhere to all rules covering the situation, particularly those involving blocking.
- Do not tip off the fake.
- Know all of their assignments and fulfill them to the best of their ability.
- Take advantage of an opponent's tendencies/weakneses.

SPECIAL TEAMS SPECIALISTS

Special teams units employ several players who have a unique array of skills and abilities, including placekickers, punters, snappers, and holders. Each role has its own set of techniques that must be mastered.

Placekickers

Teams kick off using either a straight-on or a soccer-style technique.

☐ *Straight-On Kickoff Technique:*

Alignment:

- Align 10 yards deep on a straight line with the tee.
- Keep the shoulders slightly in front of his tee with his head down and his eyes focused on the ball.
- Hang his arms loosely at his side.

Approach:

- Start his movement to the ball with his kicking foot.
- Gain momentum in his first five yards, as his steps gradually become quicker.
- In the second five yards, increase his momentum, as he approaches the ball.
- Cover these last five yards with three steps.
- Contact the ground with his plant foot, four to six inches to the side and eight inches behind the tee.

Kick and Follow-Through:

- Keep his shoulders forward and his head down at the point of contact.
- Lock the ankle of the kicking foot.
- Keep the toes in a flat or neutral position, as opposed to pointed up or down.

- Contact the ball an inch below the center of the ball.
- Follow through smoothly and extended with the head focused on the tee.

☐ *Soccer-Style Kickoff Technique:*

Alignment:

- Place the ball on the tee at a slightly backward angle, with the laces facing away from him.
- Align himself by taking nine backward steps away from the tee and five steps to the side.
- Place his kicking foot six inches in front of his plant foot.
- Keep some flexion in his knees with his shoulders in front of his hips and his arms loose, hanging to his side.

Approach:

- Start his approach by taking a short, relaxed step toward the ball with his kicking foot.
- Make each step progressively quicker as he approaches the ball.
- Position the kicker's plant foot two to four inches behind the ball, six inches to the side of the tee.
- Point the plant toe in the direction of the kick.

Kick and Follow-Through

Photo 13-1

- As he contacts the ball, keep his head down and focused on the ball.
- Keep his shoulders in front of his hips at the point of contact.
- Move the kicking leg in a high arc with the kicking toe pointed down and the knee preceding the foot.
- Strike the ball with the inside part of the instep, one inch below the center of the ball.
- Having executed the correct approach and maintaining proper body balance, feel himself being lifted off the ground.
- Land one or two feet in front of the tee.

☐ *Straight-On Field Goal/PAT Technique*

Alignment:

- Put his plant foot to the side of the launch point with his kicking foot placed directly behind the spot.
- Take three natural steps backward.
- Take the first step with his kicking foot.
- After the third step, shift his feet so that the instep of the kicking foot is even with the toe of the plant foot.
- Keep his feet six to eight inches apart with most of his weight on the non-kicking foot.
- Hang his arms down and forward.

Approach:

- Use a two-step motion.
- First, start the body forward by taking a natural, relaxed step with his kicking foot.
- Second, explosively step with the non-kicking (plant) foot, landing eight inches behind and to the left (for a right-footed kicker) of the kicking spot.
- Keep the shoulders forward throughout both steps.

Kick and Follow-Through:

- Bring the kicking leg forward in a big arc as the plant foot hits the ground.
- Lock the ankle so that the sole of the foot is even with the ground at the point of contact.
- Use his momentum to carry himself straight ahead over the spot.
- Bend and spread the arms naturally during the kick to provide balance.

☐ *Soccer-Style Field Goal/PAT Technique*

Alignment:

- Place his non-kicking (plant) foot to the side of the tee or launch point, which is usually seven yards from the center.
- With his kicking foot positioned directly behind the spot, take three normal steps backward, starting with the kicking foot.
- End up with the kicking foot in a direct line with the ball.
- Take two sideways steps at a 90-degree angle and then turn and face the launch point.
- Place his plant foot slightly ahead of his kicking foot with his feet slightly less than shoulder width apart.
- Keep his weight distributed equally on the balls of the feet with a slight bend in the knees.
- Bend at the waist so that his shoulders are in front of the knees and his arms are hanging loosely by his side.
- Focus his eyes on the kicking spot.
- From this pre-snap position, shift his weight forward and signal to the holder that he is ready.
- See the ball peripherally, in order to time-up the kick.

Approach:

- On his first step, take a step with the kicking foot in a smooth, relaxed manner.
- On his second step, take a longer step and come down even with and six inches from the ball.

Kick and Follow-Through:

- Once the plant foot hits the ground, start the kicking leg forward, following a high arc, with the leg almost fully extended.
- With a slight knee bend, point the kicking toe forward and lock the ankle.
- Contact the ball with the top inside part of the kicking foot.
- Strike the ball with the shoe-laced portion of the foot (the area of big hard bone), not the toe.
- Contact the ball one inch below the center of the ball.
- On contact, open his hips and have them pointed to the goal post.
- Be aware that a good follow-through brings the body straight down the target line, with the shoulders remaining square with the target.
- At the point of contact, keep his head down and his eyes focused on the launch point. Do not look up.

Punters

Photo 13-2

The two most common approaches to punting entail taking either two steps or three steps before kicking the ball. Advantages exist with either method. The primary advantage of the two-step approach is that the ball is punted more quickly, which makes it more difficult to block. The main advantage of the three-step method is that it provides better balance and offers more momentum into the ball.

☐ *Stance:*

- Assume a stance that is relaxed and comfortable.
- Position the feet no wider than shoulder width apart.
- Place his kicking foot forward, with toe-to-instep relationship.
- Distribute the weight on the instep of both feet, which will enable the punter to move nimbly to either side in the event of an errant snap.
- Bend at the knees, with his upper body tilted forward.
- Anticipate a bad snap every time he lines up.
- Do not allow his knee to touch the ground.

☐ *Steps (Two-Step Approach):*

- Take his first step with the forward or kicking foot.
- Step into the snap by moving his body to keep it in front of the ball.
- Look the ball all the way into his hands.
- Make his first step a short, controlled step, slightly open, which allows his hips to open. Land on the ball of the foot.
- Take his second step (a normal stride) with his back foot.

- Have the toe of the back foot follow the same angle as the toe of the kicking foot.
- Have the trail foot contact the ground on the ball of the foot.
- Maintain the upper body in the pre-snap position throughout the movement.
- Keep the hips over the feet.
- As the trail foot hits the ground, swing the kicking foot forward with the ankle locked and the kicking toe pointed downward.

☐ *Hands:*

- To receive the ball, extend the hands waist high with the palms up and the little fingers touching.
- As he steps into the ball, bend the elbows slightly and help soften the blow of the ball striking the hands.
- Catch the ball just inside the hip of the kicking leg.
- Be careful on a low snap that the knees don't touch the ground. On a low snap, bend at the waist and knees.
- Do not bring the ball into the body.
- Extend the hands to help get the ball off quickly.
- Present the laces of the ball at 12 o'clock.
- Grip the ball with light pressure.
- Extend the ball on a direct line with the outer edge of the punting leg.

☐ *Dropping the Ball (Two-Handed Method):*

Some punters present the ball with both hands. Others choose to drop the ball with one hand. The main advantage of the two-handed method is that it offers better ball security.

- Grip the back tip of the ball with the dominant hand (using the thumb and forefinger).
- Rest the off-hand lightly on the inside lower panel of the ball.
- Tilt the front point of the ball slightly downward and inward.
- Rotate the ball so that the laces face straight up.
- As he takes this second step, remove his off-hand and allow it to fall away and then swing back above and outside the hip.
- Drop the ball slightly to the outside of the punting leg, from a height between the bottom of the jersey numbers and the waist.
- As the ball is dropped, swing the kicking leg through and contact the ball with the kicking foot.

☐ *Contacting the Ball:*

Photo 13-3

- Once the ball is dropped, swing the kicking leg in a smooth, controlled manner.
- As he swings, lock out his kicking ankle and point the toe downward. See the ball strike the top of his foot.

- On the follow-through, swing the kicking leg straight downfield and upward toward the same-side shoulder.
- At the moment of contact, lock the support leg and generate power from the ground up.

Snappers

Differences exist between snapping the ball for a punt and snapping the ball for a field goal/PAT. Accordingly, the snapper has to make adjustments for those differences. The major factor, in this regard, is the distance the ball must travel. Most punters set up approximately 15 yards deep. In contrast, a snap for a field gold/PAT usually covers about seven yards, which is less than half the distance it must travel on a punt. Another difference is the height of the snap. The target for a punt is considerably higher than a snap for a field goal/PAT.

☐ *Grip:*

Photo 13-4

- Grasp the ball with his dominant hand, just forward of the center of the ball.
- Contact the laces of the ball with the ring finger and pinkie.
- Keep the thumb on the underside of the ball, about the same distance from the back tip of the ball as the middle finger.
- Place the off-hand (guide hand) on the opposite side of the ball, with the fingers pointed toward the line of scrimmage.
- Grip the ball only with the finger pads of the off-hand.
- Avoid palming the ball.

☐ *Stance:*

- Assume a stance slightly wider than shoulder width.
- Position the toes on the right foot even with the instep of the left foot (right-handed snapper).
- Keep his weight on the balls of the feet with the feet firmly planted.
- To grip the ball, bend his knees and reach out.

☐ *Addressing the Ball:*

- Exert little or no weight on the ball.
- Keep his shoulders square and the back level when he bends over the ball.
- Assume a position in which the ball is at arm's length after he settles in his stance. The arms should be 90 to 95 percent extended.
- Pre-position the ball so that the laces are rotated toward the right and facing down toward the ground.
- Reach out and grip the ball, positioning his dominant hand underneath it.

☐ *Snapping the Ball:*

- Use the holder's hands as the target on a field goal/PAT snap (a short snap). In contrast, the target on a snap for a punt (long snap) is usually the punter's kicking leg, thigh, and hip.
- After the holder gives the ready signal, snap the ball when ready.
- Look through his legs to focus on the target.
- When snapping the ball, pull both arms through the legs with equal effort.
- Graze the grass with the dominant hand, as the ball moves toward the target.
- Keep the guide hand on the top of the ball, as the arms extend toward the target.
- Concurrently, use the dominant hand to essentially throw the ball to the target.
- Supply spin and velocity to the ball with the dominant hand.
- Roll the dominant wrist so that the forefinger goes over the top and points toward the target.
- As the arms extend backward, flex the fingers and the hands toward the forearm to get full extension.
- Use the guide hand to steer the ball in a straight line during and after the snap.
- End the snap with the arms fully extended toward the target, with the fingers pointing toward the holder and the palms facing up and out.
- Try to drive the shoulders between the legs to get good follow-through as well as get his body weight behind the ball.

Holders

Photo 13-5

The holder receives the snap from the long snapper on field goal/PAT attempts and is responsible for placing the ball on the turf and balancing it until it is kicked.

- Set up just to the right of the tee or the launch point for the field goal/PAT (for a right-footed kicker).
- Position his left knee on the ground just behind and to the side of the tee or launch point.
- Place his right foot comfortably and naturally in front of him.
- Extend his arms out naturally in front of the tee or launch point, giving the center a target to hit with his hands.
- Have his thumbs and index fingers face each other, and slightly spread apart. Naturally spread the rest of his fingers apart.
- Receive the snap right between both hands.
- With the momentum of the catch, bring the hands and the ball back just over the tee or launch point.

- Set the ball quickly for the kick with the laces facing out, whenever possible.
- Hold the ball lightly in place with the index finger on the ball. Some holders use more than one finger to hold the ball.
- Do not apply too much pressure down on the ball.
- Lean the ball slightly backward on the tee or launch point.
- Concentrate on getting the ball correctly on the tee or launch point and holding it there until it is kicked.

SECTION V

ENHANCING LIFE SKILLS FOR SUCCESS

CHAPTER 14

HOW TO TEACH AND REINFORCE VALUES IN YOUR ATHLETES

A major reason some individuals are more effective in life, as well as in coaching football, is who they are as people. All factors considered, they are driven by forces that help define how they think and behave. Those forces reflect a person's highest priorities and most deeply held beliefs. Those principles and qualities that people hold in high regard are commonly known as values.

As a football coach, your values provide a moral dimension to what you do. They enable you to know the difference between merely doing your best and doing what is right. Not only do they help guide the way you coach, they also affect how your players and members of your staff see you as a person. In essence, they are the blueprint of who you are.

Beyond serving as a moral compass, your values are important to you for a number of reasons. Values help you determine your purpose. Your values also help you behave in a way that is compatible with who you want to be. In addition, your values enable you to make decisions in a more composed, less emotionally influenced way. Your values help you to prioritize what's really important in life. They enable you to know what's important to you—what you want in your life. Your values also help you to be more self-confident given the sense of stability that they help foster.

As a football coach, adhering to and living your values is one of the most powerful options you have to help you become the person you want to be and to help you lead and influence others. In the latter instance, your values provide you with an exceptional opportunity to affect the social-emotional growth of your players. As a coach, your job is to teach them more than to simply play the game. Your role also includes having a positive impact on who they become as people—as members of society.

INSTILLING VALUES IN YOUR ATHLETES

Without question, as their coach, you are not the only source from which your players learn values. You, however, can be an integral part of a plethora of factors (e.g., peer pressure, family, school, Internet, television, video games, media, etc.) that can contribute to the values-based development of your athletes. Once you understand and accept your role in that regard, your next step is to determine how you can best undertake such a responsibility.

The reality is that you are teaching values to your players every minute that they are spending with you. The real issue isn't whether you should be teaching values, but whether a better way exists for you to teach them. The key point to remember is that teaching values is too important to leave to chance. Among the steps that you can embark on in this regard are the following:

- ☐ Set a good example for your athletes. Model the values you hold dear. Be consistent in how you behave. Your players observe what you do in different situations. They see how you treat them. They overhear how you interact with others. Never forget that it isn't what you say; it's what you do that really counts.

- ☐ Use everyday experiences as a springboard to talk explicitly about your values with your athletes and detail why they are important to you and for them.

- ☐ Whenever it's appropriate, share with your players why you make decisions affecting them based on your values. Discuss how you utilize your values in your role as a coach.

- ☐ Applaud good behavior. Reinforce any expression of a key value. If an athlete demonstrates an essential value, recognize him for it, being as specific as possible.

- ☐ Consciously teach positive values, e.g., good sportsmanship. One way to accomplish that is to develop a structured program for the team for focusing on a specific value within a particular timeframe, such as having a "value theme" for a particular week.

- ☐ Make your efforts to instill values in your players as relevant as possible. On occasion, values can seem almost theoretical to your athletes unless you take the opportunity to explain how they apply to their lives.

DEFINING YOUR VALUES

When you take the time to determine your values, you are ascertaining what's important to you in life. While no two football coaches are exactly the same, one commonality that exists among almost all "successful" coaches is the presence of ethically grounded principles: their values. These principles not only enable these individuals to exercise good judgment, make sound decisions, and reach appropriate choices, they also serve as a roadmap for the growth and development of their young players.

In reality, hundreds of distinct values exist. Some are more important than others to a specific individual. The key is to decide which ones are important to you, particularly in your role as coach of young and impressionable athletes. Among the values that many coaches deep down deem significant are the following:

- ☐ *Accountability.* You accept responsibility for your actions, not only for what you do specifically as a coach, but also for what those individuals under your direction do or not do.

- ☐ *Commitment.* You have made a commitment to your athletes and their families to apply the best version of yourself to the task at hand.

- ☐ *Courage.* You have the strength of mind to address a number of situations that you and your team encounter during the season.

- ☐ *Honesty.* You tell the truth and foster an atmosphere of fun and trust.

- ☐ *Honor.* You have a keen sense of ethical conduct and act in a highly principled manner, one that includes fairness, worthiness, and respect.

- ☐ *Integrity.* You think and do what is right, no matter the consequences. You live by your standards and beliefs, even when no one is watching.

- ☐ *Leadership.* You have the capacity to develop a vision for what your team will accomplish and can motivate members of your program (athletes and staff) to achieve it together within a fun team sport.

- ☐ *Loyalty.* You exhibit unwavering allegiance to your team, your staff, your vision, and your principles. You refuse to compromise your values for personal gain.

- ☐ *Passion.* You have enthusiasm for football and for what you do (coach young athletes). You pour your heart, mind, and soul into your role as a coach.

- ☐ *Pride.* You have a feeling of gratification for being part of something that is meaningful and inherently good. You should be able to take pride in your behavior, your accomplishments, and the actions of those whom you lead.

- ☐ *Professionalism.* You conduct yourself in a manner that shows you have the ability, interest, and willingness to do your job. How you think, act, and speak elicits respect.

- ☐ *Respect.* You treat or think about someone or something with deference. You respect your players, their parents, your fellow coaches, and the sport.

- ☐ *Self-control.* You have the ability to exercise restraint over your impulses, emotions, and desires. As a coach, your ability to control your behavior can also entail managing your time wisely, accepting responsibility for your actions (or the lack thereof), and maintaining an appropriate level of focus.

- ☐ *Selflessness.* You exhibit more concern with the needs of others, than you do for your own. In other words, you put your team first.

- ☐ *Teamwork.* You have the ability to get your players to work together to achieve a common goal. You create an environment in which your players have a shared mindset, i.e., having an "us," rather than "me," way of thinking.

- ☐ *Thoughtfulness.* You show consideration for others. Not only are you polite and respectful toward them, you also make time for them.

- ☐ *Trustworthiness.* You inspire others (your players and your staff) to take you at your word. You are someone in whom they can believe. You keep your commitments. You can be counted on. You do what you say you will do.

APPENDICES

APPENDIX A
GLOSSARY OF TERMS

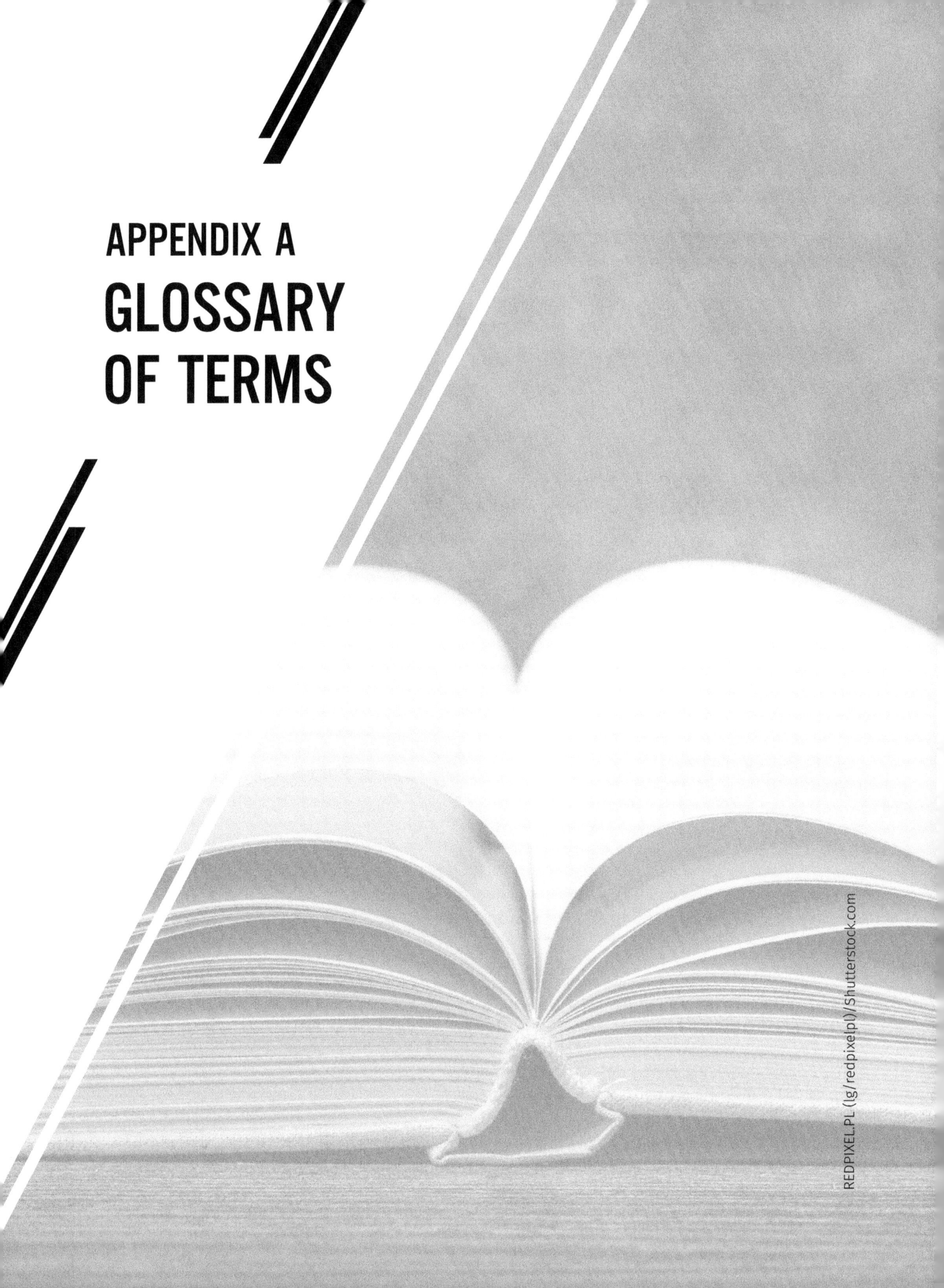

The following compilation of football terms defines the basic nomenclature associated with the game.

3-4: A defensive scheme that utilizes three defensive linemen, four linebackers, and four defensive backs

3-5-3: A defensive scheme that employs three defensive linemen, five linebackers, and three defensive backs

4-2-5: A defensive scheme that employs four defensive linemen, two linebackers, and five defensive backs

4-3: A defensive scheme that involves four defensive linemen, three linebackers, and four defensive backs

4-4: A defensive scheme that utilizes four defensive linemen, four linebackers, and three defensive backs

46 defense: Bear defense; a defensive formation with eight men in the box that entails six players along the line of scrimmage—four playing defensive line technique and two in a linebacker technique—plus two players at linebacker depth and three defensive backs

Across-the-middle: The course of a pass route bisecting the middle of the field

A-gap: The lateral spacing between the center and the offensive guards when aligned at the line of scrimmage

Angle run: A sideways run with the runner opened or angled sideways to the line of scrimmage, looking over his shoulder

Area block: A type of blocking in which the blocker takes one step to the onside and blocks that area

Audible: A play call made by the quarterback prior to the snap after analyzing the defense or receiving a play call from the sideline

Away: A blocking term in which the offensive lineman blocks the seam away from the point of attack

Backpedal: Running backward

Backside: The side of the offensive formation away from the action of an offensive play

Balanced formation: A 2 x 2 (balanced) offensive alignment in which there are two receiver-type players to each side of the formation

Ball control offense: The efforts of an offense to hold on to the football for as much of the game as possible by utilizing heavy run game play and high-percentage passes

Ball security: The execution of techniques that are designed to help guarantee ball possession by whomever has the ball

Ball-stripping: The act of a defensive player dislodging the football from a ballcarrier in an effort to cause a fumble

Base defense: The basic defensive design that a team utilizes

Base offense: The basic offensive design that a team utilizes

Belly: An inside running play in which the quarterback reverse pivots, quickly faking a toss-sweep action

B-gap: The lateral spacing between an offensive guard and an offensive tackle when aligned at the line of scrimmage

Blindside: The side of the offense away from a quarterback as he turns his back and sets up to pass

Blitz: Action in which a secondary player or a linebacker rush the quarterback in an effort to sack or disrupt him

Bomb: A slang term for a deep streak route

Boot: Short for bootleg pass

Boundary: The lines that indicate out-of-bounds

Boundary help: Because a pass cannot be completed out-of-bounds, the boundary can serve as an extra defender depending on the situation

Box: An area from tackle to tackle, two to three yards on each side of the line of scrimmage

Bubble screen: A quickly thrown screen pass

Bump-and-run: A secondary pass coverage technique in which a defensive back legally joins a receiver he is covering man-to-man for up to five yards past the line of scrimmage

Bunch: Any three eligible receivers aligned close together on one side of the formation

Burst: The first steps of a player, normally either a defender changing direction to close on a receiver or a receiver trying to gain separation

Button hook: A route pattern in which a receiver runs straight downfield for approximately five yards, stops quickly, and heads back toward the quarterback for a short distance to receive the pass

Buzz: An ultimate flat player sprinting to be in the wide flat under the widest receiver (i.e., in the throwing lane between the receiver and the quarterback)

Cadence: The words of the signal caller that initiate a play

C-gap: The lateral spacing between the tackle and tight end when aligned at the line of scrimmage

Check-down: Another name for a dump pass, sit route, or a safety valve read-and-throw

Check-with-me: A huddled-up play call for the offense

Chest plate: The portion of the shoulder pads that covers the chest area

Chop block: An illegal high-low or low-high combination block by any two players against an opponent (not the ballcarrier)

Close: A pass defender's sprint toward the receiving area of a receiver

Cloud: An assignment of corner force and flat

Coffin corner: The area of the field on the sideline between the goal line and the five-yard line, to which the punter attempts to punt the ball

Combo coverage: Short for combination coverage

Complementary routes: Pass routes that help to set up prime-read pass routes

Contain: The defensive effort of trying to prevent an offense from successfully gaining yardage to the outside, whether by a run or a pass

Counter: A play in which the ballcarrier starts off in one direction and then purposely breaks back in the opposite direction

Cover 0: Four-across blitz man coverage with no deep zone coverage

Cover 1: Man-free coverage

Cover 2: Two-deep zone coverage

Cover 3: Three-deep zone coverage

Cover 4: Quarters coverage

Crack: A blocking term in which the wideout blocks the first player inside him

Crackback block: A block by an offensive player usually spread out away from the main body of the formation, who comes back toward the ball to block an opponent; legal as long as the defender is not blindsided and the blocker makes initial contact with hands to the shoulders or below

Crosser: A receiver who runs a route from one side of a formation to the other

Crossing route: A pass route in which a receiver starts on one side of an offensive formation and then works his route across the formation to the opposite side

Crossover: An initial step to one side that gains only lateral distance

Curl: A pass route that stems anywhere from 10 to 22 yards deep, before a receiver plants his outside foot and sharply works back to the quarterback; an interchangeable term for a hook route

Cushion: The vertical distance between the receiver and the defender

Cut: Either a change of direction by a receiver or an illegal block—except in specific cases—in which the blocker engages with the defender below the waist

Cut-back: The action of a ballcarrier breaking sharply to the opposite side of his initial run course

Defensive coordinator (DC): The leader or coach of the defense

Defensive front: The portion of the defense that entails the defensive line and the linebackers

Delay routes: Passing routes in which running backs and tight ends delay two to three seconds before releasing into their underneath routes

Dig route: A pass route in which a wide receiver breaks hard to the inside on a square-in type route action

Dime coverage: When a fifth and sixth defensive back is added to the defensive pass coverage scheme

Disguise: The alignment of a defensive secondary designed to avoid tipping the assigned coverage

Dive play: A quick-hitting, straight-ahead run play by a running back

Dog: A commonly used term for a blitzing linebacker in combination with other defenders

Double eagle: Bear defense

Double-cut: A receiver making one cut and then a second cut, while running a route

Double-move routes: Most often associated with such route combinations as "hitch and go," "out and up," etc. in which the receiver fakes a base route action and then explodes deep on a second cut/break

Double-team block: the action of two blockers who both block one defender together

Down: A period in which a play transpires

Down block: A block by an offensive lineman or a tight end to the inside, designed to produce a significant blocking angle

Down-and-distance tendency: The relative percentage of an offense doing a certain thing on a particular down-and-distance situation

Downhill running: North-south running

Drag route: A shallow crossing route in which a receiver works flat across the formation to throttle down and work into a zone void or to separate from man-to-man coverage and stay on the move

Draw: A delayed run play that usually comes off a fake dropback pass-action by the quarterback

Draw down: A tendency, usually second- or third-and-long, in which an offense might run a draw instead of a pass

Drive block: The most common run game block; for the most part, the blocker takes the defender in whatever direction the block allows

Drop: The backward steps of the quarterback in the passing game

Edge: The area outside of a tight end or a tackle who has no tight end aligned to him

Empty formation: A formation with no offensive player in the backfield, except the quarterback

End line: The end zone boundary, 10 yards from and parallel to the goal line

Even: A defensive alignment with no defender lined up over the center

Fade: A quickly thrown, short, floating, streak-type pass that pushes the receiver toward the sideline

Fair catch: The act of a punt returner waving his hand over his head from side to side, signaling that he will not attempt to run with the ball after making the catch

False step: An extra step initially taken by a player out of a stance or to execute a change of direction

Fire: A man who aggressively blocks the onside gap and anyone else who crosses his path

Fit: A situation after the snap of the ball in which a player (offensive or defensive) is in contact with the frontal surface of the player against whom he is playing

Flat: An area approximately 10 to 12 yards deep, from outside the tackle to the out-of-bounds line (boundary)

Flex: A defensive concept in which a defensive lineman is back off the line of scrimmage two to three yards, as he aligns over a specific offensive lineman

Flood pattern: The passing action of distributing three or four receivers and their routes in a specific area of the field

Fly sweep: A fast-developing outside sweep run in which the quarterback gives the football to a fast-motioning wide receiver

Force: A player whose assignment is to turn in or stop an outside running play

Force area: The area a defender must play to cover either the flat on a pass or the pitchman versus option

Freeze: The technique of a runner to follow a blocker, without showing his intentions until the block is initiated

Front: The players (offensive or defensive) who are positioned on the line of scrimmage prior to the snap

Frontside gap: The space between two adjacent offensive linemen to the playside of an offensive run or pass play

Gaps: The spaces offensive linemen and tight ends that can act as landmarks for offensive and defensive alignments

Hail Mary: A last-second, desperation pass play in which the quarterback throws a deep, high-floating streak pass into, or toward, the end zone

Halfback pass: A pass play that is usually designed to look like a sweep or option, with a halfback subsequently passing the ball

Hands team: A kicking game special unit that is loaded up with skill position players with good hands to enhance the likelihood of the kicking team recovering an onside kick

Head-up: A defensive alignment in which a defender aligns directly on the nose of an offensive blocker

Help: Assistance provided by another defender or a boundary

Hidden yardage: A term used to denote yardage gains or losses as a result of the kicking game and its play during the course of a game

High/low read: A passing game concept in which an offense tries to isolate a defender with a receiver both in front and behind him

Hitch route: A quick game pass route in which a wide receiver takes five quick steps (about six yards), plants his outside foot, and throws back to stop and face the quarterback

Hitch-and-go route: A quickly thrown deep pass (go route) to a receiver who first fakes a hitch route

Hole: Either the area on the line of scrimmage at which the play is directed or an area in the secondary about 8 to 12 yards deep between the hook areas of the receivers

Hook: Either a type of blocking action in which the player rotates his hips to the outside, after he contacts his opponent, or an inside receiver running a route just outside his tackle and curling or hooking at a depth of 10 to 12 yards

Hook route: Interchangeable term for a curl route

Horizontal relationship: A man-to-man defender keeping an alignment either a yard inside or outside a receiver who is running vertical before his final cut

Hot route: A quick, short, possibly adjusted-on-the-run control-type pass route used to counter defensive blitz actions

I formation: An alignment in which the quarterback, fullback, and tailback are stacked in a straight "I" line behind the center

Inside alignment: The positioning of a defender on the inside portion of an offensive player

Isolation run play: A run play design, such as a blast, in which the offensive line double-team blocks a defensive tackle at the point of contact and leaves an isolated linebacker (alone) to be blocked by a fullback-type player

Jam: A term used to denote the hand and arm action of shoving, pushing, or stuffing an offensive player to prevent him from properly executing his assigned techniques

Key: Something that tips a certain movement, play, coverage, or defense

Landmark: The designated point-of-attack on a run play

Lateral pursuit: The ability of a defender to chase a ballcarrier on sideways, sideline-to-sideline courses

Lateral shuffle: A sideways movement, while facing straight ahead; the feet come together without executing crossover steps

Launch point: The spot from which a quarterback attempts to throw a pass

Lead: The down part of a double-team block

Lead option: A run, pitch-option play that has a backfield blocker lead the way for the pitch back

Leverage: The mechanical advantage gained by a football player who gets in a position (usually lower than his opponent) to best exert force

Line of scrimmage (LOS): An imaginary line from each end of the football, from sideline to sideline, prior to the snap

Log block: A type of block in which the blocker pulls and hooks his opponent, who is normally trapped

Look-off: The action of the quarterback who fixes his eyes away from the intended area to which he plans to throw the ball

Man (man-to-man) blocking: The assignment and techniques of an offensive player blocking a defender by himself

Man (man-to-man) coverage: Assignment and techniques of a defender who covers a receiver wherever the receiver goes

Man free coverage: Man-to-man pass coverage in which five defenders cover five potential receivers, one-on-one

Max protection: The use of seven to eight blockers in pass protection in an effort to provide the quarterback an extended amount of time to throw long, developing routes

Middle: A zone that starts at the line of scrimmage, from tackle to tackle, that widens, with depth, to the end zone

Midline: The imaginary line that splits the axis of the ball and the middle of both the center and the quarterback

Mike linebacker: A common term for the middle linebacker

Misdirection: An action in which the offense starts a run play in one direction and then cuts back or hands off to another offensive player to run to the opposite side of the formation

Motion: Legal lateral or backward movement by an offensive player prior to the snap of the ball

Naked bootleg: A quarterback run play fake to one side, followed by the quarterback breaking to the opposite side to throw a pass, usually on the move by design

Near back: The running back closest to the point of contact on a sweep or an off-tackle play

Neutral zone: The area at the line of scrimmage that is the width of the ball, from nose to nose, when the ball is spotted on the field prior to the snap

Nickel coverage: Pass coverage involving five defensive backs

No-huddle offense: A fast-paced offensive system in which the offense does not huddle between plays

North/south: A direction on the field that is perpendicular to the end zone

Odd: A defensive alignment in which a defender is lined up over the center

Offensive coordinator (OC): The leader and coach of the offense

Offside: Starting at the center, the area opposite the direction of the play; also, crossing the neutral zone prior to the snap

Onside: Starting at the center, the area toward the direction of the play

Onside kick: An extremely short kickoff kick that is designed to travel at least 10 yards and be recovered by the kicking team

Open hips: While running backward or backpedaling, turning the hips to an angle

Option: A run play designed to give the quarterback the option of giving the ball to a dive running back, keeping it himself, or pitching it to another back

Out of phase: A man-to-man defender near the receiving area but not in position to make a play if the ball is delivered properly and on time

Out route: A pass route to the outside in which the receiver rolls over his initial 10-yard, north-south stem action to work toward the sideline

Outlet: A formational pass pattern designed to have an optional backside or underneath route

Out-out call: A call by a wide, deep-zone defender to alert an underneath zone player that the widest receiver has made an outside cut that eliminates any inside curl, dig, or post

Over front: A defensive front that slides its linebackers weak and its defensive linemen strong to create a strongside front overload

Package: A term that refers to a specific design or philosophy of an offensive, defensive, or kicking game play

Pass route release: The effort of a pass receiver to produce an effort start (i.e., release) off of the line of scrimmage

Pass skeleton (skelly): A practice scenario consisting of pass-coverage players (usually linebackers and defensive backs), normally working pass defense versus receivers and the quarterback

Passing progression: The systematic scanning from one receiver to a second, third, and possibly a fourth or fifth receiver who are all part of a pass pattern system

Penetration: The ability to get depth past the line of scrimmage into the offensive backfield to disrupt offensive line blocking schemes

Perimeter force: The defensive action that contains an offense with a strong outside-in run support by the linebackers and secondary

Pistol: An offensive backfield set in which the quarterback is in a shotgun set, approximately four yards behind the center with the tailback stacked behind him

Plant step: The final step in a quarterback's initial dropback set-up action

Plaster: The effort that must be made in the secondary versus a broken pass play or scramble; e.g., in man-to-man, defenders must hustle to cover receivers; in zone, they must get width and depth, and not run out of their areas

Play call sheet: A pre-game determined list of plays that are planned to be called during a game

Play-action pass: A pass play in which the quarterback first fakes a run to a running back in an effort to influence the linebackers to step up on the run fake

Playside: Starting at the center, the area toward the direction of the play

Pocket: The area that is three to nine yards deep off the line of scrimmage behind the center from which a dropback quarterback throws the ball

Pooch kick: A high, looping kick on the kickoff that is intended to help prevent the normal, deep kickoff returners from returning the ball

Pooch punt: A high, floating punt that is aimed toward the sideline, ideally inside the 10-yard line, in an attempt to put the opponent in poor field position

Post: Either the stabilizing part of a double-team block; or a pass route on which the receiver runs at one of the goal posts

Post route: A pass route in which a receiver stems vertically for five to nine steps and then breaks off at an angle toward the nearest goal post

Power "I": A loaded-up backfield alignment that utilizes an I formation backfield set, with a fullback and a tailback set behind the quarterback and an extra fullback offset right or left (weak or strong)

Pre-snap: The period of time after an offense leaves the huddle and lines up at the line of scrimmage, until the ball is snapped to the quarterback

Press: An alignment of a defender on a receiver in which the defender lines up as close to the receiver as possible without being offside

Press man coverage: Man-to-man coverage in which the coverage defenders apply tight man-to-man coverage techniques wherever the receiver they are covering goes

Pressure: The act of hurrying or sacking a passer

Prevent defense: Defensive action that is designed to try to stop an offense from passing the ball deep

Pull check: A blocking term in which the offensive blocker covers the area of the man next to him who is pulling

Pull the ball: An option read action by the quarterback

Pursuit: A defensive player taking proper angles to chase and tackle an offensive player with the ball

Quick pass game: A pass game package that focuses on the three-step drop quarterback pass action, as well as quickly run short pass routes

Quick-out route: A quick speed-out route that is part of the three-step drop, quick-pass action of the quarterback, in which a receiver initially breaks up the field for three steps and then rolls his route course over, building to a depth of six yards

Rake-and-rattle: A coverage technique that involves trying to dislodge the ball as it arrives to a receiver

Reach block: The effort of a blocker to seal/cut off defenders who are moving toward the run landmark course of the ballcarrier

Read option: The run play-action of the quarterback analyzing the defensive player on the end of the line of scrimmage to see if he closes down hard to the inside. If he doesn't, the quarterback gives the ball to a running back who is on a more inside course for a run play. If he does, the quarterback keeps the ball and runs it.

Red zone: An imaginary area of the football field that extends from the 20-yard line to the goal line

Reverse: A run play in which a ballcarrier or quarterback runs laterally in one direction and then hands off or pitches the ball to a ballcarrier who is running laterally in the opposite direction

Reverse pivot: The first step of the quarterback that is opposite the direction of the play

Ride: the quarterback action of deeply placing the ball on the belly of a running back during run option action

Robber: A defender taking away a possible route (curl) by reacting to a key of another receiver

Route tree: A numbering system employed by both the offense and the defense to identify specific stems/breaks/directions that receivers run on pass plays

Rule: The blocking assignments of the offensive linemen

Run-and-shoot: A pass-oriented offense in which the receivers run their routes in relation to the type of defensive pass coverage they see, making their subsequent decisions while on the move

Run support: The action of a secondary player, usually a safety, providing extra help at, or near, the line of scrimmage in an effort to help stop the opponent's run game

Run-pass option (RPO): An offensive concept that gives an offense the option to either run the ball or pass it, depending on what kind of looks it gets from the defense

Sam linebacker: The linebacker who lines up on the tight end side (strongside) of the formation

Scheme: A term that refers to the personnel plans, alignments, stunts, and blitzes of the defense

Scoop block: A block in which the offensive lineman takes a flat, initial inside or outside step to get his body across the body of a defensive lineman, which seals him away from the point of attack of a run play

Screen: A short pass thrown to a back, tight end, or receiver in an area near the line of scrimmage behind a wall of blockers

Screen down: A down-and-distance tendency in which an offense might throw a screen, usually on second- or third-and-long

Seal block: A blocking assignment that is designed to wall off a defender on a run play

Seam route: A quickly thrown streak/go-type route in which two vertical laterally route running receivers isolate (two-on-one) a single deep safety

Seat the ball: When quarterbacks take a snap from center and immediately draw the ball into their stomach

Shade: A tight defensive alignment of a defensive lineman or linebacker in which the defender's nose aligns with an offensive blocker's inside or outside armpit

Shift: The action of an offense and/or offensive players moving from one offensive alignment to another

Shotgun: An offensive backfield alignment set in which the quarterback aligns anywhere from four to seven yards deep in the backfield behind the center

Sideline hole throw: A pass thrown to a wide receiver who is running a sideline streak route, with the ball thrown in the area above the cover Z zone hole over the top of a squatted cornerback and outside of the two-deep safety

Single back set: An offensive formation with only one running back, besides the quarterback, in the backfield

Single wing: A four-running-back formation in which the center's snap is to a deep running back or a running quarterback

Sky: When a safety forces on run and/or delivers the flat in a zone coverage

Slant and go: A quickly thrown deep pass (go route) to a receiver who first fakes a slant route

Slant route: A short, quick-pass game route in which a wide receiver or a flexed tight end drives up the field for one to three steps and then breaks on an approximately 45-degree angle course to receive a pass

Slide protection: The actions of an offensive line, or portions of it, to set up on an angle to one side of the formation or the other to zone pass protection block

Smash: A commonly used deep post-corner/flat route combination to counter either cover Z coverage or man-to-man coverages

Snake route: An inside receiver running a route to the flat outside a #1 receiver and then breaking deep down the boundary

Solid: A blocking term that calls off other blocks

Speed option: A quick developing run option play in which either the quarterback or the designated pitch back carries the ball in relation to the reaction of the defender on the end of the line

Split: The distance between linemen in their stance at the line of scrimmage

Spread offense: The use of a spread-out formation in an effort to thin out defenses while opening up the offense

Sprint-out: The pass action when the quarterback runs wide after taking the snap from the center

Square-in route: A 10 to 12 yard route (or more) in which the receiver breaks to the inside off of an initial vertical route stem

Square-out route: A 10 to 12 yard route (or more) in which the receiver breaks to the outside off of an initial vertical route stem

Squat: A two-deep zone, with the corner and the safety on the strongside playing under zones (flat and curl), with the other safety and corner playing halves

Squeeze: An assigned technique to defeat a blocker, involving a defender engaging with the outside shoulder of a blocker while keeping his outside leg and arm free

Stack: The action of aligning linebackers directly behind defensive linemen to help free up the linebackers

Stalk block: A block by the wide receiver on a secondary defender

Stance: A player assuming a motionless position (with two, three, or four points of contact with the field) for a designated count before the play snap

Stick route: A short, quick-pass game route normally run by a tight end

Streak route: A pass route (e.g., go, fly, etc.) in which the receiver runs a deep, vertical route

Strongside: A term that denotes the strength of a formation, normally the side on which the tight end lines up

Stuff: A technique to defeat a blocker in which the defender attacks the blocker in a head-up alignment

Sweep: A lateral run course to the outside

Swing route: A control-type of pass route that is normally run by a running back

System: A term that refers to the personnel plans, formations, shifts, motions, and blocking designs of the offense

Tackle box: An area two or three yards (or more) on both sides of the line of scrimmage, from tackle to tackle

Taking an edge: The concept of a defender working to tightly maneuver through the inside or outside of an offensive blocker to get past that blocker as quickly as possible

Tampa 2: A form of a two-deep (cover 2) pass coverage in which a linebacker or a nickel defender plays in a deepened coverage area in the middle of the field

Tapioca: Very short, but very quick, movement of the feet

Tendencies: A propensity of the opponent's offense, defense, or kicking game to play in a certain way in a given circumstance

Three-step drop: A quarterback taking three steps before throwing a pass

Throwback pass: A passer (quarterback or halfback) rolling out one direction and throwing back to a receiver in the other direction

Thud: A method of practice in which offensive and defensive fundamentals are practiced at a live, or close to live, tempo

Touch pass: A finesse pass by a quarterback that is dropped over the top of a defender, into an open area for the receiver to catch

Trail technique: A technique in coverage that includes following underneath the route of a receiver

Trap: A run play in which a backside offensive lineman pulls out laterally toward the opposite side of the formation to block a defender inside-out, who has been set up by being left unblocked

Triple option: A run play in which there are three option possibilities

Trips: A formation structure in which there are three receivers to one side of the formation and one to the other

Twist: The action of the defensive linemen using a designated rush lane course through gaps, with other defensive linemen looping around them to attack through other gaps

Two-minute offense: A special, hurry-up, no-huddle offense designed for use in the last two minutes of either the end of the first half or the end of the game

Unbalanced formation: An offensive formation in which an imbalance of offensive players exists to one side of the formation

Uncovered lineman: An offensive lineman who does not have a defender directly in front of him on the line of scrimmage

Under front: A defensive front in which the linebackers slide strong and the defensive linemen slide weak in order to create a weakside front overload

Under route: A short, quick pass route in which a wide receiver takes five vertical steps and then squares off to probe the underneath area of the defense in front of him

Underneath zones: Area on the defensive side of the ball from the line of scrimmage back to approximately 15 yards

Veer offense: A split-back, triple-option offense

Wall-off block: A type of blocking in which the blocker pulls and puts himself in a position to cut off penetration from the middle

Weakside: A common term for the side away from the tight end (strength) side of the formation

West Coast offense: A passing-oriented offensive system that entails an emphasis on throwing the ball frequently in a nickel-and-dime fashion

Wildcat: A specialized formation that looks similar to the old-fashioned, single-wing formation in which the ball is snapped to a back deep in the backfield

Will linebacker: A common term for the outside, weakside linebacker

Wishbone offense: A triple-option offense that has three running backs and a quarterback in the backfield, aligned in a wishbone-type set

Yards after contact (YAC): The amount of yards gained by an offensive player with the ball after contact with a defender before being stopped on the play

Zone: Refers to an area of responsibility

Zone blocking: The action of offensive players, particularly offensive linemen, to block defenders in an adjacent inside or outside area in front of them

Zone coverage: A type of pass coverage in which defenders cover a specific zone or area of the field

APPENDIX B

USA FOOTBALL

NATIONAL PRACTICE GUIDELINES FOR YOUTH TACKLE FOOTBALL

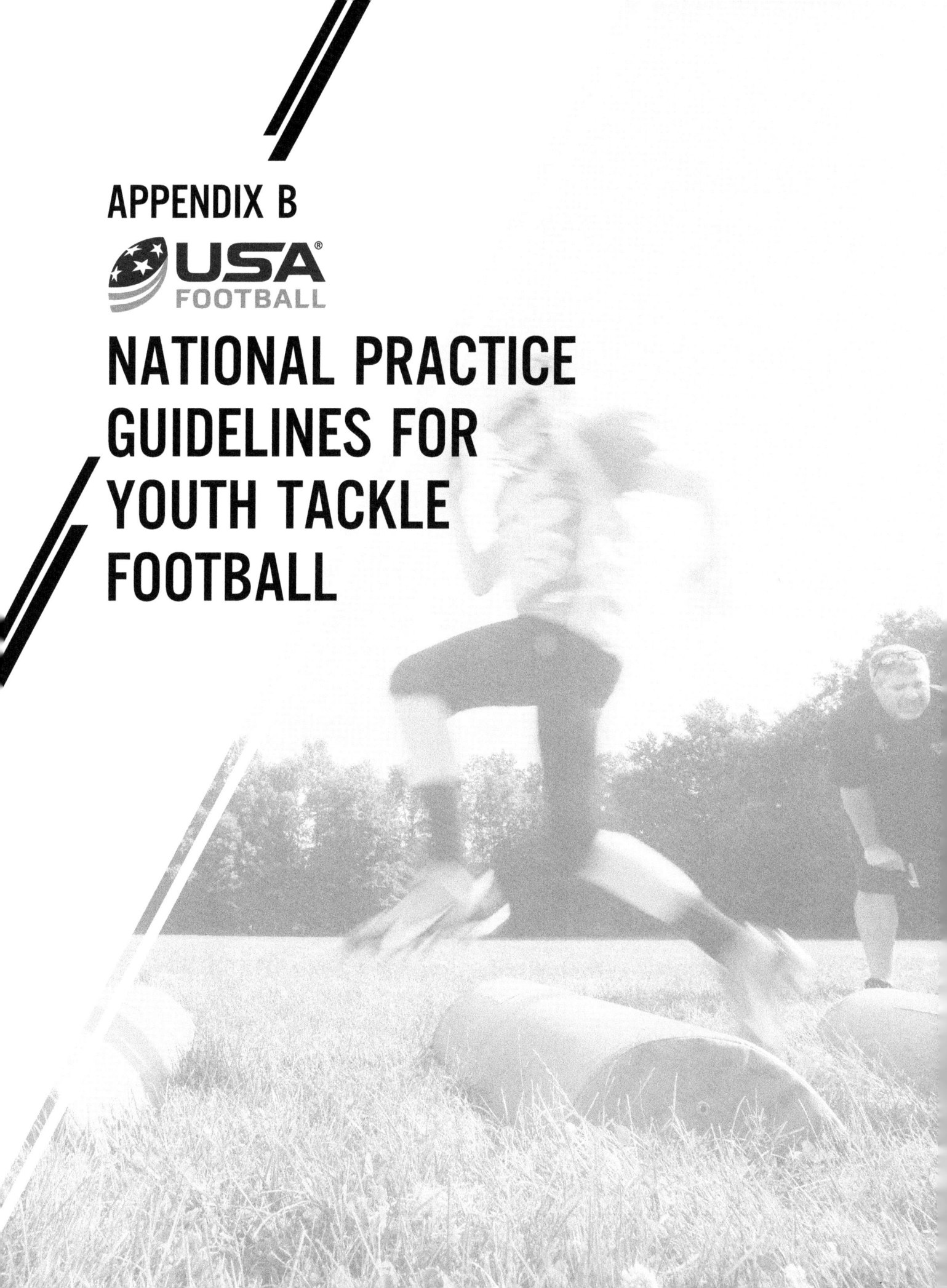

BACKGROUND

USA Football is committed to advancing player safety to protect the health and well-being of every child. In addition to coaching education, a key element of player health and safety is the responsibility of all coaches to conduct organized practices and teach proper fundamentals in a safer environment. There are approximately 9,300 youth tackle football organizations in the United States. Within these are approximately 2.5 million young athletes who play and 400,000 adults who coach.

PURPOSE

The purpose of these guidelines is to provide youth football organizations (players age 6 to 14) with recommendations to establish consistent methods designed to limit the chance for injury during structured practice sessions. This document provides youth football commissioners and coaches with heat acclimatization guidelines, clear definitions of contact, and recommendation on the number of practices per week and time limits on player-to-player full contact.

There is much to be learned about helmet impacts in youth sports. We remain committed to adopting the best evidence-based practices. We recognize that even with the latest research available, there is no clear consensus in this area. Accordingly, we will update these recommendations and guidelines in accordance with the evidence. Ideally, this emerging data will help us understand the potential for long-term adverse cognitive, emotional, and/or neurological effects from concussions and/or other repeated head contact without associated symptoms. Based on what is known about concussions today, the guiding principles in developing these recommendations were to reasonably limit head contact and thus concussion risk.

GUIDELINE 1

Implementing a pre-season youth football heat acclimatization period

Reported cases of exertional heat stroke (EHS) currently rank among the top three causes of sport participation fatalities. Setting mandatory guidelines for heat acclimatization provides a vital standard to protect athletes against exertional heat illnesses and possibly save lives. The majority of EHS cases occur during summer workouts when athletes are unprepared to cope with environmental conditions and physiological demands placed upon them. Heat acclimatization guidelines recommend that athletes be introduced slowly to environmental stresses during practice sessions, resulting in a lowered risk for EHS. These guidelines call for a two-week period (10-14 days) when coaches gradually increase the length and intensity of practice and the amount of equipment that can be worn. At all times, athletes should have access to fluids and have periods of rest throughout a practice.

Recommendations include:

1. At no time throughout the pre-season or regular season should teams practice more than once per day (no two-a-day practices). Teams should be allowed to practice a maximum of four times per week during the pre-season.

2. During practice days 1 and 2 of the heat-acclimatization period, no more than 90 minutes

of practice are allowed. A helmet should be the only protective equipment permitted. No form of player-to-player contact should occur during the first two practices.

3. During practice days 3 and 4, two hours of total practice time is allowed. Only helmets and shoulder pads should be worn. No full contact drills should be allowed. USA Football defines full contact as drills being run at "Thud" and "Live" tempo. Coaches are encouraged to limit player-to-player contact up to "Control" using USA Football's Levels of Contact.

4. On practice days 5 and 6, two hours of practice time is allowed which would occur within the second week of a youth organization's pre-season schedule according to these guidelines. Teams have the option to wear full pads and full contact drills can begin and should be utilized within the recommended time allocation discussed below.

5. If a practice is interrupted by inclement weather or heat restrictions on any of the practice days, the practice should resume once conditions are deemed safe.

6. On days when environmental conditions (heat index or WBGT) are extreme, modifications should be made to the work-to-rest ratio (to allow for cool-down periods and rehydration) or practice should be rescheduled to cooler parts of the day (i.e., before 10 a.m. or after 6 p.m.).

GUIDELINE 2

Ensure all youth coaches understand the definition of "full contact"

Full contact drills should be limited during the pre-season and regular season as the number of exposures may increase the chance for injury to youth players. For purposes of these guidelines, full contact consists of both "Thud" and "Live Action" using USA Football's definitions of Levels of Contact.

Rationale: By definition, "Thud" involves initiation of contact at full speed with no predetermined winner, but no take-down to the ground. Initial contact, particularly with linemen, is just as physical with "Thud" as with "Live Action." USA Football recognizes that "Live Action" likely carries a higher injury risk to the body than does "Thud." The first three levels of USA Football Levels of Contact—"Air," "Bags," and "Control"—are considered no or controlled contact, and thus no limitations are placed on their use in practice.

GUIDELINE 3

Recommended number of team practices and amount of "full contact" drills per week

Pre-Season Recommendation

Following the pre-season acclimatization period, it is recommended youth teams conduct no more than four practices per week. Coaches are to limit the amount of full contact to no more than 30 minutes per day and no more than 120 minutes per week. No two-a-day practices should be allowed at any point throughout the pre-season.

Rationale: USA Football recognizes pre-season practices may require more full contact time than practices occurring in the regular season to allow for teaching fundamentals with sufficient repetition to prepare for the season. Coaches are encouraged to introduce contact through a progressive manner to ensure players are using proper technique before full contact (Thud and Live Action) drills are allowed.

Regular Season Recommendation

Once the regular season begins and games commence, USA Football recommends the number of practices per week is decreased to three to account for the weekly game. Coaches are to limit the amount of full contact to no more than 30 minutes per day and no more than 90 minutes per week.

Rationale: At this point in the season, games have begun and full contact exposure rates have increased on a weekly basis for players. To account for this, the recommendation to eliminate one practice per week and decrease the amount of time dedicated to full contact drills decreases the number of exposures per week.

GUIDELINE 4

Coaches need to use a practice plan and assign a "level of contact" for every drill according to USA Football's Levels of Contact chart

USA Football defines contact using its Levels of Contact chart (see below) to help coaches assign a level of resistance for each drill period within their practice plan.

Properly employing the levels of contact during a football practice is an important skill for youth coaches to learn. This is completed by adjusting the distance between players, adjusting the speed at which they conduct a drill, and modifying the "winner" of a drill. In doing this, coaches can better accomplish specific teaching objectives during practices and decrease the chance for injury.

Planning when to teach, when to compete, and when to adjust contact promotes a better experience for players and coaches. Proper usage of the Levels of Contact system will help players perform their contact skills at a high level while instilling confidence. Employing the Levels of Contact system also helps reduce player fatigue, which can advance player safety.

Explaining Levels of Contact

Levels of Contact focuses on varying intensity levels throughout practices to build player confidence, ensure their safety, and prevent both physical and mental exhaustion.

Five intensity levels are used to introduce players to practice drills which position them to master the fundamentals and increase skill development.

CONTACT	INTENSITY	DESCRIPTION
Air	0	Players run a drill unopposed without contact.
Bags	1	Drill is run against a bag or another soft-contact surface.
Control	2	Drill is run at assigned speed until the moment of contact; one player is predetermined the "winner" by the coach. Contact remains above the waist and players stay on their feet.
Thud	3	Drill is run at assigned speed to competitive speed through the moment of contact; no predetermined "winner." Contact remains above the waist, players stay on their feet, and a quick whistle ends the drill.
Live Action	4	Drill is run in game-like conditions and is the only time that players are taken to the ground.

Practice Plan Example Within 30-Minute Full Contact Allocation

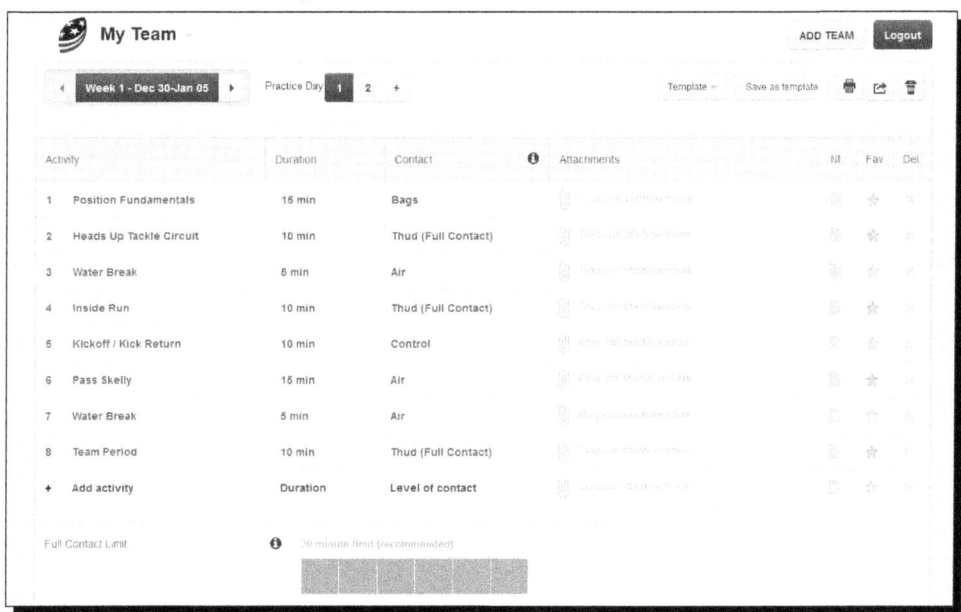

Practice Plan Example Exceeding 30-Minute Full Contact Allocation

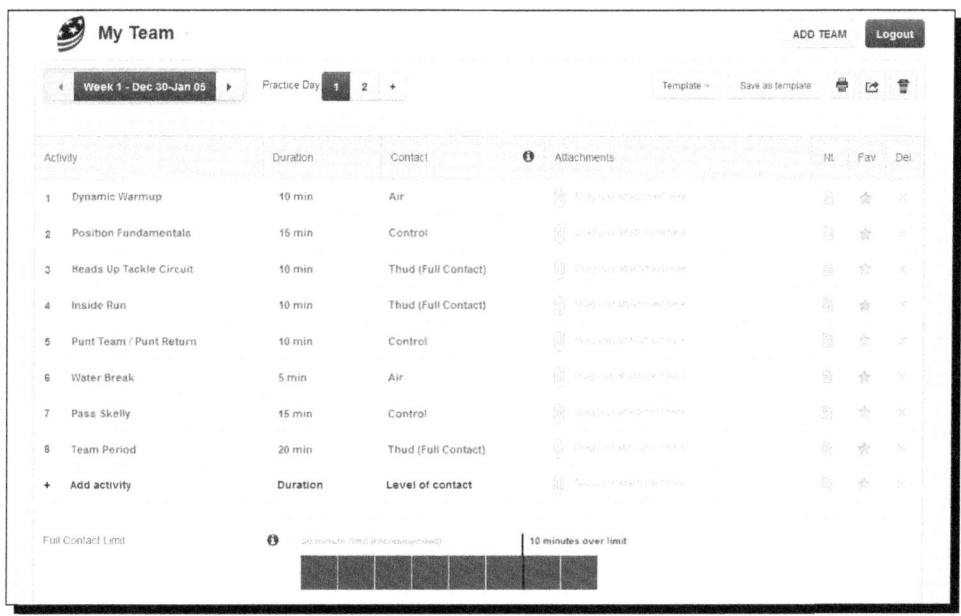

* USA Football recommends athletes be able to drink fluids at any time during a practice beyond designated breaks.

REFERENCES

1. Armstrong LA, Casa D, Millard-Stafford MMS, Moran DM, Pyne SP, Roberts WR. "Exertional Heat Illness During Training and Competition." Med. Sci. Sports Exerc. 556-572, 2007.

2. Casa D, Csillan D. "Pre-season Heat-Acclimatization Guidelines for Secondary School Athletics." Journal of Athletic Training 44(3): 332–333, 2009.

3. Casa D, Guskiewicz K, Anderson S, Courson R, Heck J, Jimenez C, McDermott B, Miller M, Stearns R, Swartz E, Walsh K. "National Athletic Trainers' Association Position Statement: Preventing Sudden Death in Sports." Journal of Athletic Training 96-118, 2012.

4. Broglio SP, Martini DN, Kasper L, Eckner JT, Kutcher JS. "Estimation of Head Impact Exposure in High School Football: Implications for Regulating Contact Practices." Am J Sport Med 41(12): 2877-2884, 2013.

5. Martini DJ, Eckner JT, Kutcher JS, Broglio SP. "Sub Concussive Head Impact Biomechanics: Comparing Differing Offensive Schemes." Med. Sci. Sports Exerc. 45(4): 755-761, 2013.

6. National Federation of State High School Associations Recommendations and Guidelines for Minimizing Head Impact Exposure and Concussion Risk in Football, http://www.nfhs.org/media/1014079/2014-nfhs-recommendations-and-guidelines-for-minimizing-head-impact-final- october-2014.pdf.

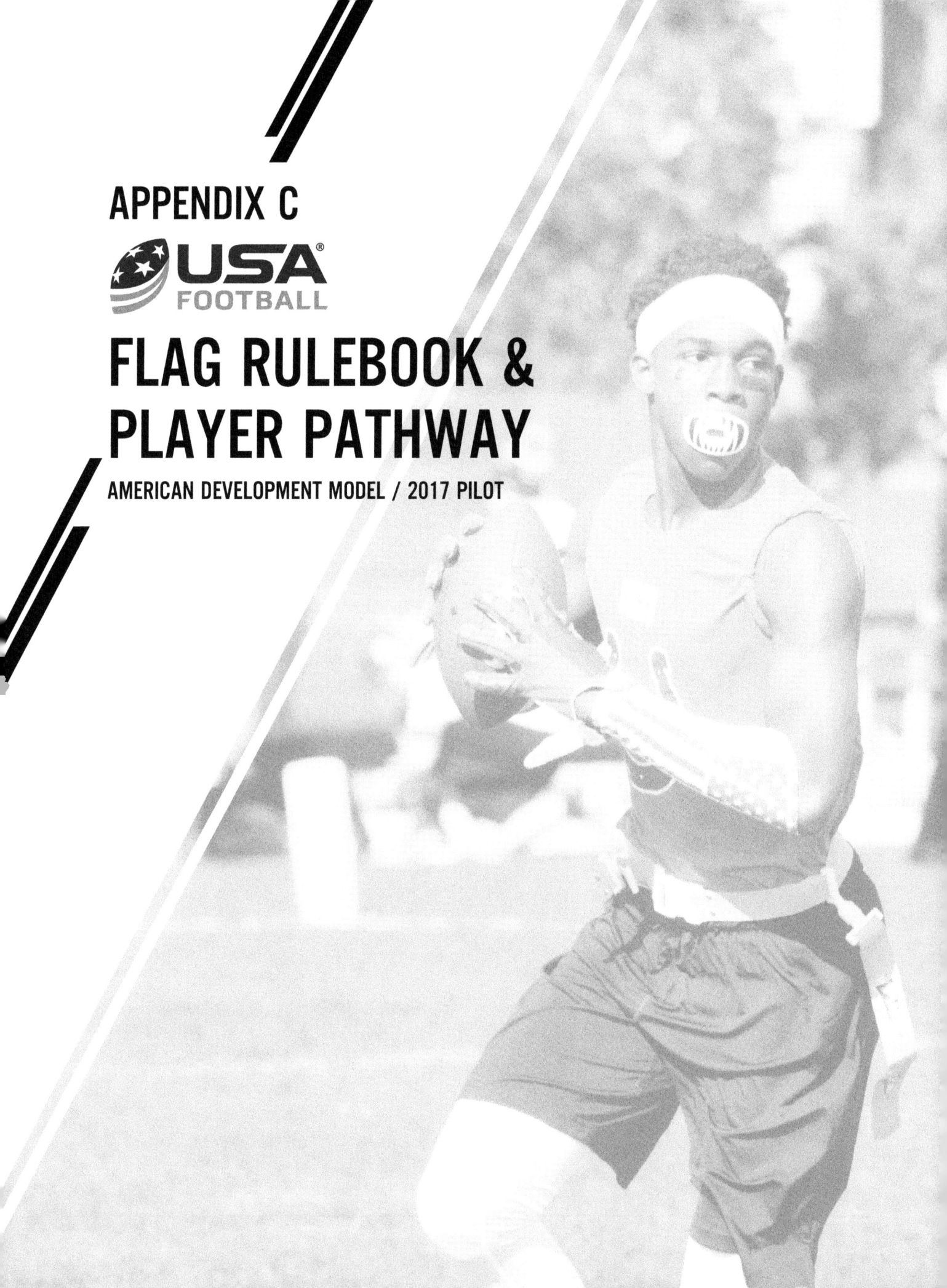

CONTENTS

1. Rules
2. Terminology
3. Equipment
4. Field
5. Rosters
6. Timing and Overtime
7. Scoring
8. Coaches
9. Live Ball/Dead Ball
10. Running
11. Passing
12. Receiving
13. Rushing the Passer
14. Flag Pulling
15. Formations
16. Unsportsmanlike Conduct
17. Penalties
    i. General
    ii. Defensive Spot Fouls
    iii. Offensive Spot Fouls
    iv. Defensive Penalties
    v. Offensive Penalties

1 / RULES

1. At the start of each game, captains from both teams meet at midfield for the coin toss to determine who starts with the ball. The visiting team calls the toss.

2. The winner of the coin toss has the choice of offense or defense. The loser of the coin toss has the choice of direction. Possession changes to start the second half to the team that started the game on defense.

3. The offensive team takes possession of the ball at its five-yard line and has three plays to cross midfield. Once a team crosses midfield, it has three plays to score a touchdown.

4. If the offense fails to score, the ball changes possession and the new offensive team starts its drive on its own five-yard line.

5. If the offensive team fails to cross midfield, possession of the ball changes and the opposition starts its drive from its own five-yard line.

6. All possession changes, except interceptions, start on the offense's five-yard line.

7. Teams change sides after the first half. Possession changes to the team that started the game on defense.

2 / TERMINOLOGY

Boundary lines	The outer perimeter lines around the field. They include the sidelines and back of the end zone lines.
Line of scrimmage	An imaginary line running through the point of the football and across the width of the field.
Line-to-gain	The line the offense must pass to get a first down or score.
Rush line	An imaginary line running across the width of the field seven yards (into the defensive side) from the line of scrimmage.
Offense	The team with possession of the ball.
Defense	The team opposing the offense to prevent it from advancing the ball.
Passer	The offensive player that throws the ball and may or may not be the quarterback.
Rusher	The defensive player assigned to rush the quarterback to prevent him/her from passing the ball by pulling his/her flags or by blocking the pass.
Downs (1-2-3)	The offensive team has three attempts or "downs" to advance the ball. It must cross the line-to-gain to get another set of downs or to score.
Live ball	Refers to the period of time that the play is in action. Generally used in regard to penalties. Live ball penalties are considered part of the play and must be enforced before the down is considered complete.
Dead ball	Refers to the period of time immediately before or after a play.
Whistle	Sound made by an official using a whistle that signifies the end of the play or a stop in the action for a timeout, halftime, or the end of the game.
Inadvertent whistle	Official's whistle that is performed in error.
Charging	An illegal movement of the ballcarrier directly at a defensive player who has established position on the field. This includes lowering the head or initiating contact with a shoulder, a forearm, or the chest.
Flag guarding	An illegal act by the ballcarrier to prevent a defender from pulling the ballcarrier's flags by stiff arm, lowering elbow or head, or by blocking access to the runner's flags with a hand or arm.
Shovel pass	A legal pitch attempted beyond the line of scrimmage.
Lateral	A backward or sideway toss of the ball by the ballcarrier.
Unsportsmanlike conduct	A rude, confrontational, or offensive behavior or language.

3 / EQUIPMENT

1. The league provides each player with an official flag belt and team jersey. Teams will use footballs provided by their league.

2. Players must wear shoes. Cleats may not be allowed at certain locations. However, cleats with exposed metal are never allowed and must be removed.

3. Players may tape their forearms, hands, and fingers. Players may wear gloves, elbow pads, and knee pads. Braces with exposed metals are not allowed. Players are encouraged to wear mouth pieces during practices and games.

4. Players must remove all jewelry, hats, and do-rags. Winter beanies are allowed.

5. Players' jerseys must be tucked into shorts or pants if they hang below the belt line.

6. We recommend players wear shorts or pants that do not have pockets. Shorts or pants with belt loops or pockets must be taped. Games will not be delayed for a player to tape up pockets.
   a. **Flag belts cannot be the same color as shorts or pants.**

4 / FIELD

1. The field dimensions are 30 yards by 53 1/3 yards with two 10-yard end zones, and a midfield line-to-gain. No-run zones precede each line-to-gain by five yards. However, some organizations may use smaller fields because of field space available or to complete tournament scheduling on time.

2. No-run zones are in place to prevent teams from conducting power run plays. While in the no-run zones (a five-yard imaginary zone before midfield and before the end zone), teams cannot run the ball in any fashion. All plays must be pass plays, even with a handoff.

3. Stepping on the boundary line is considered out of bounds.

> USA Football Recommendation: The no-run zones may be removed at the junior division for players who are still learning basic passing and catching skills.

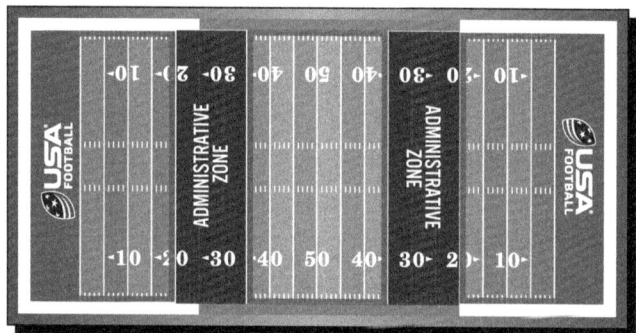

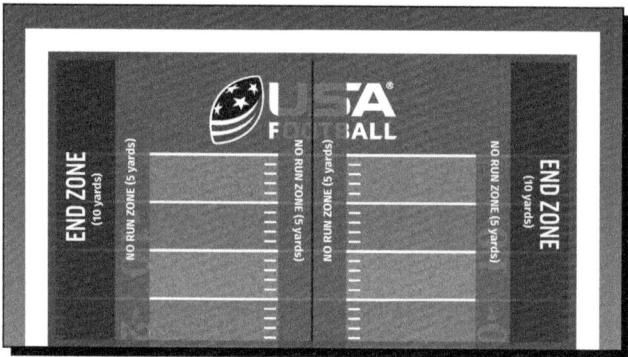

5 / ROSTERS

1. Home teams wear dark color jerseys. Visiting teams wear light color jerseys.
2. Teams must consist of at least five players with a maximum of 10 players.
3. Teams must start games with a minimum of five players. In the event of an injury, a team with insufficient substitute players may play with four players on the field but no fewer than four.

6 / TIMING AND OVERTIME

1. Games are played on a 40-minute continuous clock with two 20-minute halves unless one team gains a 28-point advantage, at which point, the score is no longer kept. Clock stops only for timeouts or injuries.
2. Halftime is one minute.
3. Each time the ball is spotted, a team has 30 seconds to snap the ball. Teams will receive one warning before a delay-of-game penalty is enforced.

> USA Football Recommendation: Officials should use discretion with junior level teams who may need more time to line up and get a playoff.

4. Each team has one 30-second timeout per half.
5. Officials can stop the clock at their discretion.
6. In the event of an injury, the clock will stop then restart when the injured player is removed from the field of play and both teams are lined up ready to restart the play.
7. In playoff games only, if the score is tied at the end of 40 minutes, an overtime period will be used to determine a winner. **Overtime format** is as follows:
    a. A coin flip will determine the team that chooses to be on offense or defense first.
        i. If a second round of overtime must be played, the team that lost the coin toss will get to choose offense or defense for the start of the second round of overtime. This process continues with teams alternating who gets to choose to be on offense or defense to start out during every round of overtime.
        ii. The referee will determine which end of the field the overtime will take place on.
    b. Each team will take turns getting one play from the defense's five-yard line for one point or the defense's 10-yard line for two points. Whether to go for one or two points is up to the offensive team. Whether or not the team that begins on offense converts, the team that started on defense gets a chance on offense to win or tie by converting a one- or two-point play of their own.
        i. Example: Team A starts on offense and chooses to go for one point from the five-yard line and is successful. Team B is then on offense and can choose to either go for one point from the five-yard line to tie and force a second round of overtime or to go for two points from the 10-yard line for the win.
        ii. If the second team on offense in an overtime round fails to beat or match the team that went first, the team that went first wins.
    c. Both teams must "go for two" from the 10-yard line starting with the third round of overtime.

d. The final points earned by the winning team in the final overtime will be added onto the winning team's total score. The losing team will not receive any additional points.

   i. Example: End of regulation time, score is 14-14. Team A scores one point and Team B scores two points. Team B wins with a final score of 16-14. Points are only added to total score from final round of overtime.

e. All regulation period rules and penalties are in effect.

f. There are no timeouts.

7 / SCORING

1. Touchdown: Six points
2. PAT (point after touchdown): One point (five-yard line) or two points (10-yard line)

   a. Note: One-point PAT is pass only; two-point PAT can be run or pass.

   > USA Football Recommendation: At the junior level, one-point tries can be run or pass.

   b. A team that scores a touchdown must declare whether it wishes to attempt a one-point conversion (from the five-yard line) or a two-point conversion (from the ten-yard line). Any change, once a decision is made to try for the extra point, requires a charged timeout. A decision cannot be changed after a penalty. Interceptions on conversions cannot be returned.

3. Safety: Two points

   a. A safety occurs when the ballcarrier is declared down in his/her own end zone. Runners can be called down when their flags are pulled by a defensive player, a flag falls out, they step out of bounds, their knee or arm touches the ground, a fumble occurs in the end zone, or a snapped ball lands in or beyond the end zone.

   > USA Football Recommendation: Safeties can be eliminated at the junior level. For flag pulls in the end zone or players running out of the back or sides of the end zone, the ball returns to the original spot or the five-yard line and a down is lost.

4. After one team is winning by 28 points or more, score is no longer kept. Once a 28 or more point advantage is gained, no PAT will be attempted. The game will continue in scrimmage mode for the remainder of the game.

5. **Forfeits are scored 28-0 for the winning team.**

8 / COACHES

1. Coaches are allowed on the field to direct players according to need and division. Upon the snap, coaches must be behind the deepest offensive and defensive players and out of the action. Coaches can assist in the alignment of their team to facilitate a fast-paced game but may not provide extra instruction or make audibles to play calls once the huddle is broken.

9 / LIVE BALL/DEAD BALL

1. The ball is live at the snap of the ball and remains live until the official whistles the ball dead.
2. The official will indicate the neutral zone and line of scrimmage.
   a. It is an automatic dead ball foul if any player on defense or offense enters the neutral zone. In regard to the neutral zone, the official may give both teams a "courtesy" neutral zone notification to allow their players to move back behind the line of scrimmage.
3. A player who gains possession in the air is considered inbounds as long as one foot comes down in the field of play.
4. The defense may not mimic the offensive team signals by trying to confuse the offensive players while the quarterback is calling out signals to start the play. This will result in an unsportsmanlike conduct penalty.
5. Substitutions may be made on any dead ball.
6. Any official can whistle the play dead.
7. Play is ruled "dead" when:
   a. The ball hits the ground
      i. If the ball hits the ground as a result of a bad snap, the ball is then placed where the ball hit the ground.
   b. The ballcarrier's flag is pulled
   c. The ballcarrier steps out of bounds
   d. A touchdown, PAT, or safety is scored
   e. Any part of the body other than feet or hands touches the ground
   f. The ballcarrier's flag falls out
   g. The receiver catches the ball while in possession of one or no flag(s)
   h. The seven-second pass clock expires
   i. An inadvertent whistle occurs
8. In the case of an inadvertent whistle, the offense has two options:
   a. Take the ball where it was when the whistle blew, and the down is consumed.
   b. Replay the down from the original line of scrimmage.
9. A team is allowed to use a timeout to question an official's rule interpretation. If the official's ruling is correct, the team will be charged a timeout. If the rule is interpreted incorrectly, the timeout will not be charged and the proper ruling will be enforced. Officials should all agree upon any controversial call in order to give each team the full benefit of each call.

10 / RUNNING

1. The ball is spotted where the runner's feet are when the flag is pulled, not where the ballcarrier has the ball. Forward progress will be measured by the player's front foot.
2. The quarterback cannot directly run with the ball. The quarterback is the offensive player who receives the snap.
3. Only direct handoffs behind the line of scrimmage are permitted. Handoffs may be in front of, behind, or to the side of the offensive player but must be behind the line of scrimmage. The offense may use multiple handoffs.
   a. **"Center sneak" play is not allowed. The quarterback is not allowed to hand off to the center on the first handoff of the play.**
4. Absolutely NO laterals of any kind.

5. No-run zones are located five yards before each end zone and five yards on either side of midfield and are designed to avoid short-yardage power-running situations. Teams are not allowed to run in these zones if the subsequent line is *live*. (Reminder: Each offensive team approaches only *two* no-run zones in each drive—one five yards from midfield to gain the first down and one five yards from the goal line to score a touchdown.)

> USA Football Recommendation: The no-run zones may be removed at the junior division for players who are still learning basic passing and catching skills.

6. Any player who receives a handoff can throw the ball from behind the line of scrimmage.

7. Once the ball has been handed off in front of, behind, or to the side of the quarterback, all defensive players are eligible to rush.

8. Runners may not leave their feet to advance the ball. Diving, leaping, or jumping to avoid a flag pull is considered flag guarding.

9. Spinning is allowed, but players cannot leave their feet to avoid a flag pull. Players spinning out of control will be called for flag guarding.

10. Runners may leave their feet if there is a clear indication that they have done so to avoid collision with another player without a flag guarding penalty enforced.

11. No blocking or "screening" is allowed at any time.

12. Offensive players without the ball must stop their motion once the ball has crossed the line of scrimmage. No running with the ballcarrier.

13. Flag obstruction: All jerseys *must* be tucked in before play begins. The flags must be on the player's hips and free from obstruction. Deliberately obstructed flags will be considered flag guarding.

11 / PASSING

1. All passes must be from behind the line of scrimmage, thrown forward, and received beyond the line scrimmage.

    a. All passes that do not cross the line of scrimmage, whether received or not, are illegal forward passes.

    b. The quarterback may throw the ball away to avoid a sack. Pass must go beyond the line of scrimmage.

> USA Football Recommendation: At the junior level, officials should use their discretion for balls that do not reach the line of scrimmage as long as the player made an honest effort to make it there.

2. Shovel passes are allowed but must be received beyond the line of scrimmage.

3. The quarterback has a seven-second "pass clock." If a pass is not thrown within the seven seconds, the play is dead, the down is consumed, and the ball is returned to the line of scrimmage. Once the ball is handed off, the seven-second rule is no longer in effect.

    a. If the quarterback is standing in the end zone at the end of the seven-second clock, the ball is returned to the line of scrimmage.

b. Officials count off the seven-second rule as they would visually signaling a three-second call in basketball with the final three seconds counted off verbally so the quarterback can hear it.

> USA Football Recommendation: For the junior level, eliminate pass rushers to allow young players the full seven seconds to throw the ball without pressure.

12 / RECEIVING

1. All players are eligible to receive passes (including the quarterback if the ball has been handed off behind the line of scrimmage).

2. Only one player is allowed in motion at a time. All motion must be parallel to the line of scrimmage and no motion is permitted toward the line of scrimmage.

3. A player must have at least one foot inbounds when making a reception.

4. In the case of simultaneous possession by both an offensive and defensive player, possession is awarded to the offense.

5. Interceptions change possession at the point of the interception. Interceptions are returnable and are the only changes of possession that do not result with starting on the five-yard line.

6. The play is blown dead immediately if an interception is made on an extra-point try. There are no returns on that play.

13 / RUSHING THE PASSER

1. All players who rush the passer must be a minimum of seven yards from the line of scrimmage when the ball is snapped. Any number of players can rush the quarterback. Players not rushing the quarterback can defend on the line of scrimmage.

2. Once the ball is handed off, the seven-yard rule no longer is in effect and all defenders may go behind the line of scrimmage.

3. A special marker, or the referee, will designate a rush line seven yards from the line of scrimmage. Defensive players should verify they are in the correct position with the official on every play.

   a. A legal rush is:
      i. Any rush from a point seven yards from the defensive line of scrimmage.
      ii. A rush from anywhere on the field *after* the ball has been handed off by the quarterback.
      iii. If a rusher leaves the rush line early (breaks the seven-yard area), they may return to the rush line, reset, and then legally rush the quarterback.
      iv. If a rusher leaves the rush line early and the ball is handed off before he/she crosses the line of scrimmage, he/she may legally rush the quarterback.

   b. A penalty may be called if:
      i. The rusher leaves the rush line before the snap crosses the line of scrimmage before a handoff or pass—illegal rush (five yards from the line of scrimmage and first down).
      ii. Any defensive player crosses the line of scrimmage before the ball is snapped—offside (five yards from the line of scrimmage and first down).

iii. Any defensive player not lined up at the rush line crosses the line of scrimmage before the ball is passed or handed off—illegal rush (five yards from the line of scrimmage and first down).

c. Special circumstances:

i. Teams are not required to rush the quarterback with the seven-second clock in effect.

ii. Teams are not required to identify their rusher before the play.

4. Players rushing the quarterback may attempt to block a pass; however, *no* contact can be made with the quarterback in any way. Blocking the pass or attempting to block the pass and then making contact with the passer will result in a roughing the passer penalty.

5. The offense cannot impede the rusher in any way. The rusher has the right to a clear path to the quarterback, regardless of where they line up prior to the snap. If the "path or line" is occupied by a moving offensive player, then it is the offense's responsibility to avoid the rusher. Any disruption to the rusher's path and/or contact will result in an impeding the rusher penalty. If the offensive player does not move after the snap, then it is the rusher's responsibility to go around the offensive player and to avoid contact.

6. A sack occurs if the quarterback's flags are pulled behind the line of scrimmage. The ball is placed where the quarterback's feet are when the flags are pulled.

a. A safety is awarded if the sack takes place in the offensive team's end zone unless playing the junior rule exception of returning the ball to the offense on the line of scrimmage or five-yard line with a loss of down.

b. See junior recommendation above.

14 / FLAG PULLING

1. A legal flag pull takes place when the ballcarrier is in full possession of the ball.

2. Defenders can dive to pull flags but cannot tackle, hold, or run through the ballcarrier when pulling flags.

3. It is illegal to attempt to strip or pull the ball from the ballcarrier's possession at any time.

4. If a player's flag inadvertently falls off during the play, the player is down immediately upon possession of the ball and the play ends. The ball is placed where the flag lands.

5. A defensive player may not intentionally pull the flags off a player who is not in possession of the ball.

6. Flag guarding is an attempt by the ballcarrier to obstruct the defender's access to the flags by stiff arming, dropping the head, hand, arm, or shoulder, or intentionally covering the flags with the football jersey.

15 / FORMATIONS

1. Offenses must have a minimum of one player on the line of scrimmage (the center) and up to four players on the line of scrimmage. The quarterback must be off the line of scrimmage.

a. One player at a time may go in motion one yard behind and parallel to the line of scrimmage. Example: An offensive player lined up three yards deep in the backfield can never go in motion. A player in motion must either start from a set position on the line of scrimmage or one yard off to adhere to the rule.

b. No motion is allowed toward the line of scrimmage.

2. Movement by a player who is set or a player who runs toward the line of scrimmage while in motion is considered a false start.

3. The center must snap the ball with a rapid and continuous motion between his/her legs to a player in the backfield, and the ball must completely leave his/her hands.

16 / UNSPORTSMANLIKE CONDUCT

1. If the field monitor or referee witnesses any acts of intentional tackling, elbowing, cheap shots, blocking, or any unsportsmanlike act, the game will be stopped and the player will be ejected from the game. The decision is made at the referee's discretion. No appeals will be considered. FOUL PLAY WILL NOT BE TOLERATED!

> USA Football Recommendation: At the junior level, move any player who commits an unsportsmanlike or dangerous act from the field to receive instruction from a coach and a cooling off period. Officials can eject the player at their discretion if there are continued infractions that are deemed intentional.

2. Offensive or confrontational language is not allowed. Officials have the right to determine offensive language. If offensive or confrontational language occurs, the referee will give one warning. If it continues, the player or players will be ejected from the game.

3. Players may not physically or verbally abuse any opponent, coach, or official.

4. Ballcarriers *must* make an effort to avoid defenders with an established position.

5. Defenders are not allowed to run through the ballcarrier when pulling flags.

6. Fans must also adhere to good sportsmanship:

    a. Yell to cheer on players, not to harass officials or other teams.

    b. Keep comments clean and profanity-free.

    c. Compliment *all* players, not just one child or team.

7. Fans are required to keep fields safe and kid-friendly:

    a. Keep younger kids and equipment such as coolers, chairs, and tents a minimum of 10 yards off the field in the end zone area.

    b. Stay in the end zone area, not between fields. The administration zone is reserved for league administration, game officials, medical personnel, coaches, and players only.

    c. Dispose of *all* trash in designated trash cans.

8. Unsportsmanlike conduct penalties:

    a. Defense: +10 yards from the line of scrimmage and automatic first down

    b. Offense: -10 yards from the line of scrimmage and loss of down

17 / PENALTIES

i. General

1. The officials will call all penalties.
2. Game officials determine incidental contact that may result from normal run of play.
3. All penalties will be assessed from the line of scrimmage, except as noted. (Spot fouls)
4. Only the team captain or head coach may ask the referee questions about rule clarification and interpretations. Players may not question calls.
5. Games may not end on a defensive penalty unless the offense declines it.
6. Penalties are assessed live ball then dead ball. Live ball penalties must be assessed before play is considered complete.
7. Penalties will be assessed half the distance to the goal yardage when the penalty yardage is more than half the distance to the goal.
8. Penalties may not move the ball past the 40-yard line and into the Administrative Zone.
9. Penalties occurring on the 40-yard line result in loss of down and no yards lost.

ii. Defensive Spot Fouls

Defensive pass interference	Automatic first down
Holding	Automatic first down
Stripping	+10 yards and automatic first down

iii. Offensive Spot Fouls

Screening, blocking, or running with the ball	-10 yards and loss of down
Charging	-10 yards and loss of down
Flag guarding	-10 yards and loss of down

iv. Defensive Penalties

Defensive unnecessary roughness	+10 yards and automatic first down
Defensive unsportsmanlike conduct	+10 yards and automatic first down
Offside	+5 yards from line of scrimmage and automatic first down
Illegal rush (starting rush from inside seven-yard marker)	+5 yards from line of scrimmage and automatic first down
Illegal flag pull (before the receiver has the ball)	+5 yards from line of scrimmage and automatic first down
Roughing the passer	+5 yards from line of scrimmage and automatic first down
Taunting	+5 yards from line of scrimmage and automatic first down

v. Offensive Penalties

Offensive unnecessary roughness	-10 yards and loss of down
Offensive unsportsmanlike conduct	-10 yards and loss of down
Offside/false start	-5 yards from line of scrimmage and loss of down
Illegal forward pass (any pass that is received or lands behind the line of scrimmage or throwing a pass after crossing the line of scrimmage)	-5 yards from line of scrimmage and loss of down
Offensive pass interference	-5 yards from line of scrimmage and loss of down
Illegal motion (more than one person moving)	-5 yards from line of scrimmage and loss of down
Delay of game	-5 yards from line of scrimmage and loss of down
Impeding the rusher	-5 yards from line of scrimmage and loss of down

ABOUT THE AUTHORS

Tony Dungy is a former NFL player, Super Bowl-winning NFL coach, and *New York Times* best-selling author. After playing collegiately as a quarterback for the University of Minnesota, Dungy played in the NFL for three seasons as a defensive back for the Pittsburgh Steelers and San Francisco 49ers.

Dungy began his NFL coaching career in 1980 at the age of 25, making him the youngest assistant coach in NFL history. He then went on to serve as the head coach of the Tampa Bay Buccaneers (1996-2001) and subsequently the Indianapolis Colts (2002-2008), whom he guided to a Super Bowl victory in 2007.

Dungy and his wife, Lauren, are the parents of seven children. Since his retirement in 2008, Dungy has served as an analyst for NBC's "Football Night in America," as well as remained active in a number of charitable causes.

James A. Peterson, Ph.D., FACSM, is a sports medicine consultant and author who resides in Monterey, CA. He has written or co-authored over 100 books, including *Finding the Winning Edge* with Bill Walsh and Brian Billick and *Competitive Leadership* with Brian Billick. Currently, he is working on *Coaching Football's 3-4 Defense* with Wade Phillips.

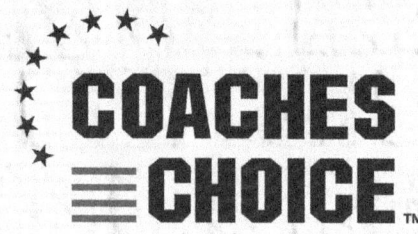